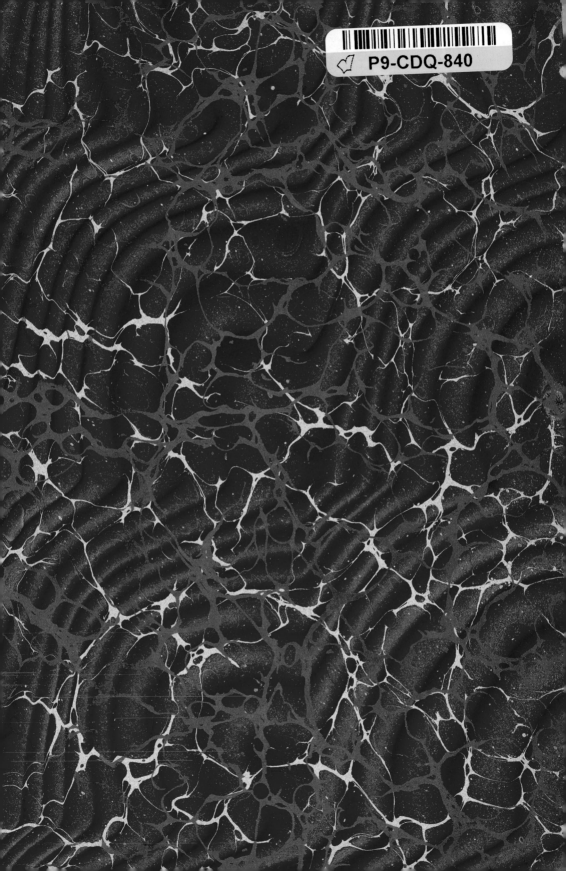

COLLECTION OF VASES, MODELLED AND PAINTED IN THE
GRAND TEMPLE. PHILAE ISLAND.

History of Egypt

From 330 B. C. to the Present Time

By S. RAPPOPORT, Doctor of Philosophy, Basel;
Member of the Ecole Langues Orientales, Paris;
Russian, German, French Orientalist and Philologist

VOL. III

*Containing over Twelve Hundred
Colored Plates and Illustrations*

THE GROLIER SOCIETY

PUBLISHERS △ △ △ LONDON

CONTENTS

CHAPTER I.

THE CRUSADERS IN EGYPT

CHAPTER II.

THE FRENCH IN EGYPT

CHAPTER III.

THE RULE OF MEHEMET ALI

CHAPTER IV.

THE BRITISH INFLUENCE IN EGYPT

CONTENTS

CHAPTER V.

THE WATERWAYS OF EGYPT

CHAPTER VI.

THE DECIPHERMENT OF THE HIEROGLYPHS

CHAPTER VII.

THE DEVELOPMENT OF EGYPTOLOGY

CHAPTER VIII.

IMPORTANT RESEARCHES IN EGYPT

1313

LIST OF ILLUSTRATIONS

——

MODERN EGYPT

— ◆ —

EGYPT DURING THE CRUSADES — RISE OF THE OTTOMAN POWER — NAPO-
LEON IN EGYPT — THE RULE OF THE KHEDIVES — DISCOVERING THE
SOURCE OF THE NILE — ARCHÆOLOGICAL RESEARCH AND DISCOVERY.

*Spread of Muhammedanism — Spirit of the Crusades — The Fati-
mite Caliphs — Saladin's brilliant reign — Capture of Damietta —
Conquests of Beybars — Mamluks in power — Wars with Cyprus —
Turkish misrule — Napoleon invades Egypt — Battle of the Pyramids
— Policy of conciliation — Nelson destroys the French fleet — Napoleon
in Syria — Battle at Mount Carmel — Napoleon returns to France
— Negotiations for surrender — Kléber assassinated — French army
surrenders — Rise of Mehemet Ali — Massacre of the Mamluks —
Egyptian army reorganized — Ibrahim Pasha in Greece — Battle of
Navarino — Revolt against Turkey — Character of Mehemet Ali —
Reforms under his Rule — Ismail Pasha made Khedive — Financial
difficulties of Egypt — England and France assume control — Tewfik
Pasha becomes Khedive — Revolt of Arabi Pasha — The Mahdist in-
surrection — Death of General Gordon — Kitchener's campaign against*

the Dervishes — Prosperity of Egypt under English control — Abbas Pasha becomes Khedive — Education, courts, and government of modern Egypt — The Nile; its valley, branches, and delta — Ancient irrigation systems — The Suez Canal, its inception and completion — The great dam at Aswan — Ancient search for the sources of the Nile — Modern discoveries in Central Africa — The Hieroglyphs — Origin of the alphabet — Egyptian literature — Mariette's discoveries — The German Egyptologists — Jeremiah verified — Maspero, Naville, and Petrie — Palæolithic man — Egyptian record of Israel — Egypt Exploration Fund — The royal tombs at **Abydos** — Chronology of the early kings — Steles, pottery, and jewelry — The temples of Abydos — Seals, statuettes, and ceramics.

CHAPTER I.

THE CRUSADERS IN EGYPT

The Ideal of the Crusader : Saladin's Campaign : Richard I. in Palestine : Siege of Damietta : St. Louis in Egypt : The Mamluks : Beybars' Policy.

ORNAMENT FROM THE
PORCH OF HASAN.

THE traditional history of the Christian Church has generally maintained that the Crusades were due solely to religious influence and sprang from ideal and moral motives: those hundreds of thousands of warriors who went out to the East were religious enthusiasts, prompted by the pious longings of their hearts, and Peter the Hermit, it was claimed, had received a divine message to call Christendom to arms, to preach a Crusade against the unbelievers and take possession of the Holy Sepulchre. That such ideal reasons should be

3

attributed to a war like the Crusades, of a wide and far-reaching influence on the political and intellectual development of mediæval Europe, is not at all surprising. In the history of humanity there have been few wars in which the combatants on both sides were not convinced that they had drawn their swords for some noble purpose, for the cause of right and justice. That the motives prompting the vast display of arms witnessed during the Crusades, that the wanderings of those crowds to the East during two centuries, and the cruelties committed by the saintly warriors on their way to the Holy Sepulchre, should be attributed exclusively to ideal and religious sources is therefore quite natural. It is not to be denied that there was a religious factor in the Crusades; but that the religious motive was not the sole incentive has now been agreed upon by impartial historians; and in so far as the motives animating the Crusaders were religious motives, we are to look to powerful influences which gradually made themselves felt from without the ecclesiastical organisations. It was by no means a movement which the Church alone had called into being. On the contrary, only when the movement had grown ripe did Gregory VII. hasten to take steps to enable the Church to control it. The idea of a Crusade for the glory of religion had not sprung from the tenets of Christianity; it was given to mediæval Europe by the Muhammedans.

History can hardly boast of another example of so gigantic a conquest during so short a period as that gained by the first adherents of Islam. Like the fiery wind of the desert, they had broken from their retreats, animated by the promises of the Prophet, and spread the new doctrine far and wide. In 653 the scimitar of the Saracens enclosed an area as large as the Roman Empire under the Cæsars. Barely forty years elapsed after the death of the Prophet when the armies of Islam reached the Atlantic. Okba, the wild and gallant leader, rode into the sea on the western shore of Africa, and, whilst the seething waves reached to the saddle of his camel, he exclaimed: " Allah, I call thee as witness that I should have carried the knowledge of Thy name still farther, if these waves threatening to swallow me would not have prevented me from doing so." Not long after this, the flag of the crescent was waving from the Pyrenees to the Chinese mountains. In 711 the Saracens under General Tarik crossed the straits between the Mediterranean and the Atlantic, and landed on the rock which has since been called after him, " the hill of Tarik," Jebel el-Tarik or Gibraltar. Spain was invaded and captured by the Moslems. For awhile it seemed as if on the other side of the Garonne the crescent would also supplant the cross, and only the victory of Charles Martel in 732 put a stop to the wave of Muhammedan conquest.

Thus in a brief period Muhammedanism spread from the Nile Valley to the Mediterranean. Muhammed's trenchant argument was the sword. He gave a distinct command to his followers to convince the infidels of the power of truth on the battle-field. " The sword is a surer argument than books," he said. Accordingly the Koran ordered war against unbelievers: " The sword is the key to heaven and hell; a drop of blood shed in the cause of Allah, a night spent in arms, is of more avail than two months of fasting and prayer; whoever falls in battle, his sins are forgiven, and at the day of judgment his limbs shall be supplied with the wings of angels and cherubim." Before the battle commenced, the commanders reminded the warriors of the beautiful celestial houris who awaited the heroes slain in battle at the gates of Paradise.

The first efforts having been crowned with success, the Moslems soon became convinced of the fulfilment of the prophecy that Allah had given them the world and wished them to subdue all unbelievers. Under the Caliph Omar, the Arabs had become a religious-political community of warriors, whose mission it was to conquer and plunder all civilised and cultured lands and to unfurl the banner of the crescent. They believed that " Paradise is under the shadow of the sword." In this belief the followers of Muhammed engaged in battle without fear or anxiety, spurred to great deeds, reckless in the face of danger, happy to die and pass to the delights of Paradise. The " holy war " became an armed propaganda pleasing to Allah. It was, however, a form of propaganda quite unknown and amazing to Christendom. In the course of two centuries the crescent had supplanted the cross. Of what avail was the peaceful missionary's preaching if province after province and country after country were taken possession of by the new religion that forced its way by means of fire and sword?

Was it not natural that Christian Europe should conceive the idea of doing for their religion what the Moslems did for Islam? and that, following the example of Moslems in their " holy war," Christians should emulate them in the Crusades?

It must not be forgotten also that the Arabs, almost from the first appearance of Muhammedanism, were under the refining and elevating influences of art and science. While the rest of Europe was in the midnight of the Dark Ages, the Moorish universities of Spain were the beacon of the revival of learning. The Christian teacher was still manipulating the bones of the saints when the Arab physician was practising surgery. The monachal schools and monasteries in Italy,

ARABIC DECORATIVE PAINTING.

France, and Germany were still grappling with poor scholastic knowledge when Arab scholars were well advanced in the study of Aristotle and Plato. Stimulated by their acquaintance with the works of Ptolemy and Euclid, Galenus and Hippocrates, they extended their researches into the dominions of astronomy, mathematics, and medicine.

The religious orders of the knights, a product of the Crusades, found their antitype in similar organisations of the Moslems, orders that had exactly the same tend-

encies and regulations. Such an order established **for**
the spread of Islam and the protection of its followers
was that of the Raabites or boundary-guards in the Pyre-
nean peninsula. These knights made a vow to carry,
throughout their lives, arms in defence of the faith; they
led an austere existence, were not allowed to fly in battle,
but were compelled either to conquer or fall. Like the
Templars or the Hospital Knights their whole endeavour
was to gain universal dominion for their religion. The
relation existing between the Moslems and the Christians before the Crusades was much closer than is generally imagined. Moslem soldiers often fought in the
ranks of the Christian armies; and it was by no means
rare to see a Christian ruler call upon Moslem warriors
to assist him against his adversary. Pope Gregory rescued Rome from the hands of his imperial opponent,
Henry of Germany, only with the aid of the Saracen
soldiers.

When, therefore, the influence of Muhammedanism
began to assert itself throughout the south of Europe,
it was natural that in a crude and stirring age, when
strife was the dominant passion of the people, the idea
of a holy war in the cause of faith was one in which
Christian Europe was ready to take an example from
the followers of Islam. The political, economical, and
social state of affairs, the misery and suffering of the
people, and even the hierarchy and the ascetic spirit of
the time certainly made the minds of the people acces-
sible to the idea of war; the spirit of unrest was per-
vasive and the time was ripe, but the influence of Islam

was a prominent factor in giving to it an entirely religious aspect.

But even in the means employed to incite the Christian warriors and the manner in which the Crusades were carried on, there is a great similarity between the Christian and the Muhammedan procedure. The Church, when espousing the cause of the Crusader, did exactly what Muhammed had done when he preached a holy war. The Church addressed itself to the weaknesses and passions of human nature. Fallen in battle, the Moslem, so he was told, would be admitted—be he victor or vanquished—to the joys of Paradise. The same prospect animated the Crusader and made him brave danger and die joyfully in defence of Christianity. " Let them kill the enemy or die. To submit to die for Christ, or to cause one of His enemies to die, is naught but glory," said Saint Bernard. Eloquently, vividly, and in glowing colours were the riches that awaited the warriors in the far East described: immense spoil would be taken from the unbelievers. Preachers did not even shrink from extolling the beauty of the women in the lands to be conquered. This fact recalls Muhammed's promise to his believers that they would meet the ever-beautiful dark-eyed houris in the life after death. To the material, sensual allurements, the Church added spiritual blessings and eternal rewards, guaranteed to those who took the red cross. During the Crusades the Christians did their utmost to copy the cruelties of the Moslems. That contempt for human life, that entire absence of mercy and the sense of pity which is familiar in all countries where Islam has gained sway is characteristic also of the Crusades.

Although the narrative of the Crusades belongs rather to the history of Europe than of any one country, it is so closely intertwined with the history of Egypt at this period that some digression is necessary. About twenty years after the conquest of Jerusalem by the Turks, in 1076, the Holy Sepulchre was visited by a hermit of the name of Peter, a native of Amiens, in the province of Picardy, France. His resentment and sympathy were excited by his own injuries and the oppression of the Christian name; he mingled his tears with those of the Patriarch, and earnestly inquired if no hope of relief from the Greek emperors of the East could be entertained. The Patriarch exposed the vices and weakness of the successors of Constantine. "I will rouse," exclaimed the hermit, "the martial nations of Europe in your cause;" and Europe was obedient to the call of the hermit. The astonished Patriarch dismissed him with epistles of credit and complaint; and no sooner did he land at Bari than Peter hastened to kiss the feet of the Roman pontiff. Pope Urban II. received him as a prophet, applauded his glorious design, promised to support it in a general council, and encouraged him to proclaim the deliverance of the Holy Land. Invigorated by the approbation of the pontiff, this zealous missionary traversed with speed and success the provinces of Italy and France. He preached to innumerable crowds in the churches, the streets, and the highways: the hermit entered with equal confidence the palace and the cottage; and the people of all classes were impetuously moved by his call to repentance and arms.

The first Crusade was headed by Godefroy de Bouillon, Duke of Lower Lorraine; Baldwin, his brother; Hugo the Great, brother of the King of France; Robert, Duke of Normandy, son of William the Conqueror; Raymond of St. Gilles, Duke of Toulouse; and Bohemond, Prince of Tarentum. Towards the end of 1097 A. D. the invading force invested Antioch, and, after a siege of nine months, took it by storm. Edessa was also captured by the Crusaders, and in the middle of the summer of 1098 they reached Jerusalem, then in the hands of the Fatimites.

El-Mustali b'Illah Abu'l Kasim, son of Mustanssir, was then on the throne, but he was only a nominal ruler, for El-Afdhal, a son of El-Gemali, had the chief voice in the affairs of the kingdom. It was the army of Kasim that had captured Jerusalem. The city was besieged by the Crusaders, and it surrendered to them after forty days. Twice did new expeditions arrive from Egypt and attempt to retake the city, but with disastrous results, and further expeditions were impossible for some time, owing to the internal disorders in Egypt. Mustali died after a reign of about four years; and some historians record, as a truly remarkable circumstance, that he was a Sunnite by creed, although he represented a Shiite dynasty.

The next ruler, El-Amir, was the five-year-old son of Mustali, and El-Afdhal conducted the government until he became of age to govern. His first act was to put

El-Afdhal to death. Under El-Amir the internal condition of Egypt continued unsatisfactory, and the Crusaders, who had been very successful in capturing the
towns of Syria, were only deterred from an advance on
Egypt by the death of their leader, Baldwin. In A. H.
524, some of the surviving partisans of El-Afdhal, it is
said, put El-Amir to death, and a son of El-Afdhal assumed the direction of affairs, and appointed El-Hafiz,
a grandson of Mustanssir as caliph. Afdhal's son, whose
name was Abu Ali Ahmed, perished in a popular tumult.
The new caliph had great trouble with his next three
viziers, and at length abolished the office altogether.
After reigning twenty years, he was succeeded by his
licentious son, Dhafir, whose faults led to his death at
the hand of his vizier, El-Abbas.

For the ensuing six years the supreme power in Egypt
was mainly the bone of contention between rival viziers,
although El-Faiz, a boy of five, was nominally elected
caliph on the death of Dhafir. El-Abbas was worsted
by his rival, Tataë, and fled to Syria with a large sum
of money; but he fell into the hands of the Crusaders,
was returned to Tataë, and crucified.

The last of the Fatimite caliphs, El-Adid, in 555 A. D.,
was raised to the throne by Tataë, but his power was
merely the shadow of sovereignty. Tataë's tyranny,
however, became so odious that the caliph had him assassinated a year after his accession, but he concealed the
fact that he had instigated the murder. The caliph appointed Tataë's son, El-Adil, as vizier in his stead. The
governorship of Upper Egypt was at this time in the

hands of the celebrated Shawir, whom El-Adil dispos-
sessed, but in a test of battle, El-Adil was defeated and
put to death. In his turn, Shawir yielded to the more
powerful Ed-Durghan, and fled to Damascus. There he
enlisted the aid of the Atabeg Sultan Nur ed-Din, who

ENAMELLED GLASS CUP FROM ARABIA.

sent his army against Ed-Durghan, with the result that
Shawir was reinstated in power in Egypt. He thereupon
threw off his promised allegiance to Nur ed-Din, whose
general, Shirkuh (who had led the Damascenes to
Egypt), took up a strategic position. Shawir appealed

for aid to the Crusaders, and with the help of Amaury, King of Jerusalem, Shawir besieged his friend Shirkuh. Nur ed-Din was successfully attacking the Crusaders elsewhere, and in the end a peace was negotiated, and the Damascenes left Egypt.

Two years later, Nur ed-Din formulated a plan to punish the rebellious Shawir. Persecuted by Shirkuh, Nur ed-Din sent him with his army into Egypt. The Franks now joined with Shawir to defend the country, hoping thereby to baffle the schemes of Nur ed-Din. The Christian army was amazed at all the splendour of the caliph's palace at Cairo. Shawir retreated to entice the invaders on, who, advancing beyond their base, were soon reduced to straits. Shirkuh then tried to come to terms with Shawir against the Christians as a common foe, but without success. He next thought of retreating, without fighting, with all his Egyptian plunder. Persuaded at length to fight, he defeated the Franks and finally came to terms with Shawir, whereby the Franco-Egyptian alliance came to an end, and he then left Egypt on receiving an indemnity, Shawir still remaining its ruler.

The peace, however, did not last long, and Nur ed-Din sent Shirkuh again with many Frankish free-lancers against the ill-fated country. On the approach of the army towards Cairo, the vizier set fire to the ancient city of Fostât, to prevent it from falling into the hands of the invaders, and it burned continually for fifty days. El-Adid now sought aid of Nur ed-Din, who, actuated by zeal against the Franks, and by desire of conquest, once more despatched Shirkuh. In the meantime negotiations

had been opened with Amaury to raise the siege of Cairo
on payment of an enormous sum of money. But, before
these conditions had been fulfilled, the approach of the

GATE OF EL FUTUH AT CAIRO.

Syrian army induced Amaury to retreat in haste. Shirkuh and Saladin entered the capital in great state, and
were received with honour by the caliph, and with obse-
quiousness by Shawir, who was contriving a plot which

was fortunately discovered, and for which he paid with his life. Shirkuh was then appointed vizier by El-Adid, but, dying very shortly, he was succeeded in that dignity by his nephew Saladin (A. D. 1169).

Saladin inaugurated his reign with a series of brilliant successes. Egypt once again took an important place among the nations, and by the wars of Saladin it became the nucleus of a great empire. Military glory was never the sole aim of Saladin and his successors. They continued to extend to letters and the arts their willing patronage, and the beneficial effects of this were felt upon the civilisation of the country. Though ruler of Egypt, Saladin gained his greatest renown by his campaigns against the Crusaders in Syria. The inability of Nur ed-Din's son, El-Malik es-Salih Ismail, to govern the Syrian dominions became an excuse for Saladin's occupation of Syria as guardian of the young prince, and, once having assumed this function, he remained in fact the master of Syria. He continued to consolidate his power in these parts until the Crusaders, under Philip, Count of Flanders, laid siege to Antioch. Saladin now went out to meet them with the Egyptian army, and fought the fierce battle of Ascalon, which proved to be disastrous to himself, his army being totally defeated and his life endangered. After this, however, he was fortunate enough to gain certain minor advantages, and continued to hold his own until a famine broke out in Palestine which compelled him to come to terms with the Crusaders, and two years later a truce was concluded with the King of Jerusalem, and Saladin returned to Egypt.

In the year 576 A. H., he again entered Syria and made war on Kilidj-Arslan, the Seljukide Sultan of Anatolia, and on Leon, King of Armenia, both of whom he forced to come to terms. Soon after his return, Saladin again left Egypt to prosecute a war with the Crusaders, since it was plain that neither side was desirous of remaining at peace. Through an incident which had just occurred, the wrath of the Crusaders had been kindled. A vessel bearing fifteen hundred pilgrims had been wrecked near Damietta, and its passengers captured. When the King of Jerusalem remonstrated, Saladin replied by complaining of the constant inroads made by Renaud de Châtillon. This restless warrior undertook an expedition against Eyleh, and for this purpose constructed boats at Kerak and conveyed them on camels to the sea. But this flotilla was repulsed, and the siege was raised by a fleet sent thither by El-Adil, the brother of Saladin, and his viceroy. A second expedition against Eyleh was still more unfortunate to the Franks, who were defeated and taken prisoners. On this occasion the captives were slain in the valley of Mina. Saladin then threatened Kerak, encamped at Tiberias, and ravaged the territory of the Franks. He next made a futile attempt to take Beirut. He was more successful in a campaign against Mesopotamia, which he reduced to submission, with the exception of Mosul. While absent here, the Crusaders did little except undertake several forays, and Saladin at length returned towards Palestine, winning many victories and conquering Aleppo on the way. He next ravaged Samaria, and at last received the fealty of the lord of Mosul, though he did not succeed in actually conquering the city.

In the year 1186 war broke out again between Saladin and the Christian hosts. The sultan had respected a truce which he had made with Baldwin the Leper, King of Jerusalem, but the restless Renaud, who had previously attacked Eyleh, had broken through its stipulations. His plunder of a rich caravan enraged Saladin, who forthwith sent out orders to all his vassals and lieutenants to prepare for a Holy War. In the year 1187 he marched from Damascus to Kerak, where he laid close siege to Renaud. At the same time a large body of cavalry was sent on towards Nazareth under his son El-Afdhal. They were met by 730 Knights Hospitallers and Templars, aided by a few hundred foot-soldiers. Inspired by the heroic Jacques de Maillé, marshal of the Temple, they defied the large Saracen army. In the conflict which ensued, the Crusaders immortalised themselves by fighting until only three of their number were left alive, who, after the conflict was over, managed to escape.

Soon after this, Saladin himself approached with a great army of eighty thousand men, and the Christians with all their forces hastened to meet him upon the shores of Lake Tiberias. The result of this battle proved to be the most disastrous defeat which the Christians had yet suffered. They were weakened by thirst, and on the second day of the conflict a part of their troops fled. But the knights nevertheless continued to make a heroic defence until they were overwhelmed by numbers and forced to flee to the hills of Hittûn. A great number of Crusaders fell in this conflict, and Guy de Lusignan, King of Jerusalem, and his brother, Renaud de Châtillon, were among the prisoners of war. The number of those taken was very great, and Saladin left an indelible stain upon a reign otherwise re-

ARAB DRINKING - VESSELS.

nowned for mercy and humanity by allowing the prisoners to be massacred. Tiberias, Acre, Nabulus, Jericho, Ramleh, Cæsarea, Arsûr, Jaffa, Beirut, and many other places now fell into the hands of the conqueror. Tyre successfully resisted Saladin's attacks. Ascalon surrendered on favourable conditions, and, to crown all,

Jerusalem itself fell a prey to his irresistible arms. The great clemency of Saladin is chronicled on this occasion by Christian historians, but the same was an offence to many of the Moslems and is but little referred to by their historians.

Tyre was now again besieged and was on the point of capture when the besieged were relieved by the arrival of Conrad, son of the Marquis of Monferrat. The defence was now fought with such vigour that Saladin abandoned it and made an attack upon Tripoli, but with no better success, although he succeeded in forcing Bohemond, Prince of Antioch, and ruler of Tripoli, to submit on terms favourable to himself. After this, Saladin took part in the defence of the ever-memorable siege of Acre, which called forth deeds of gallantry and heroism on both sides, and which lasted for two years, during which it roused the interest of the whole of the Christian world. The invading army were in time reinforced by the redoubtable Richard Cœur de Lion, King of England, and Philip II. of France, and, breaking down all opposition, they captured the city, and floated upon its walls the banners of the cross in the year 1191 A. D. Unfortunately for the good name of the Christians, an act of ferocious barbarity marred the lustre of their triumph, for 2,700 Moslems were cut down in cold blood in consequence of the failure of Saladin to fulfil the terms of the capitulation; and the palliative plea that the massacre was perpetrated in the heat of the assault can scarcely be urged in extenuation of this enormity. While many historians have laid the blame on King Richard, the historian Michaud believes it rather to have been decided on in a council of the chiefs of the Crusade.

After a period of rest and debauchery, the army of the Crusaders, led on by King Richard, began to march towards Jerusalem. Saladin harassed his advance and rendered the strongholds on the way defenceless and ravaged the whole country. Richard was nevertheless ever victorious. His great personal bravery struck terror into the Moslems, and he won an important victory over them at Arsûr. Dissensions now broke out among chiefs of the Crusaders, and Richard himself proved to be a very uncertain leader in regard to the strategy of the campaign. So serious were these drawbacks that the ultimate aim of the enterprise was thereby frustrated, and the Crusaders never attained to their great object, which was the re-conquest of Jerusalem. At the time when the Christian armies were in possession of all the cities along the coast, from Jaffa to Tyre, and the hosts of Saladin were seriously disorganised, a treaty was concluded and King Richard sailed back on the return journey to England. The glory acquired by Saladin, and the famous campaigns of Richard Cœur de Lion, have rendered the Third Crusade the most memorable in history, and the exploits of the heroes on both sides shed a lustre on the arms of both Moslems and Christians.

Saladin died about a year after the conclusion of this peace, at Damascus, A. D. 1193, at the age of fifty-seven. With less rashness and bravery than Richard,

Saladin possessed a firmer character and one far better calculated to carry on a religious war. He paid
more attention to the results of his enterprises; more
master of himself, he was more fit to command others.
When mounting the throne of the Atabegs, Saladin
obeyed rather his destiny than his inclinations; but,
when once firmly seated, he was governed by only two
passions,—that of reigning and that of securing the triumph of the Koran. On all other subjects he was mod-
erate, and when a kingdom or the glory of the Prophet
was not in question, the son of Ayyub was admired as
the most just and mild of Muhammedans. The stern
devotion and ardent fanaticism that made him take up
arms against the Christians only rendered him cruel and
barbarous in one single instance. He displayed the
virtues of peace amidst the horrors of war. " From the
bosom of the camps," says an Oriental poet, " he covered the nations with the wings of his justice, and poured
upon his cities the plenteous showers of his liberality."
During his reign many remarkable public works were
executed. The Muhammedans, always governed by fear,
were astonished that a sovereign could inspire them with
so much love, and followed him with joy to battle. His
generosity, his clemency, and particularly his respect for
an oath, were often the subjects of admiration to the
Christians, whom he rendered so miserable by his victories, and of whose power in Asia he had completed
the overthrow. Previous to his death, Saladin had
divided the kingdom between his three sons; El-Afdhal
received Damascus, Southern Syria, and Palestine, with

the title of sultan; El-Aziz obtained the kingdom of Egypt, and Ez Zahir the princedom of Aleppo.

El-Aziz undertook a campaign against Syria, but was defeated and obliged to retreat to Cairo on account of a mutiny among his troops. El-Afdhal pursued him, and had already pressed forward as far as Bilbeis, when El-Adil, who had hitherto espoused his cause, fearing that he might become too powerful, forced him to conclude a peace. The only advantage he obtained was that he regained possession of Jerusalem and the southern part of Syria. Soon after, El-Adil prevailed upon his nephew Aziz, with whom he stood on friendly terms, to renew the war and to take Damascus; El-Afdhal was betrayed, and only Sarchod was left to him, whereas El-Adil occupied Damascus and forced Aziz to return to Egypt again (June, 1196). After Aziz's death, in November, 1198, El-Afdhal was summoned by some of the emirs to act as regent in Egypt. Others called upon El-Adil to adopt the same course. El-Afdhal, however, became master of Egypt, and besieged Damascus, reinforced by his brother Zahir, who feared his uncle's ambition no less than himself. The agreement between the brothers, however, did not last long; their armies separated, and El-Afdhal was obliged to raise the siege and retreat to Egypt. He was pursued by his uncle, and forced, after several skirmishes, to surrender the capital and content himself once more with Sarchod and one or two towns on the Euphrates (February, 1200). El-Adil ruled for a short time in the name of El-Aziz's son; he soon came forward as sultan, forced Zahir to recognise him as his suzerain, and appointed his son El-Muzzain as governor of Damascus; the towns which belonged to him in Mesopotamia were distributed among his other sons, and he thus became, to a certain extent, the over-lord of all the lands conquered by Saladin. His son, El-Ashraf, later became lord of Chelat in Armenia, and his descendant, Masud, Kamil's son, obtained pos-session of happy Arabia; so that the name Malik Adil was pronounced in all the Moslem chancels from the borders of Georgia to the Gulf of Aden.

El-Adil was so much engaged with wars against the Moslem princes,—the princes of Nissibis and Mardin,— and also with repulsing El-Afdhal, who wished to re-cover his lost kingdom, that he was unable to proceed with any force against the Crusaders; he took unwilling measures against them when they actually broke the peace, and was always ready to conclude a new treaty. He took Jaffa by storm when the pilgrims, armed by Henry VI., came to Palestine and interfered with the Moslem devotions, and when the chancellor Conrad there-upon seized Sidon and Beirut, El-Adil contented himself with laying waste the former town and hindering the capture of the fortress Joron; Beirut he allowed to fall into the enemy's hands. Still later he permitted several attacks of the Christians—such as the devastation of the town Fuah, situated on the Rosetta arm of the Nile— to pass unnoticed, and even bought peace at the expense of the districts of Ramleh and Lydda, which had formerly belonged to him. It was not until the year 1206 that he acted upon the offensive against the regent, John of

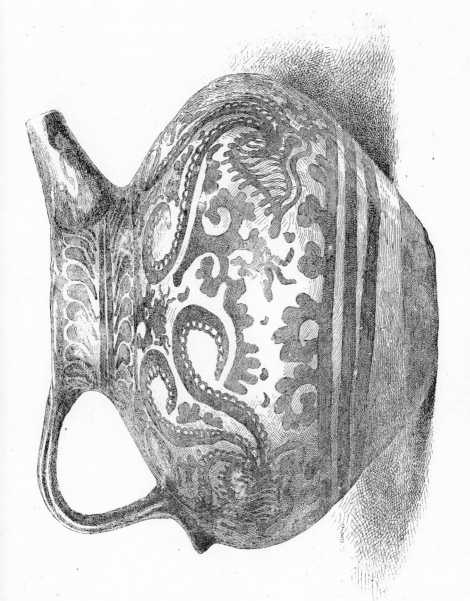

VASE IN THE ABBOTT COLLECTION, NEW YORK.

Ibelin, and even then he contented himself with slight advantages and concluded a new truce for thirty years.

Shortly before his death, El-Adil, like his brother Saladin, narrowly escaped losing all his glory and the fruits of so many victories. Pope Honorius III. had successfully aroused the zeal of the Western nations for a new Crusade. Numerous well-armed and warlike-minded pilgrims—among whom were King Andreas of Hungary and Duke Leopold of Austria—landed at Acre in 1217, and King John of Jerusalem led them against the Moslems. El-Adil hastened from Egypt to the scene of action, but was forced to retreat to Damascus and to give up the whole of the southern district, with the exception of the well-fortified holy town, to be plundered by the Christians. In the following spring, whilst El-Adil was in Syria, a Christian fleet sailed to Damietta, and besieged the town. The attacking forces were composed of Germans and Hungarians, who had embarked at Spalato on the Adriatic for St. Jean d'Acre, where they spent a year in unfortunate expeditions and quarrels with the Christians of Syria. They were joined by a fleet of three hundred boats furnished by North Germans and Frisians, who, leaving the banks of the Rhine, had journeyed there by way of the Straits of Gibraltar, prolonging the journey by a year's fighting in Portugal.

The Christians then in Palestine had persuaded the Crusaders to begin with an attack on Egypt, and they had therefore chosen to land at Damietta. This was a large commercial town to the east of one of the arms of the Nile, which was defended by three walls and a large tower built on an island in the middle of the Nile, from which started the chains that barred the river.

The Frisian sailors constructed a castle of wood, which was placed between the masts of two ships, and from which the Crusaders were able to leap to the tower, and thus they were able to blockade and starve the town. The siege was long, and an epidemic breaking out among the besiegers carried off a sixth of their number. The sultan tried to succour the besieged by floating down the stream corpses of camels, which were stuffed with provisions, but the Christians captured them. He then offered to give the Crusaders, on condition they would depart, the True Cross and all he possessed of the kingdom of Jerusalem; but Pelagius, the papal legate,—a Spanish monk who had himself named commander-in-chief,—rejected the offer.

El-Adil was so stunned by the news of the success of the Christians that he died a few days after (August, 1218). El-Kamil, however, was not discouraged; he not only defended Damietta, but also harassed the enemy in their own camp by means of hordes of Bedouins. Not until he was forced, by a conspiracy of his troops in favour of his brother El-Faiz, to fly to Cairo, did the Christians succeed in getting across the Nile and completely surrounding Damietta. Order was soon restored in Egypt, owing to the arrival of Prince Muzzain, who had taken over the government of Damascus on the death of his father. The rebels were chastised, and both brothers proceeded towards Damietta: they could not succeed, however, in raising the siege, and the garrison dimin-

ished daily through hunger, sickness, and constant attacks, and the fortress soon fell into the hands of the
Crusaders, almost without a blow (November 5, 1219).
The Crusaders pillaged the town, taking from it four
hundred thousand gold pieces. The Italians also settled
there, and made it the seat of their commerce with Egypt.

This conquest caused excite-
ment in Europe, and the
Pope called Pelagius " the
second Joshua."

If the Franks had been
more at peace among them-
selves, they might easily
have pushed forward to
Cairo after the fall of Damietta. But the greatest discontent prevailed between
the papal legate, Pelagius,
and King John of Brienne,
so that the latter soon after
left Egypt, while Pelagius
was forced to wait for reinforcements before he could
get away from Damietta.

PUBLIC FOUNTAIN, CAIRO.

El-Kamil, meanwhile, reinforced his army with the help
of the friendly Syrian princes, and, by destroying the
channels and dams of the Nile canals, so endangered the
Christian camp that they were soon forced to sue for
peace, and offered to quit Damietta on the condition of
an unmolested retreat. El-Kamil, equally anxious for

peace, accepted these conditions (August, 1221). Scarcely had the Ayyubites thus warded off the threatening danger when they proceeded to fall out among themselves.

After the death of El-Kamil, who in the end was generally regarded as overlord, a new war broke out, in March, 1238, between his son El-Adil II., who was reigning in Egypt, and his brother Ayyub, who occupied Damascus. Ayyub conquered Egypt, but, in his absence, his uncle Ismail, Prince of Balbek, seized upon Damascus and made a league with the Franks in Palestine and several of the Syrian princes. Through this unnatural league, Ismail, however, estranged not only the Moslem inhabitants of Syria, but also his own army. Part of the army deserted in consequence to Ayyub, who was thus enabled easily to subdue the allied army (1240). Another coalition was formed against him a few years later, and this time Da'ud of Kerak was one of the allies. Ayyub sent a strong army of Egyptians, negroes, and Mamluks under the future sultan, Beybars, to Syria. The Syrian troops fought unwillingly against their fellow-believers in the opposite ranks, and the wild Charizmites, who had also joined the ranks, inspired them with terror, so that they deserted the field of battle in the neighbourhood of Gaza (October, 1244). The Christians, left to themselves, were not in a position to resist the enemy's attacks; and the Egyptians made themselves masters of Jerusalem and Hebron, and in the following year obtained Damascus, Balbek, Ascalon, and Tiberias. In 1248 Ayyub came again into Syria, in order to

chastise El-Malik en-Nasir, Prince of Aleppo, who had
seized upon Hemessa when he heard of the coming Crusaders under Saint Louis. To this end he made peace
with the natives of Aleppo, and returned to Jerusalem in
order to make the necessary preparations for defence.
The pilgrims, however, succeeded in landing, for Emir
Fakhr ed-Din, the Egyptian commander, had taken to
flight after a short skirmish, and the fortress was allowed
to fall into the hands of the enemy (June, 1249). Ayyub
now established a firm footing in the town of Cairo—
which his father had founded—in a district intersected
by canals, and harassed the Christian camp with his light
cavalry. Louis was expecting reinforcements, but they
did not arrive until the inundations of the Nile made any
advance into the interior almost impossible. At last,
on the 21st of December, the Christian army arrived at
the canal of Ashmum Tanah, which alone separated them
from the town of Mansuria. The Egyptians were now
commanded by Emir Fakhr ed-Din. Ayyub had died a
month before, but his wife, Shejret ed-Durr, kept his
death a secret until his son Turan Shah should arrive
from Mesopotamia. Fakhr ed-Din did everything in his
power to retrieve his former error. He attacked the
Christians when they were engaged in building a dam
across the canal, hindering their work on the southern
bank with his throwing-machines, destroying their towers with Greek fire; and when, in spite of all discourage-
ments, their toilsome work was nearly finished, he rendered it useless by digging out a new basin, into which
he conducted the water of the Ashmum canal.

1313

On the 8th of February, 1250, the French crossed the canal, but, instead of collecting there, as the king had commanded, so as to attack the enemy *en masse*, several troops pressed forward against the Egyptians, and many, including the Count of Artois, the king's brother, were killed by the valiant enemy under Beybars. The battle remained long undecided, for the Egyptians had barricaded Cairo so well that it could only be stormed at the cost of many lives, and after the capture the army needed rest. The Egyptians took advantage of this delay to bring a fleet up in the rear of the Egyptian ships, which, in combination with the fleet stationed near Mansuria, attacked and completely destroyed them. As soon as they were masters of the Nile, the Egyptians landed troops below the Christian camp, which was thus completely cut off from Damietta, and soon suffered the greatest hardships from lack of provisions. Under these circumstances, Louis opened negotiations with Turan Shah, and when these proved fruitless, nothing remained for him but to return to Damietta. Although they began their retreat by night, they did not thus escape the vigilance of the Egyptians. The fugitives were overtaken on the following morning, and so shut in by the enemy that resistance was impossible. A large portion of the army was cut to pieces, in spite of their surrender; the rest, together with the king and his brother, were taken prisoners and brought in triumph to Cairo. Turan Shah treated the king with consideration and hastened to conclude peace with the Bahritic Mamluks,—so called because they had been brought up on the Nile (Bahr), on the island Rhodha,—as soon as the ransom money of his prisoners was assured. The Bahrites grumbled at this peace because it left the Christians in Palestine in possession of their towns, and they forthwith murdered Turan Shah, with the help of Shejret ed-Durr, whom he had maltreated (May 2, 1250).

After Turan Shah's death, his mother was proclaimed sultana, and the Mamluk Aibek became general of the army. Later, when the caliph of Baghdad revolted against the rule of a woman, Aibek assumed the title of sultan and married Shejret ed-Durr. He ruled again after some time in the name of a young descendant of Kamil, so as to be able to fight against the Ayyubids in Syria, who, with En-Nasir at their head, had taken possession of Damascus, with an appearance of right. A battle took place between Aibek and the Syrians (February, 1251), which was decided in favour of Aibek in consequence of the treachery of the Turks under Nasir. Aibek again assumed the title of sultan after the victory, but was soon after to be murdered by the Mamluks, who were unwilling to be subject to any control. He anticipated their plot, however, and slew their leader, the Emir Aktai, putting his followers to flight. He then demanded the diploma of investiture and the insignia of his office from the caliph, and also pressed the Prince of Mosul to grant him his daughter in marriage. His own wife, unable to endure such perfidy, had him murdered in his bath (April 10, 1257).

When Beybars first ascended the throne, he assumed the name of Sultan Kahir (the over-ruler), but afterwards, when he was informed that this name had always brought misfortune to its bearer, he changed it to that of Sultan Zahir (the Glorious). Now that he was absolute master of Syria and Egypt, Beybars tried to obliterate the remembrance of the misdeeds he had formerly been guilty of by means of undertakings for the general good and for the furtherance of religion. He had the mosques repaired, founded pious institutions, designed new aqueducts, fortified Alexandria, had all the fortresses repaired and provisioned which the Mongols had razed to the ground, had a large number of great and small war-ships built, and established a regular post between Cairo and Damascus. In order to obtain a semblance of legitimacy, since he was but a usurper, Beybars recognised a nominal descendant of the house of Abbas as caliph, who, in the proper course of things, ought to invest him with the dominions of Syria and Egypt. Beybars bade his governors receive this descendant of the house of the Prophet with all suitable marks of honour, and invited him to come to Egypt. When he approached the capital, the sultan himself went out to meet him, followed by the vizier, the chief cadi, and the chief emirs and notabilities of the town. Even the Jews and Christians had to take part in the procession, carrying respectively the Tora and the Gospel. The caliph made his entrance into Cairo with the greatest pomp, rode through the town amidst the shouts of the multitude, and proceeded to the citadel, where Beybars had appointed him a magnificent dwelling. Some days afterwards the caliph had a reception of the chief cadi, the most celebrated

An Egyptian Café

After the painting by Gerome

theologians and lawyers of Egypt, and many notables of the capital. The Arabs who formed his escort and an eunuch from Baghdad testified to the identity of the caliph's person, the chief cadi recognised their assertion as valid, and was the first to do homage to him as caliph. Thereupon the sultan arose, took the oath of allegiance to him and swore to uphold both the written laws of the Koran and those of tradition; to advance the good and hinder the evil, to fight zealously for the protection of the faith only, to impose lawful taxes, and to apply the taxes only to lawful purposes. After the sultan had finished, homage was done by the sheiks, the emirs, and the other chief officers of the kingdom. The caliph invested the sultan with power over all the kingdoms subject to Islam, as well as over all future conquests, whereupon the people of all classes were admitted to do homage likewise. Then command was sent out to all the distant princes and governors to do homage to the caliph, who has assumed the name of El-Mustanssir, and to place his name beside that of the sultan in their prayers and also on their coins.

Beybars' treatment of his viziers, governors, and other important emirs, one or other of whom he either imprisoned or executed on every possible occasion, was merciless, but he proceeded even more shamelessly against Malik Mughith, Prince of Kerak and Shaubek, whom he feared so much as one of the bravest descendants of the house of Ayyub that he stamped himself publicly as a perjured assassin, in order to get him out of the way. Beybars had at first, without any declaration of war, in fact, without any notification of it in Egypt, suddenly sent a detachment of troops under the leadership of Emir Bedr ed-Din Aidimri, which took the fortress Shaubek by surprise, and placed the Emir Saif ed-Din Bilban el-Mukhtasi in it as governor. In the next year, in order to win over Mughith, he liberated his son Aziz, whom Kotuz had captured at Damascus and imprisoned at Cairo; he also assured Mughith of his friendly intentions towards him and repeatedly urged him to arrange a meeting. El-Malik el-Mughith did not trust Beybars, and invented all kinds of reasons not to accept his invitations. Beybars resolved at last to calm the fears of his intended victim by means of a written oath. The fears of Mughith, however, were not allayed, and he hesitated to fall in with the wish of the sultan and to appear at his court. The following year, when the sultan came to Syria and again urged a meeting, he was at a loss for an excuse, and was forced either to acknowledge his mistrust or risk everything. He sent his mother first to Gaza, where she was received with the greatest friendliness by the sultan, and sent back laden with costly presents; on her return to Kerak, corrupted by the hospitality and generosity of the sultan, she persuaded her son to wait on him, as did also his ambassador Alamjad with equal zeal. Finally he set out from Kerak—when he had made his troops do homage to his son El-Malik el-Aziz—on a visit to the sultan, who was then in Tur. The sultan rode out to meet him as far as Beisan. Malik Mughith wished to dismount when he perceived the sultan, but he would not permit this, and rode beside

Mughith till he reached his own tent. Here he was separated from his followers, thrown into chains, and brought into the citadel of Cairo (A. H. 660). In order to palliate this crime, the sultan made public the correspondence of the Prince of Kerak with the Mongols, which it was thought would stamp the former as a traitor to Islam. The judges whom he brought with him, and amongst whom we find the celebrated historian Ibn Khallikan, who was then chief judge of Damascus, declared him guilty, but we only have historical proof of the sending of his son into Hulagu's camp to beg that his province might be spared, at a time when all the princes of Syria, seized with panic, threw themselves at the feet of the Mongolian general. Be that as it may, he none the less committed a piece of treachery, since he had sworn not to call him to account for his former crimes. Beybars hoped, now that he had disposed of Malik Mughith, that the fortress Kerak would immediately surrender to his emissary, Emir Bedr ed-Din Beisari, but the governor of the fortress feared to trust the promises of a perjurer and offered resistance. Beybars therefore set out for Syria with all the necessary siege apparatus, constructed by the best engineers of Egypt and Syria. The garrison saw the impossibility of a long resistance and capitulated.

The son of Malik Mughith, El-Malik el-Aziz, a boy of twelve, was honoured as prince and taken to Egypt, as also Mughith's family. His emirs and officials were treated with consideration, but the prince was later thrown into prison. Nothing certain is known with regard to the death of Mughith. According to some reports, because he offended the wife of Beybars, when as a wandering Mamluk he once was staying with him, he was delivered over to the sultan's wives and was put to death by them; another account says that he died of hunger in prison.

After the conquest of Shekif, the sultan made an attack on the province of Tripoli because Prince Bohmond, Governor of Antioch and Tripoli, was his bitterest enemy and the truest ally of the Mongolians, and had, moreover, at the time of Hulagu's attack on Syria, made himself master of several places which till then had belonged to the Mussulmans. The whole land was wasted, all the houses destroyed, all Christians who fell into the hands of the troops were murdered, and several strongholds in the mountains conquered. Laden with rich booty, the Moslem army set out for Hemessa. From here Beybars proceeded towards Hamah and divided the army into three divisions; one division, under the Emir Bedr ed-Din Khaznadar (treasurer), was to take the direction of Suwaidiya, the port of Antioch; the second, under Emir Izz ed-Din Ighan, struck the route towards Derbesak; the third, which he led himself, proceeded in a straight line over Apamaa and Schoghr towards Antioch, which was the meeting-place for the two other emirs, and would so be shut in from the north, the west, and the south. On the 16th May the sultan found himself in front of the town, which contained a population of over one hundred thousand. Fighting soon ensued between the outposts of the sultan and the constable who advanced against him at the head of the militia. The

latter was defeated, and the constable himself taken prisoner. On the 3d of Ramadhan the whole army had
united and preparations were made for the siege. Meanwhile the sultan had already attempted to persuade the
imprisoned constable to return to the town and enduce
them to surrender, and to leave his own son behind as
a hostage. But when several days had passed in fruitless
discussions, at last the sultan gave the word for the attack. In spite of the resistance of the Christians, the
walls were scaled on the same day, and the garrison
retired thereupon into the citadel; the inhabitants were
massacred or taken prisoner and all the houses plundered. No one could escape, for Beybars had blocked
all the entrances. On the next day the garrison, women
and children included, which numbered eight thousand,
surrendered on account of lack of water and meal. The
chiefs apparently made their escape during the confusion
and fled into the mountains. The garrison only saved
their lives by surrendering. Beybars had them chained
and distributed as slaves amongst his troops; he then
had the other prisoners and the rest of the booty brought
together, and proceeded with the lawful distribution.
When everything had been settled, the citadel was set
on fire, but the conflagration was so great that the whole
town was consumed.

Beybars died soon after his return from Asia Minor
(July 1, 1277). According to some reports his death
was occasioned by a violent fever; other accounts say
that he died in consequence of a poison which he had
prepared for an Ayyubid and which he accidentally took

himself. He had designated the eldest of his sons as his successor, under the name of El-Malik es-Said, and in order to give him a strong support he had married him to the daughter of the Emir Kilawun, one of his best and most influential generals. In spite of all this, however, es-Said was not able to maintain himself on the throne for any length of time.

Kilawun conspired against his master, and was soon able to ascend the throne under the title of El-Malik el-Mansur. His fame as a warrior was already established, and he added to his successes during his ten years' reign. His first task was to quell disturbances in Syria, and he despatched an army thither and captured Damascus. In the year 680 of the Hegira he took the field in person against a large force of Tatars, defeated them, and raised the siege of Rahabah. Eight years later he laid siege to Tripoli, then rich and flourishing after two centuries of Christian occupation, and the town was taken and its inhabitants killed. Other expeditions were undertaken against Nubia, but the Nubians, after they had been twice defeated, appear to have re-established themselves.

The fortress of Acre was at this time the only important stronghold still retained by the Christians, and for its conquest Kilawun was making preparations when he died, on the 10th of November, 1290. Kilawun, says the modern historian Weil, has been unduly praised by historians, most of whom lived in the reign of his son. He was certainly not so bloodthirsty as Beybars, and he also oppressed his subjects less. He, too, cared more

COURT IN THE MORISTAN OF KILAWUN.

for the increase and establishment of his kingdom than for justice and good faith. He held no agreement sacred, if he could get any advantage by breaking it, as was shown by his behaviour towards the Crusaders and the descendants of Beybars. The most beautiful monument which he left behind him was a huge building outside Cairo, which included a hospital, a school, and his own tomb. The hospital was so large that every disease had a special room allotted to it; there were also apartments for women, and large storerooms for provisions and medical requirements, and a large auditorium in which the head doctor delivered his lectures on medicine. The expenses were so great—for even people of wealth were taken without compensation—that special administrators were appointed to oversee and keep an account of the necessary outlay. Besides these officers, several stewards and overseers were appointed to control the revenues devoted to the hospital by different institutions. Under the dome of the tomb the Koran and traditional charters were taught, and both teachers and scholars received their payment from the state. A large adjacent hall contained a library of many works on the Koran, tradition, language, medicine, practical theology, jurisprudence, and literature, and was kept in good condition by a special librarian and six officials. The school building contained four audience-halls for the teachers of the Islamite schools, and in addition to these a school for children, into which sixty poor orphans were received without any charge and provided with board, lodging, and clothes.

Khalil, the son of Kilawun, who succeeded him, with the title of El-Malik el-Ashraf, was able to begin operations in the spring of 1291 against Acre, and on the 18th of May, after an obstinate resistance, the town was taken by storm. Those who could not escape by water were either cut down or taken prisoner; the town was plundered, then burnt, and the fortifications razed to the ground. After the fall of Acre, towns such as Tyre, Sidon, Beirut, and others, which were still in the hands of the Christians, offered no resistance, and were either deserted by their inhabitants or given up to the enemy. El-Ashraf, now that he had cleared Syria of the Crusaders, turned his arms against the Mongols and their vassals. He began with the storming of Kalat er-rum, a fortress on the Upper Euphrates in the neighbourhood of Bireh, the possession of which was important both for the defence of Northern Syria and for attacks on Armenia and Asia Minor. In spite of many pompous declarations that this was only the beginning of greater conquests in Asia Minor and Irak, he retired as soon as the Ilkhan Kaikhatu sent a strong detachment of troops against him. Later on he threatened the Prince of Armenia-Minor with war, and obliged him to hand over certain border towns. He also exchanged some threatening letters with Kaikhatu. But neither reigned long enough to make these threats good, for Kaikhatu was soon after dethroned by Baidu, and Baidu in his turn by Gazan (1295), after many civil wars which had continually hindered him from carrying on a foreign war. El-Ashraf was murdered in 1294, whilst hunting, by the

regent Baidara, whom he had threatended to turn out
of his office. Kara Sonkor, Lajin, El-Mansuri, and some
of the other emirs had conspired with Baidara in the

WINDOW IN THE MAUSOLEUM OF KILAWUN.

hope that, when once the deed was accomplished, all the
chiefs in the kingdom would applaud their action, since
El-Ashraf had slain and imprisoned many influential

emirs, and was generally denounced as an irreligious
man, who transgressed not only against the laws of Islam,
but also against those of nature. Baidara, however,
immediately proceeded to mount the throne, and a strong
party, with the Emir Ketboga at its head, was formed
against him. Ketboga called upon El-Ashraf's Mamluks
to take vengeance, pursued the rebels, and killed Baidara.
He then returned to Cairo, and, after long negotiations
with the governor of the capital, Muhammed, a younger
brother of El-Ashraf, was proclaimed sultan, with the
title of El-Malik en-Nasir.

Muhammed en-Nasir occupies such an important
place in the history of these times that the other Moslem
princes may easily be grouped around him. He was only
nine years old when he was summoned to be ruler of the
kingdom of the Mamluks. Naturally he was the sultan
only in name, and the real power lay in the hands of
Ketboga and Vizier Shujai. These two lived in perfect
harmony so long as they were merely occupied with the
pursuit of their rivals,—not only the friends and followers of El-Ashraf's murderer, but also the innocent ex-
vizier of El-Ashraf, because he had treated them with
contempt and was in possession of riches for which they
were greedy. He shared the fate of the king's assassins,
for, in spite of the intercession of the ladies of the royal
harem, he ended his life on the gallows. But as soon
as the two rulers had got rid of their enemies and ap-
peased their own avarice, their peaceful union was at
an end, for each wished to have complete control over
the sultan. Shujai had the Mamluks of the late sultan

on his side; while Ketboga, who was a Mongol by birth, had with him all the Mongols and Kurds who had settled in the kingdom during Beybars' reign. A Mongol warned Ketboga against Shujai, who had made all necessary preparations to throw his rival into prison, and he immediately was attacked by Ketboga and defeated after several attempts.

Ketboga's ambition was not yet fulfilled, although he was now supreme ruler. He first demanded homage as regent; as he met with no opposition, he conceived the idea of setting the sultan, Nasir, aside; and he hoped to carry out his plan with the assistance of Lajin and Kara Sonkor, El-Ashraf's murderers, and their numerous following. He had the pardon of these two emirs proclaimed, whereupon they left their hiding-places and joined Ketboga, for it was to their interest also that the sultan should be put out of the way. This *coup d'état* was a complete success (December, 1294), but in spite of these plans, Ketboga's reign was both unfortunate and brief. The old emirs were vexed with him because he raised his own Mamluks to the highest posts of honour, and the clergy were displeased because he received favourably a number of Mongols, although they were heathens. The people blamed him for the severe famine which visited Egypt and Syria and which was followed by a terrible pestilence. Several emirs, with Lajin again at their head, conspired against him, and forced their way into his tent while he was on the way to Syria; overpowering the guard, they attempted to get possession of his person. He managed to escape, however, and

so saved his life and liberty, but Lajin obtained possession of the throne, with the agreement of the other emirs.
In spite of his advantages, both as man and as pious
Moslem, and in spite of his brilliant victories over the
princes of Armenia, Lajin was murdered, together with
his successor, and Nasir, who was then living in Kerak,
was recalled as sultan (January, 1299).

Nasir was still too young to reign alone; he had to
let himself be ruled by the emirs who had already assumed a kind of regency before his return. At the head
of these emirs stood Sellar and Beybars Jashingir. Distrust and uneasiness existed between these two, one of
whom was regent and the other prefect of the palace, for
each wanted to assume the chief power; but soon their
private intrigues were put into the background by a
common danger. The Ilkhan Gazan was actively preparing for war against the Mamluk kingdom because the
Governor of Aleppo had fallen upon Mardin, a town belonging to the Mongols, and brutally maltreated the
inhabitants; also because the refugees from Egypt and
Syria assured him that the moment was favourable for
extending his dominion over these lands.

The internal history of Egypt at this period offers
nothing but tedious strifes between different emirs, and
specially between the two most powerful, Beybars and
Sellar, who would have often brought it to open warfare
had not their friends and followers intervened. They
agreed, however, on one point, namely, to keep the sultan
as long as possible from taking over the reins of government, and to keep him as secluded as possible in order

to deprive him of all influence. Whilst Sellar was wasting immense sums, the sultan was in fact almost starving. When Sellar went on a pilgrimage to Mecca, he paid the debts of all the Moslems who had retired to this town; he further distributed ten thousand malters of fruit amongst the poor people in the town, and so much money and provisions that they were able to live on it for a whole year. He also treated the inhabitants of Medina and Jiddah in an equally generous way. The sultan, who was hunting in Lower Egypt, at the same time tried in vain to obtain a small loan from the Alexandrian merchants, to buy a present for his wife. Finally, his vizier, who had granted him two thousand dinars ($5,060), was accused on Sellar's return of embezzling the public money, was led round the town on a donkey, and beaten and tortured so long that he succumbed under his torments.

In the year 1307, when Nasir was twenty-three years old, though still treated as a child, he attempted, with the help of the Emir Bektimur, who commanded the Mamluks in the palace, to seize the persons of his oppressors. The plan failed, for they had their spies everywhere, and the only result was that the sultan's faithful servants were banished to Syria, and the sultan himself was more oppressed than ever. It was two years before he succeeded in deceiving his tyrants. He expressed the wish to make a pilgrimage to Mecca; this was granted, as the emirs saw nothing dangerous in it, and, moreover, as a religious duty, it could not be resisted. As soon as he reached the fortress Kerak, with the help of those soldiers in his escort who were devoted to his cause, and having deceived the governor by means of false letters, he obtained possession of the fortress, and immediately declared his independence of the guardianship of Sellar and Beybars. Sellar and Beybars, on hearing this, immediately summoned the sultan to return to Cairo; but, even before they received his answer, they realised that their rule was over, and that either they must quit the field, or Nasir must be dethroned. After long consideration amongst themselves, they proceeded to the choice of another sultan, and the choice fell on Beybars (April, 1309). Beybars accepted the proffered throne on the condition that Sellar also retained his place. He confirmed the other emirs also in their offices, hoping thereby to gain their support.

The change of government met with no resistance in Egypt, where the majority of the emirs had long been dependent on Beybars and Sellar. In Syria, on the other hand, the emirs acting as governors refused to acknowledge Beybars, partly from devotion to Nasir's race, and partly because the choice had been made without their consent. Only Akush, Governor of Damascus, who was an old friend of Beybars, and like him a Circassian, took the oath of allegiance. . The governors of Aleppo, Hamah, and Tripoli, together with the governors of Safed and Jerusalem, called upon Nasir to join them, and, with the help of his other followers, to reconquer Egypt. The cunning sultan, who saw that the time for open resistance had not yet arrived, since Egypt was as yet too unanimous, and Damascus also had joined the enemy,

INTERIOR OF THE MOSQUE OF KILAWUN.

advised them to deceive Beybars and to take the oath
of allegiance, which they could break later, as having
been obtained by force. He himself feigned to submit
to the new government, and even had the prayers carried
on from the chancel in Beybars' name. Beybars was
deceived, although he knew with certainty that Nasir
carried on a lively intercourse with the discontented
emirs. He relied chiefly on Akush, who kept a strict
watch over Nasir's movements. The spies of Akush,
however, were open to corruption, and they failed later
to take steps to render Nasir harmless at the right moment. Beybars believed Nasir to be still in Kerak, when
he was well on the way to Damascus; and when he finally
received news of this, the rebellion had already gone so
far that some of the troops who had been sent out against
the sultan had already deserted to his side. The only
possible way of allaying the storm was for Beybars to
put himself at the head of his troops, and, joining forces
with Akush, to offer battle to Nasir. The necessary courage and resolution failed him. Instead of having re-
course to the sword, he applied to the caliph, who declared Nasir an exile, and summoned all believers to
listen to the Sultan Beybars—whom he had consecrated
—and to take part in the war against the rebel, Nasir.
But the summons of the caliph, which was read in all
the chancels, had not the slightest effect. The belief
in the caliph had long disappeared, except in so far as
he was considered a tool of the sultan on whom he
depended. Even Beybars' party mocked the caliph's
declaration, and wherever it was read manifestations

were made in favour of the exile. Beybars, also, was now deserted by Sellar, and he at length was obliged to resign. Beybars was then seized and throttled by Nasir, and Sellar was starved to death.

Nasir, who now came to the throne, had grown suspicious and treacherous on account of the many hardships and betrayals endured by him during his youth. He was, however, favourable to the Christians, and to such an extent that he received anonymous letters reproaching him for allowing Moslems to be oppressed by Christian officials. He found them to be experienced in financial matters, for, in spite of all decrees, they had never ceased to hold secretaryships in different states: they were, moreover, more unscrupulous than born Muhammedans, who always had more respect for law, custom, and public opinion. Certainly the sultan considered the ministers in whom he placed great confidence less dangerous if they were *non*-Moslems, since he was their only support, whereas comrades in religion could always find plenty of support and might easily betray him.

Nasir died on the 6th of June, 1341, at about fifty-eight years of age, after a reign of forty-three years. His rule, which did not actually begin until he mounted the throne for the third time, lasted thirty-two years. During this period he was absolute ruler in the strongest sense of the word; every important affair was decided by him alone. The emirs had to refer all matters to him, and were a constant source of suspicion and oversight. They might not speak to each other in his presence, nor visit each other without his consent. The mildest punishment for breaking such decrees was banishment to Syria. Nasir inspired them with fear rather than with love and respect, and, as soon as it was known that his illness was incurable, no one paid any further attention to him. He died as a pious Moslem and repentant sinner in the presence of some of his servants. His burial, which took place by night, was attended by a few emirs, and only one wax candle and one lamp were carried before the bier. As one of his biographers justly remarks, the rich sultan, whose dominion had extended from the borders of Abyssinia to Asia Minor and up the Euphrates as far as Tunis, and the father of a large family, ended his life like a stranger, was buried like a poor man, and brought to his grave like a man without wife or child. Nasir was the last sultan who ruled over the Bahritic Mamluk kingdom with a firm hand. After his death we read of one insurrection after another, and the sultans were either deposed or became mere slaves of the emirs.

Abu Bekr, whom Nasir had appointed his successor, did not hold his own for quite two months, because he maltreated the discontented emirs and put his favourites in their places. An insurrection, with the Emir Kausun at its head, was formed against him; he was dethroned and his six-year-old brother Kujuk was proclaimed sultan in his stead. The dethroned sultan was banished to Upper Egypt, whither his elder brother Ahmed should have been brought; Ahmed, however, refused to leave his fortress of Kerak, and, finding support among the Syrian emirs, he conspired against Kausun, who was at this moment threatened also with an insurrection in

Cairo. After several bloody battles, Kausun was forced to yield, and Ahmed was proclaimed sultan (January, 1342). Ahmed, however, preferred a quiet, peaceful life to the dangerous post of sultan, and not until he had received the most solemn oaths of allegiance did he proceed to his capital, where he arrived quite unexpectedly, so that no festivities had been prepared. After some time, he had all the Syrian emirs arrested by his Mamluks, because they tried to usurp his powers; he then appointed a regent, and himself returned to Kerak, taking with him everything he had found in the sultan's palace, and there he remained in spite of the entreaties of the faithful emirs, and lived simply for his own pleasure.

The natural consequence of all this was Ahmed's deposition in June, 1342. His brother Ismail, a good-hearted youth of seventeen years, sent troops to Kerak to demand an oath of allegiance from Ahmed, but they could effect nothing, as the fortress was well fortified and provisioned, and, moreover, many of the emirs, both in Syria and Egypt, were still in league with Ahmed. Not until fresh troops had been sent, and Ahmed himself betrayed, did they succeed in taking the fortress; and Ahmed was put to death in 1344. Ahmed's death made such a deep impression upon the weak sultan that he fell into a fit of depression which gradually increased until he died in August of the following year.

His brother and successor, Shaban, was an utter profligate, cruel, faithless, avaricious, immoral, and pleasure-loving. Gladiators played an important part at his court, and he often took part in their contests. Horse-racing, cock-fights, and such like amusements occupied him much more than state affairs, and the whole court followed his example. As long as Shaban did not offend the emirs, he was at liberty to commit any atrocities he pleased, but, as soon as he seized their riches and imprisoned and tortured them, his downfall was certain. Ilbogha, Gov-

FRIEZE IN MOSQUE OF SULTAN HASAN.

ernor of Damascus, supported by the other Syrian emirs, sent him a list of his crimes and summoned him to abdicate. Meanwhile an insurrection had broken out in Cairo, and, although Shaban expressed his willingness to abdicate, he was murdered by the rebels in September, 1346. His brother Haji met with a similar fate after a reign of fifteen months, though some accounts affirm that he was not murdered but only exiled.

Haji was succeeded by his brother Hasan, who was still a minor; the emirs who ruled in his name competed for the highest posts until Baibagharus and his brother Menjik carried off the victory. These two ruled supreme for a time. The so-called " black death " was ravaging Egypt; many families were decimated, and their riches fell to the state. The disease, which differed from the ordinary pest in the blood-spitting and internal heat, raged in Europe and Asia, and spread the greatest consternation even amongst the Moslems, who generally regarded disease with a certain amount of indifference, as being a divine decree. According to Arabic sources, the black death had broken out in China and from there had spread over the Tatar-land of Kipjak; from here it took its course towards Constantinople, Asia Minor, and Syria on the one hand, and towards Greece, Italy, Spain, France, and Germany on the other, and was probably brought to Egypt from Syria. Not only men, but beasts and even plants were attacked. The ravages were nowhere so fearful as in Egypt; in the capital alone in a few days as many as fifteen or twenty thousand people were stricken. As the disease continued to rage for two years, there was soon a lack of men to plough the fields and carry on the necessary trades; and to increase the general distress, incursions were made by the tribes of Turcomans and Bedouins, who plundered the towns and villages. Scarcely had this desperate state of affairs begun to improve when court intrigues sprang up afresh, and only ended with the deposition of the sultan in August, 1351. He was recalled after three years,

during which his brother had reigned, and he was subsequently deposed and put to death in March, 1361. Finally the descendants of Nasir, instead of his sons, began
to rule. First came Muhammed Ibn Haji, who, as soon
as he began to show signs of independence, was declared
to be of unsound mind by his chief emir, Ilbogha; then
Shaban, the son of Husain (May, 1363), who was stran-
gled in March, 1377; and finally Husain's eight-year-old
son Ali. After repeated contests, Berkuk and Berekeh,
two Circassian slaves, placed themselves at the head of
the government. Berkuk, however, wished to be absolute,
and soon put his co-regent out of the way (1389). He
contented himself at first with being simply regent, and,
even when Ali died, he declared his six-year-old brother
Haji, sultan. The following year, when he discovered
a conspiracy of the Mamluks against him, and when
many of the older emirs were dead, he declared that it
was for the good of the state that no longer a child,
but a man capable of directing internal affairs and leading an army against the enemy, should take over the
government. The assembly, whom he had bribed beforehand, supported him, and he was appointed sultan in
November, 1382.

The external history of Egypt during this time is but
scanty. She suffered several defeats at the hands of the
Turcomans in the north of Syria, lost her supremacy in
Mecca through the influence of the princes of South
Arabia, and both Alexandria and several other coast
towns were attacked and plundered by European fleets.
This last event occurred in Shaban's reign in 1365. Peter

of Lusignan, King of Cyprus, had, in league with the Genoese, the Venetians, and Knights of Rhodes, placed himself at the head of a new Crusade, and since his expedition was a secret even in Europe,—for he was thought to be advancing against the Turks,—it was easy for him to take the Egyptians by surprise, and all the more so because the Governor of Alexandria happened to be absent at the time. The militia tried in vain to prevent their landing, and the small garrison held out for but a short time, so that the prosperous and wealthy town was completely sacked and many prisoners were taken before the troops arrived from Cairo.

The Christians living in Egypt suffered from this attack of the King of Cyprus. They had to find ransom money for the Moslem prisoners and to provide means for fitting out a new fleet. All negotiations with Cyprus, Genoa, and Venice were immediately broken off. This event, however, had the effect of reconciling the Italian traders again with Egypt, and an embassy came both from Genoa and Venice, expressing regret at what had happened, with the assurance that the government had had no hint of the intentions of the King of Cyprus. Genoa also sent back sixty prisoners who had fallen to them as their share of the Alexandrian booty. As Egypt's trade would also be at a standstill if they had no further negotiations with the Franks, who imported wood, metal, arms, oil, coral, wool, manufacturing and crystal wares in exchange for spices, cotton, and sugar, the former trade relations were re-established. The war with Cyprus continued, however; Alexandria was again

INSIDE THE MOSQUE OF HASAN.

threatened and Tripoli was surprised by the Cyprian fleet, whereupon a number of European merchants in Egypt were arrested. In the year 1370, after the death of Peter of Lusignan, peace and an exchange of prisoners were finally brought about. After this peace the Egyptians were able to concentrate their whole force against Leo VI., Prince of Smaller Armenia, who was brought as a prisoner to Cairo; and with him the supremacy of the Christians in this land was at an end: henceforth Egypt was ruled by Egyptian governors.

Faraj, Berkuk's son and successor, had to suffer for his father's political mistakes. He had scarcely ascended the throne when the Ottomans seized Derenda, Albustan, and Malatia. Preparations for war were made, but given up again when it was seen that Bayazid could not advance any farther south. Faraj was only thirteen years old, and all the old intrigues amongst the emirs broke out again. In Cairo they fought in the streets for the post of regent; anarchy and confusion reigned in the Egyptian provinces, and the Syrians wished to revolt against the sultan. When at last peace was re-established in Egypt, and Syria was reduced, the latter country was again attacked by the hordes of Tamerlane.

Tamerlane conquered the two important cities of Aleppo and Hemessa, and Faraj's forces returned to Egypt. When the sultan's ally, Bayazid, was defeated, Faraj concluded a peace with Tamerlane, at the price of the surrender of certain lands. In 1405 Tamerlane died, and Faraj was collecting troops for the purpose of recovering Syria when domestic troubles caused him to flee from Egypt, his own brother Abd el-Aziz heading the insurrection. In the belief that Faraj was dead, Aziz was proclaimed his successor, but three months later Faraj was restored, and it was not until 1412 that he was charged with illegal practices and beheaded, his body being left unburied like that of a common malefactor. The fact that criminal proceedings were brought against the sultan is evidence of a great advance in the spirit of civilisation, but the event must be regarded more as a proof of its possibility than as a demonstration of its establishment.

The Caliph El-Mustain was then proclaimed sultan, but after some months he was dethroned and his former prime minister, Sheikh Mahmudi, took over the reins of government (November, 1412). Although Sheikh had obtained the throne of Egypt so easily, he experienced great difficulty in obtaining the recognition of the emirs. Newruz, Governor of Damascus, in league with the other governors, made a determined resistance, and he was obliged to send a strong army into Syria to put down the rebels. Newruz, after suffering one defeat, threw himself into the citadel of Damascus and capitulated, when Sheikh had sworn to keep the terms of the capitulation. Newruz's ambassadors, however, had not a sufficient knowledge of Arabic to perceive that the oath was not binding, and when Newruz, trusting to this oath, appeared before Sheikh, he was immediately thrown into chains, and afterwards murdered in prison because the cadis declared the oath was not binding. In the next year (1415) Sheikh was obliged to make another expedition against Syria to re-conquer some of the places of which the smaller princes had taken possession during the civil war. One of these princes was the Prince Muhammed of Karaman, who had taken the town of Tarsus. Sheikh was summoned by Muhammed's own brother to overcome him, which he easily succeeded in doing. Many other princes were forced to submit, and

MOSQUE OF BERKUK.

finally the town of Malatia, which the Turcoman Husain had stormed, was recaptured. The war against Husain and the Prince of Karaman was to have been continued, but Sheikh was forced to return home, owing to a wound in his foot. As soon as certain misunderstandings between Sheikh and Kara Yusuf had been cleared up, another army was despatched into Asia Minor, for Tarsus had been recaptured by the Prince of Karaman, who had driven out the Prince of Albustan, whom Sheikh had installed. Ibrahim, the sultan's son, took command of this army, and occupied Cæsarea, Nigdeh, and Karaman. Whilst he was occupied in the interior of Asia Minor, the Governor of Damascus had defeated Mustapha, son of the Prince of Karaman, and the Prince Ibrahim of Ramadhan, near Adana, which latter town, as well as Tarsus, he had re-conquered.

The Prince of Karaman, who now advanced against Cæsarea, suffered a total defeat. Mustapha remained on the field of battle, but his father was taken prisoner and sent to Cairo, where he lingered in confinement until after the death of the sultan.

Once again was Syria threatened by Kara Yusuf, but he was soon forced to return to Irak by the conspiracy of his own son, Shah Muhammed, who lived in Baghdad. As soon as this insurrection was put down, Kara Yusuf was obliged to give his whole attention to Shah Roch, the son of Tamerlane, who had raised himself to the highest power in Persia, and was now attempting to re-conquer the province of Aderbaijan. Kara Yusuf placed himself at the head of an army to protect this province, but suddenly died (November, 1420) on the way to Sultania, and his possessions were divided among his four sons, Shah Muhammed, Iskander, Ispahan, and Jihan Shah, who all, just as the descendants of Tamerlane had done, immediately began to quarrel among themselves.

The sultan was already very ill when the news of Kara Yusuf's death reached him. The death of Ibrahim,

his son, whom he had caused to be poisoned, on his
return from Asia Minor, weighed heavily upon him and
hastened his death, which took place on January 13, 1421.
He left immense riches behind him, but could not obtain
a proper burial; everything was at once seized by the
emirs, who did not trouble themselves in the least about

THE TOMB OF BERKUK.

his corpse. He had been by no means a good sultan;
he had brought much misery upon the people, and had
oppressed the emirs. But in spite of all he had many
admirers who overlooked his misdeeds and cruelty, because he was a pious Moslem; that is, he did not openly
transgress against the decrees of Islam, favoured the
theologians, and distinguished himself as an orator and

poet; he also founded a splendid mosque, a hospital, and a school for theology. His whole life abounds in contrasts. After he had broken his oath to Newruz, he spent several days in a cloister to make atonement for this crime, and was present at all the religious ceremonies and dances. Although he shed streams of blood to satisfy his avarice, he wore a woollen garment, and bade the preachers, when they mentioned his name after that of Muhammed, to descend a step on the staircase of the chancel. Under a religious sultan of this stamp, the position of the non-Muhammedans was by no means an enviable one. The Jews and Christians had to pay enormous taxes and the old decrees against them were renewed. Not only were they forced to wear special colours, but the length of their sleeves and head-bands was also decreed, and even the women were obliged to wear a distinctive costume.

Sheikh appointed his son Ahmed, one year old, as his successor, and named the emirs who were to act as regents until he became of age. Tatar, the most cunning and unscrupulous of these emirs, soon succeeded in obtaining the supreme power and demanded homage as sultan (August 29, 1421); but he soon fell ill and died after a reign of about three months. He, too, appointed a young son as his successor and named the regents, but Bursbai also soon grasped the supreme power and ascended the throne in 1422. He had of course many insurrections to quell, but was not obliged to leave Egypt. As soon as peace was restored in Syria, Bursbai turned his attention to the European pirates, who had long been harassing the coasts of Syria and Egypt. They were partly Cypriots and partly Catalonians and Genoese, who started from Cyprus and landed their booty on this island. Bursbai resolved first to conquer this island. He despatched several ships with this object in view; they landed at Limasol, and, having burnt the ships in the harbour and plundered the town, they returned home. The favourable result of this expedition much encour-

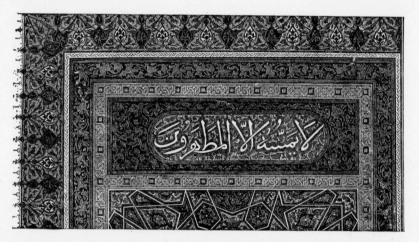

A TITLE-PAGE OF THE KORAN OF THE TIME OF SHABAN.

aged the sultan, and in the following year he sent out a large fleet from Alexandria which landed in Famagosta. This town soon surrendered and the troops proceeded to plunder the neighbouring places, and defeated all the troops which Prince Henry of Lusignan sent out against them. When they had advanced as far as Limasol, the Egyptian commander, hearing that Janos, the King of Cyprus, was advancing with a large army against him, determined to return to Egypt to bring his enormous booty into safety. In July, 1426, a strong Egyptian fleet set out for the third time, landed east of Limasol, and took this fortress after a few days' fighting. The Moslem army was, however, forced to retreat. But the Cypriots scattered instead of pursuing the enemy, and the Mamluks, seeing this, renewed their attack, slew many Christians and took the king prisoner. The capital, Nicosia, then capitulated, whereupon the Egyptian troops returned to Egypt with the captive king and were received with great jubilation. The King of Cyprus, after submitting to the greatest humiliations, was asked what ransom he could pay. He replied that he possessed nothing but his life, and stuck to this answer, although threatened with death. Meanwhile, Venetian and other European merchants negotiated for the ransom money, and the sultan finally contented himself with two hundred thousand dinars (about $500,000). Janos, however, was not set at liberty, but sent to Cyprus as the sultan's vassal. After the death of Janos in 1432, his son, John II., still continued to pay tribute to Egypt, and when he died (1458) and his daughter Charlotte became Queen of Cyprus, James II., the natural son of John II., fled to Egypt and found a friendly reception at the sultan's court. The sultan then ruling was Inal, and he promised to re-install James as King of Cyprus. Meanwhile messengers arrived from the queen, offering a higher tribute, and Inal allowed himself to be persuaded by his emirs to acknowledge Charlotte as queen, and to hand James over to her ambassadors. But as soon as the ambassadors had left the audience-chamber, a tumult

arose; the people declared that the sultan had only the
advantage of the Franks—especially of Prince Louis of
Savoy—in view, and they soon took such a threatening

PRAYER-NICHE IN THE MOSQUE OF THE SULTAN MAHMUDI.

attitude that Inal was forced to declare himself for James
again and renew his former preparations. In August,
1460, an Egyptian fleet bore James to Cyprus, and with
the help of the Egyptian troops he soon obtained

the island, with the exception of the fortress Cerines, which Queen Charlotte still had in her power. The majority of the Egyptian troops now returned to Egypt, and only some hundred men remained with James. Later, when the Genoese declared themselves on the side of Charlotte, fresh troops had to be sent out from Egypt, but, as soon as James had taken Famagosta and had no further need of them, he dismissed them (1464).

Bursbai despised no means by which he might enrich himself; he appropriated the greater part of the inheritance of the Jews and Christians; he even taxed poor pilgrims, in spite of the fact that he was a pious Moslem, prayed much, fasted, and read the Koran. He turned Mecca into a money-market. At the very moment when pious pilgrims were praying for the forgiveness of their sins, one of his heralds was proclaiming: " Whoever buys wares and does not pay toll for them in Egypt has forfeited his life." That is to say, all wares bought in Mecca or Jiddah had to go out of their way to Egypt in order to be laid under toll in this land.

In appointing his son Yusuf to the consulship, Bursbai counted on the devotedness of his Mamluks, and the Emir Jakmak, whom he appointed as his chief adviser, and, in fact, Yusuf's coronation, in June, 1438, met with no resistance. After three months, however, Jakmak, feeling himself secure, quietly assumed the sultan's place; at first he had much resistance to put down, but soon his prudence and resolution established him safely in spite of all opposition. As soon as the rebels in the interior had been dealt with, Yusuf, as a good Muham-

medan, wished to attack the Christians, and chose the
island of Rhodes as the scene of the Holy War, hoping
to obtain this island as easily as Bursbai had obtained
the island of Cyprus. But the Order of St. John, to
whom this island belonged, had its spies in Egypt, so
that the sultan's intentions were discovered and preparations for defence were made. The only result of the
sultan's repeated expeditions was the devastation of

ORNAMENTAL PAGE FROM A KORAN OF THE FOURTEENTH CENTURY.

some unimportant coast towns; all attempts on the capital failed, so that the siege was soon raised and peace
concluded with the chief master of Rhodes (1444).

Jakmak's relations with the foreign chiefs were most
friendly. He constantly exchanged letters and gifts with
both Sultan Murad and Shah Roch. The sons of Kara
Yelek and the princes of the houses of Ramadhan and
Dudgadir submitted to him; also Jihangir, Kara Yelek's

grandson and Governor of Amid, tried to secure his friendship, as did the latter's deadly enemy, Jihan Shah, the son of Kara Yusuf.

Jakmak's rule was mild compared with that of Burs-bai, and we hear less of extraordinary taxes, extortions, executions, and violence of the Mamluks. Although he was beloved by the people and priests on account of his piety, he could not secure the succession of his son Os-man, in favour of whom he abdicated fourteen days before his death (February, 1453). Osman remained only a month and a half on the throne; he made him-self odious to the emirs who did not belong to his Mam-luks. The Mamluks of his predecessors conspired against him, and at their head stood his own Atabeg, the Emir Inal, a former Mamluk of Berkuk. Osman was warned, but he only mocked those who recommended him to watchfulness, since he believed his position to be unas-sailable. He had forgotten that his father was a usurper, who, although himself a perjurer, hoped to bind others by means of oaths. His eyes were not opened until he had lost all means of defence. He managed to hold out for seven days, after which the citadel was captured by the rebels, and he was forced to abdicate on the 19th of March. Inal became, even more than his predecessors had been, a slave to those Mamluks to whom he owed his kingdom. They committed the greatest atrocities and threatened the sultan himself when he tried to hold them in check. They plundered corpses on their way to the grave, and attacked the mosques during the hours of service in order to rob the pilgrims.

MOSQUE OF KAIT BEY, CAIRO.

They were so hated and feared that, when many of them were carried off by the plague, their deaths were recorded by a contemporary historian as a benefit to all classes of society.

In the hour of his death (26th February, 1461), Inal appointed his son Ahmed as his successor, but the latter was no more able to maintain himself on the throne than his predecessors had been, in spite of his numerous good qualities. He was forced to submit in the strife with his emirs, and on the 28th of June, 1461, after a reign of four months and three days, he was dethroned, and the Emir Khosh Kadem, a former slave of the Sultan Sheikh, of Greek descent, was proclaimed in his stead. Khosh Kadem reigned for seven years with equity and benignity, and under one of his immediate successors, El-Ashraf Kait Bey, a struggle was begun with the Ottoman Turks. On the death of Muhammed II., dissensions had arisen between Bayazid II. and Jem. Jem, being defeated by Bayazid, retired to Egypt, which led to the invasion and conquest of Syria, hitherto held by the Sultan of Egypt. On surrendering Tarsus and Adana to Bayazid, Kait Bey was suffered to end his days in peace in A. D. 1495. After many dissensions, the brave and learned El-Ghuri ascended the throne, and Selim I., the Turkish sultan, soon found a pretext for an attack upon the Mamluk power. A long and sanguinary battle was fought near Aleppo, in which El-Ghuri was finally defeated through treachery. He was trampled to death by his own cavalry in their attempt to escape from the pursuing Ottomans. With his death, in A. D. 1516, Egypt lost her independence. Tuman Bey, a nephew of the deceased, fiercely contested the advance of the Ottomans, but was defeated and treacherously killed by the Turks.

A long period of Turkish misrule now opened for the ill-fated country, though some semblance of conciliation was attempted by Selim's appointment of twenty-

WADI FEIRAN, IN THE SINAI PENINSULA.

four Mamluk beys as subordinate rulers over twenty-four military provinces of Egypt. These beys were under the control of a Turkish pasha, whose council was formed of seven Turkish chiefs, while one of the Mamluk beys held the post of Sheikh el-Beled or Governor of the Metropolis. For nearly two centuries the Turkish pashas were generally obeyed in Egypt, although there were frequent intrigues and quarrels on the part of

MAUSOLEUM OF EL-GHURI.

competing Mamluk beys to secure possession of the coveted post of Sheikh el-Beled. Towards the middle of the eighteenth century the authority of the Turkish pashas had become merely nominal, while that of the beys had increased to such an extent that the government of Egypt became a military oligarchy. The weakness of the Turks left the way open for the rise of any adventurer of ability and ambition who might aspire to lead the Mamluks to overthrow the sovereignty of the Porte.

In the year 1768 the celebrated Ali Bey headed a revolt against the Turks, which he maintained for several years with complete success. A period of good but vigorous government lasted during the years in which he successfully resisted the Ottoman power. Ali's generals also gained for him considerable influence beyond the borders of Egypt. Muhammed Abu Dhahab was sent by him to Arabia and entered the sacred city of Mecca, where the sherif was deposed. Ali also despatched an expedition to the eastern shores of the Red Sea, and Muhammed Bey, after his successes in Arabia, invaded Syria and wrested that province from the power of the sultan. The victorious soldier, however, now plotted against his master and took the lead in a military revolt. As a result of this, Ali Bey fell into an ambuscade set by his own rebellious subjects, and died from poisoning in 1786. Thus terminated the career of the famous Mamluk, a man whose energy, talents, and ambition bear a strong resemblance to those of the later Mehemet Ali.

Muhammed Bey, the Mamluk who had revolted against Ali Bey, now tendered his allegiance to the Porte. To the title of Governor of the Metropolis was also added that of Pasha of Egypt. He subdued Syria, and died during the pillage of Acre.

After his death violent dissensions again broke out. The Porte supported Ismail Bey, who retained the post of Governor of the Metropolis (Sheikh el-Beled) until the terrible plague of 1790, in which he perished.

His former rivals, Ibrahim and Murad, now returned; and eight years later were still in the leadership when the news was brought to Egypt that a fleet carrying thirty thousand men, under Bonaparte, had arrived at Alexandria on an expedition of conquest.

Bonaparte in Egypt
From painting by M. Orange

ORNAMENTAL GIRDLING OF THE MORISTAN OF KILWUN.

CHAPTER II

THE FRENCH IN EGYPT

Napoleon's campaign: Battles of the Pyramids and of Abukir: Siege of Acre:
Kléber's administration : The evacuation of Egypt.

T the close of the eighteenth century
Egypt's destiny passed into the hands
of the French. Napoleon's descent upon
Egypt was part of his vast strategic
plan for the overthrow of Great Britain.
He first of all notified the Directory of
this design in September, 1797, in a letter sent from Italy.
Late in the same year and during 1798 vast preparations
had been in progress for the invasion of England. Napoleon then visited all the seaports in the north of France
and Holland, and found that a direct invasion of England
was a practical impossibility because the British held
command over the sea. The suggested invasion of Egypt
was now seriously considered. By the conquest of Egypt,
it was contended, England would be cut off from the
possession of India, and France, through Egypt, would

81

dominate the trade to the Orient. From Egypt Napoleon could gather an army of Orientals and conquer the whole of the East, including India itself. On his return, England would prove to be too exhausted to withstand the French army at home and would fall a prey to the ambitions of the First Consul. The Directory assented to Bonaparte's plans the more readily because they were anxious to keep so popular a leader, the idol of the army, at a great distance from the centre of government. While the preparations were in process, no one in England knew of this undertaking. The French fleet lay in various squadrons in ports of Italy, from which thirty thousand men were embarked.

Bonaparte arrived at Toulon on May 9, 1798. His presence rejoiced the army, which had begun to murmur and to fear that he would not be at the head of the expedition. It was the old army of Italy, rich and covered with glory, and hence had much less zeal for making war; it required all the enthusiasm with which the general inspired his soldiers to induce them to embark and proceed to an unknown destination. On seeing him at Toulon, they were inflamed with ardour. Bonaparte, without acquainting them with their destination, exhorted the soldiers, telling them that they had great destinies to fulfil, and that " the genius of liberty, which had made the republic from her birth the arbitress of Europe, decreed that she should be so to the most remote seas and nations."

The squadron of Admiral Brueys consisted of thirteen sail of the line, and carried about forty thousand men of all arms and ten thousand seamen. It had water for one month and provisions for two. It sailed on the 19th of May, amid the thunders of the cannons and the cheers of the whole army. Violent gales did some damage to a frigate on leaving the port, and Nelson, who was cruising with three sail of the line in search of the French fleet, suffered so severely from the same gales that he was

BEDOUINS IN THE DESERT.

obliged to bear up for the islands of St. Pierre to refit. He was thus kept at a distance from the French fleet, and did not see it pass. It steered first towards Genoa to join the convoy collected in that port, under the command of General Baraguay d'Hilliers. It then sailed for Corsica, to call for the convoy at Ajaccio commanded by Vaubois, and afterwards proceeded to the sea of Sicily to join the division of Civita Vecchia, under the command of Desaix.

Bonaparte's intention was to stop at Malta, and there to make by the way a bold attempt, the success of which he had long since prepared by secret intrigues. He meant to take possession of that island, which, commanding the navigation of the Mediterranean, became important to Egypt and could not fail soon to fall into the hands of the English, unless they were anticipated.

Bonaparte made great efforts to join the division from Civita Vecchia; but this he could not accomplish until he was off Malta. The five hundred French sail came in sight of the island on June 9th, twenty-two days after leaving Toulon. This sight filled the city of Malta with consternation. The following day (June 10th) the French troops landed on the island, and completely invested Valetta, which contained a population of nearly thirty thousand souls, and was even then one of the strongest fortresses in Europe. The inhabitants were dismayed and clamoured for surrender, and the grand master, who possessed little energy, and recollected the generosity of the conqueror of Rivoli at Mantua, hoping to save his interest from shipwreck, released one of the French knights, whom he had thrown into prison when they refused to fight against their countrymen, and sent him to Bonaparte to negotiate. A treaty was soon concluded, by which the Knights of Malta gave up to France the sovereignty of Malta and the dependent islands. Thus France gained possession of the best harbour in the Mediterranean, and one of the strongest in the world. It required the ascendency of Bonaparte to obtain it without fighting; and it necessitated also the risk of

THE OLD HARBOUR OF ALEXANDRIA.

losing some precious days, with the English in pursuit of him.

The French fleet weighed anchor on the 19th of June, after a stay of ten days. The essential point now was not to fall in with the English. Nelson, having refitted at the islands of St. Pierre, had returned on June 1st to Toulon, but the French squadron had been gone twelve days. He had run from Toulon to the roads of Taglia-mon, and from the roads of Tagliamon to Naples, where he had arrived on June 20th, at the very moment when Bonaparte was leaving Malta. Learning that the French had been seen off Malta, he followed, determined to attack them, if he could overtake them. At one moment, the English squadron was only a few leagues distant from the immense French convoy, and neither party was aware of it. Nelson, supposing that the French were bound for Egypt, made sail for Alexandria, and arrived there before them; but not finding them, he flew to the Dardanelles to seek them there. By a singular fate, it was not till two days afterwards that the French expedition came in sight of Alexandria, on the 1st of July, which was very nearly six weeks since it sailed from Toulon. Bonaparte immediately sent on shore for the French consul. He learned that the English had made their appearance two days before, and, supposing them to be not far off, he resolved that very moment to attempt a landing. It was impossible to enter the harbour of Alexandria, for the place appeared disposed to defend itself; it became necessary, therefore, to land at some distance on the neighbouring coast, at an inlet called the

Creek of the Marabou. The wind blew violently and the sea broke with fury over the reefs on the shore. It was near the close of the day, but Bonaparte gave the signal and resolved to go on shore immediately. He was the first to disembark, and, with great difficulty, four or five thousand men were landed in the course of the evening and the following night. Bonaparte resolved to march forthwith for Alexandria, in order to surprise the place and to prevent the Turks from making preparations for defence. The troops instantly commenced their march. Not a horse was yet landed: the staff of Bonaparte, and Caffarelli himself, notwithstanding his wooden leg, had to walk four or five leagues over the sands, and came at daybreak within sight of Alexandria.

That ancient city no longer possessed its magnificent edifices, its innumerable houses, and its immense population. Three-fourths of it was in ruins. The Turks, the wealthy Egyptians, the European merchants dwelt in the modern town, which was the only part preserved. A few Arabs lived among the ruins of the ancient city: an old wall, flanked by towers, enclosed the new and the old town, and all around extended those sands which in Egypt are sure to advance wherever civilisation recedes.

The four thousand French led by Bonaparte arrived there at daybreak. Upon this sandy beach they met with Arabs only, who, after firing a few musket-shots, fled to the desert. Napoleon divided his men into three columns. Bon, with the first column, marched on the right towards the Rosetta gate; Kléber, with the second, marched in the centre towards the gate of the Catacombs.

The Arabs and the Turks, excellent soldiers behind a
wall, kept up a steady fire, but the French mounted with
ladders and got over the old wall. Kléber was the first
who fell, seriously wounded on the forehead. The Arabs
were driven from ruin to ruin, as far as the new town,
and the combat seemed likely to be continued from street
to street, and to become sanguinary, when a Turkish
captain served as a mediator for negotiating an arrangement. Bonaparte declared that he had not come to rav-
age the country, or to wrest it from its ruler, but merely
to deliver it from the domination of the Mamluks, and
to revenge the outrages which they had committed
against France. He promised that the authorities of
the country should be upheld; that the ceremonies of
religion should continue to be performed as before; that
property should be respected. On these conditions, the
resistance ceased, and the French were masters of Alexandria. Meanwhile, the remainder of the army had
landed. It was immediately necessary to decide where
to place the squadron safely—whether in the harbour
or in one of the neighbouring roads;—to form at Alexandria an administration adapted to the manners of the
country; and also to devise a plan of invasion in order
to gain possession of Egypt.

At this period the population of Egypt was, like the
towns that covered it, a mixture of the wrecks of several
nations,—Kopts, the survivors of the ancient inhabitants
of the land; Arabs, who conquered Egypt from the
Kopts; and Turks, the conquerors of the Arabs. On the
arrival of the French, the Kopts amounted at most to

two hundred thousand: poor, despised, brutalised, they had devoted themselves, like all the proscribed classes, to the most ignoble occupations. The Arabs formed almost the entire mass of the population. Their condition was infinitely varied: some were of high birth, carrying back their pedigree to Muhammed [1] himself; and some were landed proprietors, possessing traces of Arabian knowledge, and combining with nobility the functions of the priesthood and the magistracy, who, under the title of sheikhs, were the real aristocracy of Egypt. In the divans, they represented the country, when its tyrants wished to address themselves to it; in the mosques, they formed a kind of university, in which they taught the religion and the morality of the Koran, and a little philosophy and jurisprudence. The great mosque of Jemil-Azar constituted the foremost learned and religious body in the East. Next to these grandees came the smaller landholders, composing the second and more numerous class of the Arabs; then the great mass of the inhabitants, who had sunk into the state of absolute helots. These last were hired peasants or fellahs who cultivated the land, and lived in abject poverty. There was also a class of Arabs, namely, the Bedouins or rovers, who would never attach themselves to the soil, but were the children of the desert. These wandering Arabs, divided into tribes on both sides of the valley, numbered nearly

[1] The original of the illustration upon the opposite page is to be seen in a finely illuminated MS. of the ninth century, A. D., preserved in the India Office, London. The picture is of peculiar interest, being the only known portrait of Muhammed, who is evidently represented as receiving the divine command to propagate Muhammedanism.

THE PROPHET MUHAMMED (FROM A NINTH CENTURY MANUSCRIPT).

one hundred and twenty thousand, and could furnish from twenty to twenty-five thousand horse. They were brave, but fit only to harass the enemy, not to fight him.

The third and last race was that of the Turks; but it was not more numerous than the Kopts, amounting to about two hundred thousand souls at most, and was divided into Turks and Mamluks. The Turks were nearly all enrolled in the list of janizaries; but it is well known that they frequently had their names inscribed in those lists, that they might enjoy the privileges of janizaries, and that a very small number of them were really in the service. Very few of them composed the military force of the pasha. This pasha, sent from Constantinople, was the sultan's representative in Egypt; but, escorted by only a few janizaries, he found his authority invalidated by the very precautions which Sultan Selim had formerly taken to preserve it. That sultan, judging that Egypt was likely from its remoteness to throw off the dominion of Constantinople, and that a clever and ambitious pasha might create there an independent empire, had, as we have seen, devised a plan to frustrate such a motive, should it exist, by instituting a Mamluk soldiery; but it was the Mamluks, and not the pasha, who rendered themselves independent of Constantinople and the masters of Egypt.

Egypt was at this time an absolute feudality, like that of Europe in the Middle Ages. It exhibited at once a conquered people, a conquering soldiery in rebellion against its sovereign, and, lastly, an ancient degenerate class, who served and were in the pay of the strongest.

Two beys, superior to the rest, ruled Egypt: the one, Ibrahim Bey, wealthy, crafty, and powerful; the other, Murad Bey, intrepid, valiant, and full of ardour. They had agreed upon a sort of division of authority, by which Ibrahim Bey had the civil, and Murad Bey the military, power. It was the business of the latter to fight; he excelled in it, and he possessed the affection of the Mamluks, who were all eager to follow him.

Bonaparte immediately perceived the line of policy which he had to pursue in Egypt. He must, in the first place, wrest that country from its real masters, the Mamluks; it was necessary for him to fight them, and to destroy them by arms and by policy. He had, moreover, strong reasons to urge against them; for they had never ceased to ill-treat the French. As for the Porte, it was requisite that he should not appear to attack its sovereignty, but affect, on the contrary, to respect it. In the state to which it was reduced, that sovereignty was not to be dreaded, and he could treat with the Porte, either for the cession of Egypt, by granting certain advantages elsewhere, or for a partition of authority, in which there would be nothing detrimental; for the French, in leaving the pasha at Cairo, and transferring to themselves the power of the Mamluks, would not occasion much regret. As for the inhabitants, in order to make sure of their attachment, it would be requisite to win over the Arab population. By respecting the sheikhs, by flattering their old pride, by increasing their power, by encouraging their secret desire for the re-establishment of their ancient glories, Bonaparte reckoned upon ruling the land, and attaching it entirely to him. By afterwards sparing persons and property, among a people accustomed to consider conquest as conferring a right to murder, pillage, and devastate, he would create a sentiment that would be most advantageous to the French army. If, furthermore, the French were to respect women and the Prophet, the conquest of hearts would be as firmly secured as that of the soil.

Napoleon conducted himself agreeably to these conclusions, which were equally just and profound. He immediately made his plans for establishing the French authority at Alexandria, and for quitting the Delta and gaining possession of Cairo, the capital of Egypt. It was the month of July; the Nile was about to inundate the country. He was anxious to reach Cairo before the inundation, and to employ the time during which it should last in establishing himself there. He ordered everything at Alexandria to be left in the same state as formerly; that the religious exercises should be continued; and that justice should be administered as before by the cadis. His intention was merely to possess himself of the rights of the Mamluks, and to appoint a commissioner to levy the accustomed imposts. He caused a divan, or municipal council, composed of the sheikhs and principal persons of Alexandria, to be formed, in order to consult them on all the measures which the French authority would have to take. He left three thousand men in garrison in Alexandria, and gave the command of it to Kléber, whose wound was liable to keep him in a state of inactivity for a month or two. He directed a young Frenchman of extraordinary merit, and who gave promise of becoming a great engineer, to put Alexandria in a state of defence, and to construct there all the necessary works. This was Colonel Cretin, who, in a short time, and at a small expense, executed superb works at Alexandria. Bonaparte then ordered the fleet to be put in a place of security. It was a question whether the large ships could enter the port of Alexandria. A commission of naval officers was appointed to sound the harbour and make a report. Meanwhile, the fleet was anchored in the road of Abukir, and Bonaparte ordered Brueys to see to it that this question should be speedily decided, and to proceed to Corfu if it should be ascertained that the ships could not enter the harbour of Alexandria.

After he had attended to all these matters, he made preparations for marching. A considerable flotilla, laden with provisions, artillery, ammunition, and baggage, was to run along the coast to the Rosetta mouth, enter the Nile, and ascend the river at the same time as the French army. He then set out with the main body of the army, which, after leaving the two garrisons in Malta and Alexandria, was about thirty thousand strong. He had ordered his flotilla to proceed as high as Ramanieh, on the banks of the Nile. There he purposed to join it, and to proceed up the Nile parallel with it, in order to quit the Delta and to reach Upper Egypt, or Bahireh. There were two roads from Alexandria to Ramanieh; one through an inhabited country, along the sea-coast and the Nile, and the other shorter and as the bird flies, but

across the desert of Damanhour. Bonaparte, without
hesitation, chose the shorter. It was of consequence
that he should reach Cairo as speedily as possible. Desaix marched with the advanced guard, and the main
body followed at a distance of a few leagues. They
started on the 6th of July. When the soldiers found
themselves amidst this boundless plain, with a shifting
sand beneath their feet, a scorching sun over their heads,
without water, without shade, with nothing for the eye
to rest upon but rare clumps of palm-trees, seeing no
living creatures but small troops of Arab horsemen, who
appeared and disappeared at
the horizon, and sometimes
concealed themselves behind
sand-hills to murder the lag-
gards, they were profoundly
dejected. ⁃ They found all
the wells, which at intervals

STREET DOGS.

border the road through the desert, destroyed by the
Arabs. There were left only a few drops of brackish water, wholly insufficient for quenching their
thirst. They had been informed that they should find
refreshments at Damanhour, but they met with nothing
there but miserable huts, and could procure neither bread
nor wine; only lentils in great abundance, and a little
water. They were obliged to proceed again into the
desert. Bonaparte saw the brave Lannes and Murat
take off their hats, dash them on the sand, and trample
them under foot. He, however, overawed all: his presence imposed silence, and sometimes restored cheerful-

ness. The soldiers would not impute their sufferings
to him, but grew angry with those who took pleasure
in observing the country. On seeing the men of science
stop to examine the slightest ruins, they said they should
not have been there but for them, and revenged themselves with witticisms after their fashion. Caffarelli,
in particular, brave as a grenadier, and inquisitive as
a scholar, was considered by them as the man who had
deceived the general and drawn him into this distant
country. As he had lost a leg on the Rhine, they said,
" He, for his part, laughs at this: he has one foot in
France." At last, after severe hardships, endured at
first with impatience, and afterwards with gaiety and
fortitude, they reached the Nile on the 10th of July,
after a march of four days. At the sight of the Nile
and of the water so much longed for, the soldiers flung
themselves into it, and, bathing in its waves, forgot their
fatigues. Desaix' division, which from the advance-
guard had become the rear-guard, saw two or three hundred Mamluks galloping before it, whom they dispersed
by a few volleys of grape. These were the first that
had been seen, which warned the French that they would
speedily fall in with the hostile army. The brave Murad
Bey, having received the intelligence of the arrival of
Bonaparte, was actually collecting his forces around
Cairo. Until they should have assembled, he was hover-
ing with a thousand horse about the army, in order to
watch its march.

The army waited at Ramanieh for the arrival of the
flotilla. It rested till July 13th, and set out on the same

day for Chebreiss. Murad Bey was waiting there with his Mamluks. The flotilla, which had set out first and preceded the army, found itself engaged before it could be supported. Murad Bey had a flotilla also, and from the shore he joined his fire to that of his light Egyptian vessels. The French flotilla had to sustain a very severe combat. Perrée, a naval officer who commanded it, displayed extraordinary courage; he was supported by the cavalry, who had come dismounted to Egypt, and who, until they could equip themselves at the expense of the Mamluks, had taken their passage by water. Two gunboats were retaken from the enemy, and Perrée was repulsed.

At that moment the army came up; it was composed of five divisions, and had not yet been in action with its singular enemies. To swiftness and the charge of horse, and to sabre-cuts, it would be necessary to oppose the immobility of the foot-soldier, his long bayonet, and masses presenting a front on every side. Bonaparte formed his five divisions into five squares, in the centre of which were placed the baggage and the staff. The artillery was at the angles. The five divisions flanked one another. Murad Bey flung upon these living citadels a thousand or twelve hundred intrepid horse; who, bearing down with loud shouts and at full gallop, discharging their pistols, and then drawing their formidable sabres, threw themselves upon the front of the squares. Encountering everywhere a hedge of bayonets and a tremendous fire, they hovered about the French ranks, fell before them, or scampered off in the plain at the utmost speed of their horses. Murad Bey, after losing a few of his bravest men, retired for the purpose of proceeding to the point of the Delta, and awaiting them near Cairo at the head of all his forces.

This action was sufficient to familiarise the army with this new kind of enemy, and to suggest to Bonaparte the kind of tactics which he ought to employ with them. He pursued his march towards Cairo, and the flotilla ascended the Nile abreast of the army. It marched without intermission during the following days, and, although the soldiers had fresh hardships to endure, they kept close to the Nile, and could bathe every night in its waters.

The army now approached Cairo, where the decisive battle was to be fought. Murad Bey had collected here the greater part of his Mamluks, nearly ten thousand in number, and they were attended by double the number of fellahs, to whom arms were given, and who were obliged to fight behind the intrenchments. He had also assembled some thousands of janizaries, or spahis, dependent on the pasha, who, notwithstanding Bonaparte's letter of conciliation, had suffered himself to be persuaded to join his oppressors. Murad Bey had made preparations for defence on the banks of the Nile. The great capital, Cairo, is situated on the right bank of the river, and on the opposite bank Murad Bey had pitched his tent, in a long plain extending from the river to the pyramids of Gizeh.

On the 21st of July, the French army set itself in motion before daybreak. As they approached, they saw the minarets of Cairo shooting up; they saw the pyramids increase in height; they saw the swarming multitude which guarded Embabeh; they saw the glistening arms of ten thousand horsemen resplendent with gold and steel, and forming an immense line. The face of Bonaparte beamed with enthusiasm. He began to gallop before the ranks of the soldiers, and, pointing to the pyramids, he exclaimed, " Consider, that from the summit of those pyramids forty centuries have their eyes fixed upon you."

GATHERING DATES.

In the battle of the Pyramids, as it was called, the enemy's force of sixty thousand men was almost completely annihilated. The Mamluks, bewildered by European tactics, impaled themselves upon the bayonets of the French squares. Fifteen thousand men of all arms fell upon the field. The battle had cost the French scarcely a hundred killed and wounded; for, if defeat is terrible for broken squares, the loss is insignificant for victorious squares. The Mamluks had lost their best horsemen by fire or water: their forces were dispersed, and the possession of Cairo secured. The capital was in extraordinary agitation. It contained more than three hundred thousand inhabitants, many of whom were indulging in all sorts of excesses, and intending to profit by the tumult to pillage the rich palaces of the beys.

The French flotilla, however, had not yet ascended the Nile, and there was no means of crossing to take possession of Cairo. Some French traders who happened to be there were sent to Bonaparte by the sheikhs to arrange concerning the occupation of the city. He procured a few light boats, or djerms, and sent across the river a detachment of troops, which at once restored tranquillity, and secured persons and property from the fury of the populace.

Bonaparte established his headquarters at Gizeh, on the banks of the Nile, where Murad Bey had an imposing residence. A considerable store of provisions was found both at Gizeh and at Embabeh, and the soldiers could make amends for their long privations. No sooner had he settled in Cairo than he hastened to pursue the same policy which he had already adopted at Alexandria, and by which he hoped to gain the country. The essential point was to obtain from the sheikhs of the mosque of Jemil-Azar a declaration in favour of the French. It corresponded to a papal bull among Christians. On this occasion Bonaparte exerted his utmost address, and was completely successful. The great sheikhs issued the desired declaration, and exhorted the Egyptians to submit to the envoy of God, who reverenced the Prophet, and who had come to deliver his children from the tyranny of the Mamluks. Bonaparte established a divan at Cairo, as he had done at Alexandria, composed of the principal sheikhs, and the most distinguished inhabitants. This divan, or municipal council, was intended to serve him in gaining the minds of the Egyptians, by consulting it, and learning from it all the details of the internal administration. It was agreed that similar assemblies should be established in all the provinces, and that these subordinate divans should send deputies to the divan of Cairo, which would thus be the great national divan.

Bonaparte resolved to leave the administration of justice to the cadis. In execution of his scheme of succeeding to the rights of the Mamluks, he seized their property, and caused the taxes previously imposed to continue to be levied for the benefit of the French army. For this purpose it was requisite that he should have the Kopts at his disposal. He omitted nothing to attach them to him, holding out hopes to them of an amelioration of their condition. He sent generals with detachments down the Nile to complete the occupation of the Delta, which the army had merely traversed, and sent others towards the Upper Nile, to take possession of Middle Egypt. Desaix was placed with a division at the entrance of Upper Egypt, which he was to conquer from Murad Bey, as soon as the waters of the Nile should subside in the autumn. Each of the generals, furnished with detailed instructions, was to repeat in the country what had been done at Alexandria and at Cairo. They were to court the sheikhs, to win the Kopts, and to establish the levy

of the taxes in order to supply the wants of the army.
Bonaparte was also attentive to keep up the relations
with the neighbouring countries, in order to uphold and
to appropriate to himself the rich commerce of Egypt.
He appointed the Emir Hadgi, an officer annually chosen
at Cairo, to protect the great caravan from Mecca. He
wrote to all the French consuls on the coast of Barbary
to inform the beys that the Emir Hadgi was appointed,
and that the caravans might set out. At his desire the
sheikhs wrote to the sherif of Mecca, to acquaint him that
the pilgrims would be protected, and that the caravans
would find safety and protection. The pasha of Cairo
had followed Ibraham Bey to Belbeys. Bonaparte wrote
to him, as well as to the several pashas of St. Jean d'Acre
and Damascus, to assure them of the good disposition
of the French towards the Sublime Porte. The Arabs
were struck by the character of the young conqueror.
They could not comprehend how it was that the mortal
who wielded the thunderbolt should be so merciful. They
called him the worthy son of the Prophet, the favourite
of the great Allah, and sang in the great mosque a litany
in his praise.

Napoleon, in carrying out his policy of conciliating
the natives, was present at the Nile festival, which is
one of the greatest in Egypt. It was on the 18th of
August that this festival was held. Bonaparte had ordered the whole army to be under arms, and had drawn
it up on the banks of the canal. An immense concourse
of people had assembled, who beheld with joy the brave
man of the West attending their festivals.

It was by such means that the young general, as profound a politician as he was a great captain, contrived
to ingratiate himself with the people. While he flattered
their prejudices for the moment, he laboured to diffuse
among them the light of science by the creation of the
celebrated Institute of Egypt. He collected the men of
science and the artists whom he had brought with him,
and, associating with them some of the best educated of
his officers, established the institute, to which he appropriated a revenue and one of the most spacious palaces
in Cairo.

The conquest of the provinces of Lower and Middle
Egypt had been effected without difficulty, and had cost
only a few skirmishes with the Arabs. A forced march
upon Belbeys had been sufficient to drive Ibrahim Bey
into Syria, where Desaix awaited the autumn for wrest-
ing Upper Egypt from Murad Bey, who had retired
thither with the wrecks of his army.

Fortune was, meanwhile, preparing for Bonaparte the
most terrible of all reverses. On leaving Alexandria, he
had earnestly recommended to Admiral Brueys to secure
his squadron from the English, either by taking it into
the harbour of Alexandria, or by proceeding with it to
Corfu; and he had particularly enjoined him not to leave
it in the road of Abukir, for it was much better to fall
in with an enemy when under sail than to receive him
at anchor. A warm discussion had arisen on the question
whether the ships of 80 and 120 guns could be carried into the harbour of Alexandria. As to the smaller
ships, there was no doubt; but the larger would re-

quire lightening so much as to enable them to draw three feet less water. For this purpose it would be necessary to take out their guns, or to construct floats. On such conditions, Admiral Brueys resolved not to take his squadron into the harbour. The time which he spent, either in sounding the channels to the harbour, or in waiting for news from Cairo, caused his own destruction.

Admiral Brueys was moored in the road of Abukir. This road is a very regular semicircle, and his thirteen ships formed a line parallel to the shore, and so disposed that he believed no British ship could pass between him and the shore, if an attack were made.

Nelson, after visiting the Archipelago, and returning to the Adriatic, Naples, and Sicily, had at length obtained the certain knowledge of the landing of the French at Alexandria. He immediately steered in that direction in order to seek and put to flight their squadron. He sent a frigate to look out for it, and to reconnoitre its position. The English frigate, having made her observations, rejoined Nelson, who, being informed of all the particulars, immediately stood in for Abukir, and arrived there August 1, 1798, at about six o'clock in the evening. Admiral Brueys was at dinner. He immediately ordered the signal for battle to be given; but so unprepared was the squadron to receive the enemy, that the hammocks were not stowed away on board any of the ships, and part of the crews were on shore. The admiral despatched officers to send the seamen on board, and to demand part of those who were in the transports. He had no conception that Nelson would dare to attack him the same evening, and

THE ATAKA MOUNTAINS IN THE GULF OF SUEZ.

conceived that he should have time to receive the reinforcements for which he had applied.

Nelson resolved to attack immediately, and to push in between the French ships and the shore at all hazards. " Before this time to-morrow," said he, " I shall have gained a peerage or Westminster Abbey."

The number of vessels was equal on both sides, namely, thirteen ships of war. The engagement lasted upwards of fifteen hours. All the crews performed prodigies of valour. The brave Captain Du Petit-Thouars had two of his limbs shot off. He ordered snuff to be brought him, and remained on his quarter-deck, and, like Brueys, waited till a cannon-ball despatched him. The entire French squadron, excepting the two ships and two frigates carried off by Villeneuve, was destroyed. Nelson had suffered so severely that he could not pursue the fugitives. Such was the famous battle of Abukir, the most disastrous that the French had ever sustained, and involved the most far-reaching consequences. The fleet which had carried the French to Egypt, which might have served to succour or to recruit them, which was to second their movements on the coast of Syria,—had there been any to execute,—which was to overawe the Porte, to force it to put up with false reasoning, and to oblige it to wink at the invasion of Egypt, which finally, in case of reverses, was to convey the French back to their country,—that fleet was destroyed. The French ships were burned. The news of this disaster spread rapidly in Egypt, and for a moment filled the army with despair. Bonaparte received the tidings with imperturbable composure. " Well," he said, " we must die in this country, or get out of it as great as the ancients." He wrote to Kléber: " This will oblige us to do greater things than we intended. We must hold ourselves in readiness." The great soul of Kléber was worthy of this language: " Yes," replied Kléber, " we must do great things. I am preparing my faculties." The courage of these men supported the army, and restored its confidence.

Bonaparte strove to divert the thoughts of the soldiers by various expeditions, and soon made them forget this disaster. On the festival of the foundation of the republic, he endeavoured to give a new stimulus to their imagination; he engraved on Pompey's Pillar the names of the first forty soldiers slain in Egypt. They were the forty who had fallen in the attack on Alexandria; and the names of these men, sprung from the villages of France, were thus associated with the immortality of Pompey and Alexander.

Bonaparte, after the battle of the Pyramids, found himself master of Egypt. He began to establish himself there, and sent his generals into the provinces to complete their conquest. Desaix, placed at the entrance of Upper Egypt with a division of about three thousand men, was directed to reduce the remnants of Murad Bey's force in that province. It was in the preceding year (October, 1798), at the moment when the inundation was over, that Desaix had commenced his expedition. The enemy had retired before him, and did not wait for him till he reached Sediman; there, on October 7th, Desaix fought a sanguinary battle with the desperate remainder of Murad

Bey's forces. Two thousand French had to combat with four thousand Mamluks and eight thousand fellahs, intrenched in the village of Sediman. The battle was conducted in the same manner as that of the Pyramids, and like all those fought in Egypt. The fellahs were behind the walls of the village, and the horse in the plain. The field of battle was thickly strewn with slain. The French lost three hundred men. Desaix continued his march during the whole winter, and, after a series of actions, reduced Upper Egypt as far as the cataracts. He made himself equally feared for his bravery and beloved for his clemency. In Cairo, Bonaparte had been named Sultan Kebir, the Fire Sultan. In Upper Egypt, Desaix was called the " Just Sultan."

Bonaparte had meanwhile marched to Belbeys, to drive Ibrahim Bey into Syria, and he had collected by the way the wrecks of the caravan of Mecca, plundered by the Arabs. Returning to Cairo, he continued to establish there an entirely French administration. Thus passed the winter between 1798 and 1799 in the expectation of important events. During this interval, Bonaparte received intelligence of the declaration of war by the Porte, and of the preparations which it was making against him with the aid of the English. Two armies were being formed, one at Rhodes, the other in Syria. These two armies were to act simultaneously in the spring of 1799, the one by landing at Abukir near Alexandria, the other by crossing the desert which separates Syria from Egypt. Bonaparte was instantly aware of his position, and determined, as was his custom, to disconcert

the enemy and to forestall any offensive movement by
a sudden attack. He could not cross the desert which
parts Egypt from Syria in summer, and he resolved to

A FOUNTAIN AT CAIRO.

avail himself of the winter for destroying the assemblages
of troops forming at Acre, at Damascus, and in the principal towns. Djezzar, the celebrated pasha of Acre, was
appointed seraskier of the army collected in Syria. Abd
Allah Pasha of Damascus commanded its advanced-guard,

and had proceeded as far as the fort of El Arish, which is the key to Egypt on the side next to Syria. Bonaparte resolved to act immediately. He was in communication with the tribes of the Lebanon. The Druses, Christian tribes, the Mutualis, and schismatic Muhammedans offered him assistance, and ardently wished for his coming. By a sudden assault on Jaffa, Acre, and some other badly fortified places, he might in a short time gain possession of Syria, add this fine conquest to that of Egypt, make himself master of the Euphrates, as he was of the Nile, and thus command all the communications with India.

Bonaparte commenced his march very early in February at the head of Kléber's, Regnier's, Lannes's, Bon's, and Murat's divisions, about thirteen thousand strong. He arrived before the fort El Arish on February 15th, and, after a slight resistance, the garrison surrendered themselves prisoners, to the number of thirteen hundred men. Ibrahim Bey, having attempted to relieve it, was put to flight, and, after a severe march across the desert, they reached Gaza. They took that place in the sight of Djezzar Pasha, and found there, as in the fort of El Arish, a great quantity of ammunition and provisions. From Gaza the army proceeded to Jaffa (the ancient Joppa), where it arrived on March 3rd. This place was surrounded by a massive wall, flanked by towers, and it contained a garrison of four thousand men. Bonaparte caused a breach to be battered in the wall, and then summoned the commandant, who only answered by cutting off the head of the messenger. The assault was made, and the place stormed with extraordinary intrepidity, and given up for thirty hours to pillage and massacre. Here, too, was found a considerable quantity of artillery and supplies of all kinds. There were some thousands of prisoners, whom the general could not despatch to Egypt, because he had not the ordinary means for escorting them, and he would not send them back to the enemy to swell their ranks. Bonaparte decided on a terrible measure, the most cruel act of his life. Transported into a barbarous country, he had adopted its manners, and he ordered all the prisoners to be put to death. The army consummated with obedience, but with a sort of horror, the execution that was commanded.

Bonaparte then advanced upon St. Jean d'Acre, the ancient Ptolemais, situated at the foot of Mount Carmel. It was the only place that could now stop him. If he could make himself master of this fortress, Syria would be his. But the ferocious Djezzar had shut himself up there, with all his wealth and a strong garrison, and he also reckoned upon support from Sir Sidney Smith, then cruising off that coast, who supplied him with engineers, artillerymen, and ammunition. It was probable, moreover, that he would be soon relieved by the Turkish army collected in Syria, which was advancing from Damascus to cross the Jordan. Bonaparte hastened to attack the place, in hopes of taking it, as he had done Jaffa, before it was reinforced with fresh troops, and before the English had time to improve its defences. The trenches were immediately opened. The siege artillery sent by sea from Alexandria had been intercepted by Sir Sidney Smith, who captured seven vessels out of the nine. A breach was effected, and dispositions were made for the assault, but the men were stopped by a counterscarp and a ditch. They immediately set about mining. The operation was carried on under the fire of all the ramparts, and of the fine artillery which Sir Sidney Smith had taken from the French. The mine was exploded on April 17th, and blew up only a portion of the counterscarp. Unluckily for the French, the place had received a reinforcement of several thousand men, a great number of gunners trained after the European fashion, and immense supplies. It was a siege on a large scale to be carried on with thirteen thousand men, almost entirely destitute of artillery. It was necessary to open a new mine to blow up the entire counterscarp, and to commence another covered way.

Bonaparte now ordered Kléber's division to oppose the passage of the Jordan by the army coming from Damascus. The enemy was commanded by Abd Allah Pasha of Damascus, and numbered about twenty-five thousand men and twelve thousand horse. A desperate battle was fought in the plain of Fouli, and for six hours Kléber, with scarcely three thousand infantry in square, resisted the utmost fury of the Turkish cavalry. Bonaparte, who had been making a rapid march to join Kléber, suddenly made his appearance on the field of battle. A tremendous fire, discharged instantaneously from the three points of this triangle, assailed the Mamluks who were in the midst, drove them in confusion upon one another, and made them flee in disorder in all directions. Kléber's division, fired with fresh ardour at this sight, rushed upon the village of Fouli, stormed it at the point of the bayonet, and made a great carnage among the enemy. In a moment the whole multitude was gone, and the plain was left covered with dead. During this interval the besiegers had never ceased mining and countermining about the walls of St. Jean d'Acre. The siege of Acre lasted for sixty-five days. Bonaparte made eight desperate but ineffectual assaults upon the city, which were repulsed by eleven furious sallies on the part of the besieged garrison. It was absolutely necessary to relinquish the enterprise. The strategic point in the East was lost.

For two months the army had been before Acre; it had sustained considerable losses, and it would have been imprudent to expose it to more. The plague was in Acre, and the army had caught the contagion at Jaffa. The season for landing troops approached, and the arrival of a Turkish army near the mouths of the Nile was expected. By persisting longer, Bonaparte was liable to weaken himself to such a degree as not to be able to repulse new enemies. The main point of his plan was effected, since he had rendered the enemy in that quarter incapable of acting. He now commenced his march to recross the desert.

Bonaparte at length reached Egypt after an expedition of nearly three months. It was high time for him to return; for the spirit of insurrection had spread throughout the whole Delta. His presence produced everywhere submission and tranquillity. He gave orders for magnificent festivities at Cairo to celebrate his tri-

Cairo — Eskibieh Quarter

umphs in Syria. He had to curb not only the inhabitants, but his own generals and the army itself. A deep discontent pervaded it. They had been for a whole year in Egypt. It was now the month of June, and they were still ignorant of what was passing in Europe, and of the disasters of France. They merely knew that the Continent was in confusion, and that a new war was inevitable. Bonaparte impatiently waited for further particulars, that he might decide what course to pursue, and return, in case of need, to the first theatre of his exploits. But he hoped first to destroy the second Turkish army assembled at Rhodes, the very speedy landing of which was announced.

This army, put on board numerous transports and escorted by Sir Sidney Smith's squadron, appeared on July 11th in sight of Alexandria, and came to anchor in the road of Abukir, where the French squadron had been destroyed. The point chosen by the English for landing was the peninsula which commands the entrance to the road, and bears the same name. The Turks landed with great boldness, attacked the intrenchments sword in hand, carried them, and made themselves masters of the village of Abukir, putting to death the garrison. The village being taken, it was impossible for the fort to hold out, and it was obliged to surrender. Marmont, who commanded at Alexandria, left the city at the head of twelve hundred men to hasten to the assistance of the troops at Abukir. But, learning that the Turks had landed in considerable numbers, he did not dare to attempt to throw them into the sea by a bold attack, and returned to Alexandria, leaving them to establish themselves quietly in the peninsula of Abukir.

The Turks amounted to nearly eighteen thousand infantry. They had no cavalry, for they had not brought more than three hundred horses, but they expected the arrival of Murad Bey, who was to leave Upper Egypt, skirt the desert, cross the oases, and throw himself into Abukir with two or three thousand Mamluks.

When Bonaparte was informed of the particulars of the landing, he immediately left Cairo, and made from that city to Alexandria one of those extraordinary marches of which he had given so many examples in Italy. He took with him the divisions of Lannes, Bon, and Murat. He had ordered Desaix to evacuate Upper Egypt, and Kléber and Regnier, who were in the Delta, to approach Abukir. He had chosen the point of Birket, midway between Alexandria and Abukir, at which to concentrate his forces, and to manœuvre according to circumstances. He was afraid that an English army had landed with the Turks. The next day, the 7th, he was at the entrance of the peninsula.

Bonaparte made his dispositions with his usual promptitude and decision. He ordered General D'Estaing, with some battalions, to march to the hill on the left, where the one thousand Turks were posted; Lannes to march to that on the right, where the two thousand others were; and Murat, who was at the centre, to make the cavalry file on the rear of the two hills. D'Estaing marched to the hill on the left and boldly ascended it: Murat caused it to be turned by a squadron. The Turks, at sight of

CAIRO FROM THE LEFT BANK OF THE NILE.

this, quitted their post, and fell in with the cavalry, which cut them to pieces, and drove them into the sea, into which they chose rather to throw themselves than to surrender. Precisely the same thing was done on the right. Lannes attacked the two thousand janizaries; Murat turned them, cut them in pieces, and drove them into the sea. D'Estaing and Lannes then moved towards the centre, formed by a village, and attacked it in front. The Turks there defended themselves bravely, reckoning upon assistance from the second line. A column did in fact advance from the camp of Abukir; but Murat, who had already filed upon the rear of the village, fell sword in hand upon this column, and drove it back into Abukir. D'Estaing's infantry and that of Lannes entered the village at the charge step, driving the Turks out of it, who were pushed in all directions, and who, obstinately refusing to surrender, had no retreat but the sea, in which they were drowned.

From four to five thousand had already perished in this manner. The first line was carried: Bonaparte's object was accomplished. He immediately followed up his success with desperate fighting to complete his victory on the moment. The Turks, affrighted, fled on all sides, and a horrible carnage was made among them. They were pursued at the point of the bayonet and thrust into the sea. More than twelve thousand corpses were floating in the bay of Abukir, and two or three thousand more had perished by the fire or by the sword. The rest, shut up in the fort, had no rescue but the clemency of the conqueror. Such was that extraordinary battle in which a hostile army was entirely destroyed. Thus, either by the expedition to Syria, or by the battle of Abukir, Egypt was delivered, at least for a time, from the forces of the Porte.

Having arrived in the summer before the inundation, Bonaparte had employed the first moments in gaining possession of Alexandria and the capital, which he had secured by the battle of the Pyramids. In the autumn, after the inundation, he had completed the conquest of the Delta, and consigned that of Upper Egypt to Desaix. In the winter he had undertaken the expedition to Syria, and destroyed Djezzar's Turkish army at Mount Tabor. He had now, in the second summer, just destroyed the second army of the Porte at Abukir. The time had thus been well spent; and, while Victory was forsaking in Europe the banners of France, she adhered to them in Africa and Asia. The tricolour waved triumphant over the Nile and the Jordan, and over the places which were the cradle of the Christian religion.

Bonaparte was as yet ignorant of what was passing in France. None of the despatches from the Directory or from his brothers had reached him, and he was a prey to the keenest anxiety. With a view to obtaining some intelligence, he ordered brigs to cruise about, to stop all merchantmen, and to gain from them information of the occurrences in Europe. He sent to the Turkish fleet a flag of truce, which, under the pretext of negotiating an exchange of prisoners, was for the purpose of obtaining news. Sir Sidney Smith stopped this messenger, treated him exceedingly well, and, perceiving that Bonaparte was ignorant of the disasters of France, took a spiteful pleasure in sending him a packet of newspapers. The messenger returned and delivered the packet to Bonaparte. The latter spent the whole night in devouring the contents of those papers, and informing himself of what was passing in his own country. His determination was immediately taken, and he resolved to embark secretly for Europe, and on August 22nd, taking with him Berthier, Lannes, Murat, Andréossy, Marmont, Berthollet, and Monge, and escorted by some of his guides, he proceeded to a retired spot on the beach, where boats were awaiting them. They got into them and went on board the frigates, *La Muiron* and *La Carrère*. They set sail immediately, that by daylight they might be out of sight of the English cruisers. Unfortunately it fell calm; fearful of being surprised, some were for returning to Alexandria, but Bonaparte resolved to proceed. " Be quiet," said he, " we shall pass in safety." Like Cæsar, he reckoned upon his fortune. Menou, who alone had been initiated into the secret, made known in Alexandria the departure of General Bonaparte, and the appointment which he had made of General Kléber to succeed him. This intelligence caused a painful surprise throughout the army. The most opprobrious epithets were applied to this departure. They did not consider that irresistible impulse of patriotism and ambition, which, on the news of the disasters of the Republic, had urged him to return to France. They perceived only the forlorn state in which he had left the unfortunate army, which had felt sufficient confidence in his genius to follow him.

Kléber was not fond of General Bonaparte, and endured his ascendency with a sort of impatience, and now he was sorry that he had quitted the banks of the Rhine

STATUE OF GENERAL KLÉBER AT STRASBURG.

for the banks of the Nile. The chief command did not counterbalance the necessity of remaining in Egypt, for he took no pleasure in commanding.

Kléber, however, was the most popular of the generals among the soldiery. His name was hailed by them with entire confidence, and somewhat cheered them for the loss of the illustrious commander who had just left them. He returned to Cairo, assumed the command with a sort of ostentation, and took possession of the fine Arabian mansion which his predecessor had occupied in the Ezbekieh Place. But it was not long before the solicitudes of the chief command, which were insupportable to him, the new dangers with which the Turks and the English threatened Egypt, and the grief of exile, which was general, filled his soul with the most gloomy discouragement.

Kléber, together with Poussielgue, the administrator of the army, at once prepared and addressed despatches to the Directory, placing the condition of the troops, the finances, and the number of the enemy in the most melancholy light. These despatches fell into the hands of the English, and the duplicate reports found their way into the hands of Bonaparte himself. Bonaparte had left instructions with Kléber to meet every possible contingency during his absence, even to the necessity of an evacuation of Egypt. "I am going to France," said he, "either as a private man or as a public man; I will get reinforcement sent to you. But if by next spring (he was writing in August, 1799) you have received no supplies, no instructions; if the plague has carried off more than fifteen hundred men, independently of losses by war; if a considerable force, which you should be incapable of resisting, presses you hard, negotiate with the vizier:

consent even, if it must be so, to an evacuation; subject to one condition, that of referring to the French government; and meanwhile continue to occupy. You will
thus have gained time, and it is impossible that, during
the interval, you should not have received succour.''

The instructions were very sound; but the case fore-
seen was far from being realised at the time when Kléber
determined to negotiate for the evacuation of Egypt.
Murad Bey, disheartened, was a fugitive in Upper Egypt
with a few Mamluks. Ibrahim Bey, who, under the government of the Mamluks, shared the sovereignty with
him, was then in Lower Egypt towards the frontier of
Syria. He had four hundred horse. Djezzar Pasha was
shut up in St. Jean d'Acre, and, so far from preparing
a reinforcement of men for the army of the grand vizier,
he viewed, on the contrary, with high displeasure, the
approach of a fresh Turkish army, now that his pashalik
was delivered from the French. As for the grand vizier,
he was not yet across the Taurus. The English had their
troops at Mahon, and were not at this moment aggressive.
At Kléber's side was General Menou, who viewed everything under the most favourable colours, and believed
the French to be invincible in Egypt, and regarded the
expedition as the commencement of a near and momen-
tous revolution in the commerce of the world. Kléber
and Menou were both honest, upright men; but one
wanted to leave Egypt, the other to stay in it; the clear-
est and most authentic returns conveyed to them totally
contrary significations; misery and ruin to one, abundance and success to the other.

In September, 1799, Desaix, having completed the conquest and subjugation of Upper Egypt, had left two movable columns for the pursuit of Murad Bey, to whom he had offered peace on condition of his becoming a vassal of France. He then returned to Cairo by the order of Kléber, who wished to make use of his name in those negotiations into which he was about to enter. During these proceedings, the army of the grand vizier, so long announced, was slowly advancing. Sir Sidney Smith, who convoyed with his squadron the Turkish troops destined to be transported by sea, had just arrived off Damietta with eight thousand janizaries, and on the first of November, 1799, the landing of the first division of four thousand janizaries was effected. At the first tidings of this disembarkation, Kléber had despatched Desaix with a column of three thousand men; but the latter, uselessly sent to Damietta, had found the victory won,— the Turkish division having been completely destroyed by General Verdier,—and the French filled with unbounded confidence. This brilliant achievement ought to have served to encourage Kléber; unfortunately, he was swayed at once by his own lack of confidence and that of the army. In this disposition of mind, Kléber had sent one of his officers to the vizier (who had entered Syria), to make new overtures of peace. General Bonaparte, with a view to embroiling the vizier with the English, had previously entertained the idea of setting on foot negotiations, which, on his part, were nothing more than a feint. His overtures had been received with great distrust and pride. Kléber's advances met with a favourable reception, through the influence of Sir Sidney Smith, who was preparing to play a prominent part in the affairs of Egypt. This officer had largely contributed to prevent the success of the siege of St. Jean d'Acre; he was proud of it, and had devised a *ruse de guerre* by taking advantage of a momentary weakness to wrest from the French their valuable conquest. With this view, he had disposed the grand vizier to listen to the overtures of Kléber. Kléber, on his part, despatched Desaix and Poussielgue as negotiators to Sir Sidney Smith; for, since the English were masters of the sea, he wished to induce them to take part in the negotiation, so that the return to France might be rendered possible. Sir Sidney manifested a disposition to enter into arrangements, acting as "Minister Plenipotentiary of His Britannic Majesty," and attributing to himself a power which he had ceased to hold since the arrival of Lord Elgin as ambassador at Constantinople. Poussielgue was an advocate for evacuation; Desaix just the reverse.

The conditions proposed by Kléber were unreasonable: not that they were an exorbitant equivalent for what was given up in giving up Egypt, but because they were not feasible. Sir Sidney made Kléber sensible of this. Officers treating for a mere suspension of arms could not include topics of vast extent in their negotiation, such as the demand for the possession of the Venetian Islands, and the annulment of the Triple Alliance. But it was urgently necessary to settle two points immediately: the departure of the wounded and of the scientific men attached to the expedition, for whom Desaix solicited safe-conduct; and secondly, a suspension of arms, for the army of the grand vizier, though marching slowly, would soon be in presence of the French. It had actually arrived before the fort of El Arish, the first French post on the frontiers of Syria, and had summoned it to surrender. The negotiations, in fact, had been going on for a fortnight on board *Le Tigre*, while floating at the pleasure of the winds off the coasts of Syria and Egypt: the parties had said all they had to say, and the negotiations could not be continued to any useful purpose without the concurrence of the grand vizier. Sir Sidney, availing himself of a favourable moment, pushed off in a boat which landed him on the coast, after incurring some danger, and ordered the captain of *Le Tigre* to meet him in the port of Jaffa, where Poussielgue and Desaix were to be put ashore, if the conferences were to be transferred to the camp of the grand vizier.

At the moment when the English commodore reached the camp, a horrible event had occurred at El Arish. The grand vizier had collected around him an army of seventy or eighty thousand fanatic Mussulmans. The Turks were joined by the Mamluks. Ibrahim Bey, who had some time before retired to Syria, and Murad Bey, who had descended by a long circuit from the cataracts to the environs of Suez, had become the auxiliaries of their former adversaries. The English had made for this army a sort of field-artillery, drawn by mules. The fort of El Arish, before which the Turks were at this moment, was, according to the declaration of General Bonaparte, one of the two keys of Egypt; Alexandria was the other.

The Turkish advanced-guard having reached El Arish,
Colonel Douglas, an English officer in the service of

A MODERN FANATIC.

Turkey, summoned Cazals, the commandant, to surrender. The culpable sentiments which the officers had too

much encouraged in the army then burst forth. The soldiers in the garrison at El Arish, vehemently longing, like their comrades, to leave Egypt, declared to the commandant that they would not fight, and that he must make up his mind to surrender the fort. The gallant Cazals indignantly refused, and a struggle with the Turks ensued. During this contest, the recreants, who insisted on surrendering, threw ropes to the Turks; these ferocious enemies, once hoisted up into the fort, rushed, sword in hand, upon those who had given them admission into the fort, and slaughtered a great number of them. The others, brought back to reason, joined the rest of the garrison, and, defending themselves with desperate courage, were most of them killed. A small number obtained quarter, thanks to that humane and distinguished officer, Colonel Douglas.

It was now the 30th of December: the letter written by Sir Sidney Smith to the grand vizier, to propose to him a suspension of arms, had not reached him in time to prevent the melancholy catastrophe at El Arish. Sir Sidney Smith was a man of generous feelings: this barbarous massacre of a French garrison horrified him, and, above all, it made him fearful of the rupture of the negotiations. He lost no time in sending explanations to Kléber, both in his own name and that of the grand vizier, and he added the formal assurance that all hostility should cease during the negotiations.

Kléber, when informed of the massacre of El Arish, did not manifest as much indignation as he ought to have done; he was aware that, if he was too warm upon that subject, all the negotiations might be broken off. He was more urgent than ever for a suspension of arms; and, at the same time, by way of precaution, and to be nearer to the theatre of the conferences, he left Cairo, and transferred his headquarters to Salahieh, on the very border of the desert, two days' march from El Arish.

In the meantime, Desaix and Poussielgue, detained by contrary winds, had not been able to land at Gaza till the 11th, and to reach El Arish before the 13th.

The evacuation and its conditions soon became the sole subject of negotiation. After long discussions it was agreed that all hostility should cease for three months; that those three months should be employed by the vizier in collecting, in the ports of Rosetta, Abukir, and Alexandria, the vessels requisite for the conveyance of the French army; by General Kléber, in evacuating the Upper Nile, Cairo, and the contiguous provinces, and in concentrating his troops about the point of embarkation; that the French should depart with the honours of war; that they should cease to impose contributions; but that, in return, the French army should receive three thousand purses, equivalent at that time to three million francs, and representing the sum necessary for its subsistence during the evacuation and the passage. The forts of Katieh, Salahieh, and the Belbeys, forming the frontier of Egypt towards the desert of Syria, were to be given up ten days after the ratification; Cairo forty days after.

The terms of the convention being arranged, there was nothing more to be done but sign it. Kléber, who had a vague feeling of his fault, determined, in order to cover it, to assemble a council of war, to which all the generals of the army were summoned. The council met on the 21st of January, 1800. The minutes of it still exist. Desaix, although deeply grieved, was swept along by the torrent of popular opinion, gave way to it himself, and affixed his signature on the 28th of January to the convention of El Arish.

Meanwhile preparations were being made for departure; Sir Sidney Smith had returned to his ship. The vizier advanced and took possession, consecutively, of the entrenched positions of Katieh, Salahieh, and Belbeys, which Kléber, in haste to execute the convention, faithfully delivered up to him. Kléber returned to Cairo to make his preparations for departure, to call in the troops that were guarding Upper Egypt, to concentrate his army, and then to direct it upon Alexandria and Rosetta at the time stipulated for embarkation.

While these events were occurring in Egypt, the English cabinet had received advice of the overtures made by General Kléber to the grand vizier and to Sir Sidney Smith. Believing that the French army was reduced to the last extremity, it lost no time in sending off an express order not to grant any capitulation unless they surrendered themselves prisoners of war. These orders, despatched from London on the 17th of December, reached Admiral Keith in the island of Minorca in the first days of January, 1800; and, on the 8th of the same month, the admiral hastened to forward to Sir Sidney Smith the instructions which he had just received from the government. He lost no time in writing to Kléber, to express his mortification, to apprise him honestly of what was passing, to advise him to suspend immediately the delivery of the Egyptian fortresses to the grand vizier, and to conjure him to wait for fresh orders from England before he took any definite resolutions. Unfortunately, when these advices from Sir Sidney arrived at Cairo, the French army had already executed in part the treaty of El Arish.

Kléber instantly countermanded all the orders previously given to the army. He brought back from Lower Egypt to Cairo part of the troops that had already descended the Nile; he ordered his stores to be sent up again; he urged the division of Upper Egypt to make haste to rejoin him, and gave notice to the grand vizier to suspend his march towards Cairo, otherwise he should immediately commence hostilities. The grand vizier replied that the convention of El Arish was signed; that it must be executed; that, in consequence, he should advance towards the capital. At the same instant, an officer sent from Minorca with a letter from Lord Keith to Kléber, arrived at the headquarters. Kléber, fired with indignation at the demand for surrender, caused Lord Keith's letter to be inserted in the order of the day, adding to it these few words: " Soldiers, to such insults there is no other answer than victory. Prepare for action."

Agents from Sir Sidney had hastened up to interpose between the French and the Turks, and to make fresh proposals of accommodation. Letters, they said, had

just been written to London, and, when the convention
of El Arish was known there, it would be ratified to a
certainty; in this situation, it would not be right to suspend hostilities, and wait. To this the grand vizier and
Kléber consented, but on conditions that were irrecon-
cilable. The grand vizier insisted that Cairo should be
given up to him; Kléber, on the contrary, that the vizier
should fall back to the frontier. Under these conditions,
fighting was the only resource.

On the 20th of March, 1800, in the plain of Heliopolis,
ten thousand soldiers, by superiority in discipline and
courage, dispersed seventy or eighty thousand foes.
Kléber gave orders for the pursuit on the following day.
When he had ascertained with his own eyes that the
Turkish army had disappeared, he resolved to return and
reduce the towns of Lower Egypt, and Cairo in particular, to their duty.

He arrived at Cairo on the 27th of March. Important
events had occurred there since his departure. The population of that great city, which numbered nearly three
hundred thousand inhabitants, fickle, inflammable, inclined to change, had followed the suggestions of Turkish emissaries, and fallen upon the French the moment
they heard the cannon at Heliopolis. Pouring forth outside the walls during the battle, and seeing Nassif-Pasha
and Ibrahim Bey, with some thousand horse and janizaries, they supposed them to be the conquerors. Taking
good care not to undeceive the inhabitants, the Turks
affirmed that the grand vizier had gained a complete
victory, and that the French were exterminated. At

these tidings, fifty thousand men had risen in Cairo, at Bulak, and at Gizeh, and Cairo became a scene of plunder, rapine, and murder.

During these transactions, General Friant arrived, detached from Belbeys, and lastly Kléber himself. Though conqueror of the grand vizier's army, Kléber had a serious difficulty to surmount to subdue an immense city, peopled by three hundred thousand inhabitants, partly in a state of revolt, occupied by twenty thousand Turks, and built in the Oriental style; that is to say, having narrow streets, divided into piles of masonry, which were real fortresses. These edifices, receiving light from within, and exhibiting without nothing but lofty walls, had terraces instead of roofs, from which the insurgents poured a downward and destructive fire. Add to this that the Turks were masters of the whole city, excepting the citadel and the square of Ezbekieh, which, in a manner, they had blockaded by closing the streets that ran into it with embattled walls.

In this situation, Kléber showed as much prudence as he had just shown energy in the field. He resolved to gain time, and to let the insurrection wear itself out. The insurgents could not fail at length to be undeceived respecting the general state of things in Egypt, and to learn that the French were everywhere victorious, and the vizier's army dispersed. Nassif-Pasha's Turks, Ibrahim Bey's Mamluks, and the Arab population of Cairo could not agree together long. For all these reasons, Kléber thought it advisable to temporise and to negotiate.

CITADEL OF CAIRO.

While he was gaining time, he completed his treaty of alliance with Murad Bey. He granted to him the province of Saïd, under the supremacy of France, on condition of paying a tribute equivalent to a considerable part of the imposts of that province. Murad Bey engaged, moreover, to fight for the French; and the French engaged, if they should ever quit the country, to facilitate for him the occupation of Egypt. Murad Bey faithfully adhered to the treaty which he had just signed, and began by driving from Upper Egypt a Turkish corps which had occupied it. The insurgents of Cairo obstinately refused to capitulate, and an attack by main force was, therefore, indispensable for completing the reduction of the city, during which several thousand Turks, Mamluks, and insurgents were killed, and four thousand houses were destroyed by fire. Thus terminated that sanguinary struggle, which had commenced with the battle of Heliopolis on the 20th of March, and which ended on the 25th of April with the departure of the last lieutenants of the vizier, after thirty-five days' fighting between twenty thousand French on one side, and, on the other, the whole force of the Ottoman empire, seconded by the revolt of the Egyptian towns.

In the Delta all the towns had returned to a state of complete submission. Murad Bey had driven from Upper Egypt the Turkish detachment of Dervish Pasha. The vanquished everywhere trembled before the conqueror, and expected a terrible chastisement. Kléber, who was humane and wise, took good care not to repay cruelties with cruelties. The Egyptians were persuaded that they should be treated harshly; they conceived that the loss of life and property would atone for the crime of those who had risen in revolt. Kléber called them together, assumed at first a stern look, but afterwards pardoned them, merely imposing a contribution on the insurgent villages. Cairo paid ten million francs, a burden far from onerous for so large a city, and the inhabitants considered themselves as most fortunate to get off so easily. Eight millions more were imposed upon the rebel towns of Lower Egypt. The army, proud of its victories, confident in its strength, knowing that General Bonaparte was at the head of the government, ceased to doubt that it would soon receive reinforcements. Kléber had in the plain of Heliopolis made the noblest amends for his momentary faults.

He entered upon a second conquest, showing clemency and humanity on all sides, and everywhere he laboured hard to encourage the arts and industries and agriculture. He assembled the administrators of the army, the persons best acquainted with the country, and turned his attention to the organisation of the finances of the colony. He restored the collection of the direct contributions to the Kopts, to whom it had formerly been entrusted, and imposed some new customs' duties and taxes on articles of consumption. He gave orders for the completion of the forts constructing around Cairo, and set men to work at those of Lesbeh, Damietta, Burlos, and Rosetta, situated on the sea-coast. He pressed forward the works of Alexandria, and imparted fresh activity to the scientific researches of the Institute of

Egypt, and a valuable mass of information was embodied in the great French work, the "Description de l'Egypte." From the cataracts to the mouths of the Nile, everything assumed the aspect of a solid and durable establishment. Two months afterwards, the caravans of Syria, Arabia, and Darfur began to appear again at Cairo.

But a deplorable event snatched away General Kléber in the midst of his exploits and of his judicious government. He was assassinated in the garden of his palace by a young man, a native of Aleppo, named Suleiman, who was a prey to extravagant fanaticism.

With Kléber's death, Egypt was lost for France. Menou, who succeeded him, was very far beneath such a task. The English offered to make good the convention of El Arish, but Menou refused, and England prepared for an invasion, after attempting vainly to co-operate with the Turks.

Sir Ralph Abercrombie, who had been appointed as British commissioner, landed with the English army alone at Abukir. After fierce skirmishing, the French and English met on the plains of Alexandria. In the frightful conflict which ensued, Sir Ralph Abercrombie was slain, but the battle ended with the retreat of the French. Damietta surrendered on April 19th. The French were now divided, while Menou hesitated. General Hutchinson took the place of the deceased British commander. A great battle was fought at Cairo, which was won by the British, and the capital itself now fell into their hands. General Hutchinson then closed in upon

Alexandria; and, after hard fighting, Menou at length surrendered. The French troops were allowed to return to France with all their belongings, except the artillery, August 27, 1801.

ARABIC GEOMETRIC DECORATION.

CHAPTER III

THE RULE OF MEHEMET ALI

Mehemet's rise to power: Massacre of the Mamluks: Invasion of the Morea: Battle of Navarino: Struggle with the Porte: Abbas Pasha, Muhammed Said, and Ismail Pasha: Ismail's lavish expenditure: Foreign bondholders and the Dual Control.

MEHEMET ALI.

FROM the beginning of the eighteenth century, the destiny of Egypt was the destiny of one man; he aided the political movements, and accelerated or retarded social activity; he swayed both commerce and agriculture, and organised the army to his liking; he was the heart and brain of this mysterious country. Under the watchful eyes of Europe, attentive for more than forty years, this Macedonian soldier became the personification of the nation under his authority, and, in the main, the history of the country may

143

be summed up in the biography of Mehemet Ali. If we consider the events of his life, and the diverse roads by which he reached the apogee of his fortunes, reviewing the scenes, now sombre, now magnificent, of that remarkable fate, we obtain a complete picture of Egypt itself, seen from the most intimate, real, and striking point of view.

According to the most authentic accounts, Mehemet Ali was born in 1768 (A. H. 1182), at Cavala, a seaport in Turkey in Europe. He was yet very young when he lost his father, Ibrahim Agha, and soon after this misfortune, his uncle and sole remaining relative, Tussun-Agha, was beheaded by order of the Porte. Left an orphan, Mehemet Ali was adopted by the Tchorbadji of Praousta, an old friend of his father, who brought him up with his own son. The boy spent his early youth in the discharge of unimportant military duties, where, however, he frequently found opportunity to display his intelligence and courage. He was even able to render many services to his protector in the collecting of taxes, which was always a difficult matter in Turkey, and occasionally necessitated a regular military expedition.

Anxious to reward Mehemet for all his services, and also doubtless desirous of a still closer connection, the aged Tchorbadji married him to his daughter. This was the beginning of the young man's success; he was then eighteen years old. Dealings with a French merchant of Cavala had inspired him with a taste for commerce, and, devoting himself to it, he speculated with much success, chiefly in tobacco, the richest product of his country.

This period of his life was not without its influence upon Egypt, for we know how strenuously the pasha endeavoured to develop the commercial and manufacturing industries.

The French invasion surprised him in the midst of these peaceful occupations. The Porte, having raised an army in Macedonia, ordered the Tchorbadji to furnish a contingent of three hundred men, who entrusted the command of this small force to his son Ali Agha, appointing Mehemet Ali, whose merit and courage he fully appreciated, as his lieutenant. The Macedonain recruits rejoined the forces of the pasha-captain, and landed with the grand vizier at Abukir, where was fought that battle which resulted in victory for France and the complete defeat of the sultan's army. Completely demoralised by this overthrow, Ali Agha left Mehemet Ali in command of his troops, and quitted the army.

It is well to consider in a brief survey the state of the country at the moment when the incapacity of General Menou compelled the French to withdraw from Egypt. Arrayed against each other were the troops of the sultan, numbering four thousand Albanians and those forces sent from England under the command of Admiral Keith, on one side; and on the other were the Mamluks striving for supremacy; and it was a question whether this powerful force would once more rule Egypt as before the French invasion, or whether the country would again fall under the dominion of the Porte.

There was occasion for anxiety among the Mamluks themselves; their two principal beys, Osman-Bardisi and

Muhammed el-Elfi, instead of strengthening their forces by acting in concert, as Murad Bey and Ibrahim Bey had done before the French occupation, permitted their rivalry for power so completely to absorb them that it was finally the means of encompassing their ruin and that of their party.

The first pasha invested with the viceroyalty of Egypt after the departure of the French troops was Muhammed Khusurf, who faithfully served the Porte. His government was able and zealous, but the measures he employed against his haughty antagonists lacked the lofty intelligence indispensable to so difficult a task. Muhammed Khusurf, whose rivalry with Mehemet Ali had for some years attracted European attention, found himself at last face to face with his future opponent.

Mehemet Ali, by dint of hard work and the many important services rendered to his country, had passed through successive stages of promotion to the rank of serchime, which gave him the command of three or four thousand Albanians. Foreseeing his opportunity, he had employed himself in secretly strengthening his influence over his subordinates; he allied himself with the Mamluks, opened the gates of Cairo to them, and, joining Osman-Bardisi, marched against Khusurf. He pursued the viceroy to Damietta, taking possession of the town, conducted his prisoner to Cairo, where he placed him in the custody of the aged Ibrahim Bey, the Nestor of the Mamluks (1803).

At this moment, the second Mamluk bey, Muhammed el-Elfi, returned from England, whither he had accompanied the British to demand protection when they evacuated Alexandria in March of the same year, and landed at Abukir. This arrival filled Bardisi with the gravest anxiety, for Muhammed el-Elfi was his equal in station, and would share his power even if he did not deprive him of the position he had recently acquired through his own efforts. These fears were but too well founded. Whilst Bardisi was securing his position by warfare, el-Elfi had gained the protection of England, and, as its price, had pledged himself to much that would compromise the future of Egypt.

Far from openly joining one or other of the rival parties, Mehemet Ali contented himself with fanning the flame of their rivalry. The rank of Albanian captain, which gave him the air of a subaltern, greatly facilitated the part he intended to play. He worked quietly and with unending perseverance. Flattering the ambitions of some, feeding the resentment of others, winning the weak-minded with soft words, overcoming the strong by his own strength; presiding over all the revolutions in Cairo, upholding the cause of the pashas when the Mamluks needed support, and, when the pasha had acquired a certain amount of power, uniting himself with the Mamluk against his allies of yesterday; above all, neglecting nothing which could secure him the support of the people, and making use for this end of the sheikhs and Oulemas, whom he conciliated, some by religious appearances, others by his apparent desire for the public good, he thus maintained his position during the numerous changes brought about by the respective parties.

At length, in the beginning of March, 1805, as the people were beginning to weary of disturbances as violent as they were frequent, Mehemet Ali promised the sheikhs to restore peace and order if they would assure him their co-operation and influence. He then incited a revolt against the Oulemas, besieged Kourshyd Pasha in the citadel, made himself master of Cairo in the space of a few days, and finished his work by expelling the Mamluks. The Albanians and Oulemas, completely carried away by his valour and manœuvres, proclaimed him pasha immediately. Always prudent, and anxious to establish his claims upon the favour of the Porte, Mehemet Ali feigned to refuse. After considerable hesitation, which gave way before some costly gifts, or possibly on consideration of the difficulties hitherto experienced in establishing the authority of the pashas, the Turkish government determined to confirm the choice of the Egyptian people. Mehemet Ali received, therefore, the firman of investiture on July 9, 1805; but during the ensuing seven months he governed in Lower Egypt only, Alexandria still being under the authority of an officer delegated by the sultan. As for Upper Egypt, it had remained the appanage of the Mamluk beys, who had contrived to retain possession of the Saïd.

Mehemet Ali had no sooner been proclaimed than Elfi, who had reorganised his party in Upper Egypt, did all in his power to overthrow the new pasha. He first offered to assist Kourshyd to regain his former position; he promised his allegiance to the Porte on condition of the dismissal of Mehemet Ali, and then turned his attention to England. He found difficulty in obtaining her concurrence by promising to give up the chief ports of Egypt. These negotiations, suspended the first time by M. Drovetti, the French consul at Alexandria, co-operating with the pasha, were again renewed some time after through the influence of the English ambassador, who, in the name of his country, demanded the re-establishment of the Mamluks, guaranteeing the fidelity of Elfi. The Porte at once sent a fleet to Egypt bearing a firman, appointing Mehemet Ali to the pashalic of Salonica. At this juncture, the viceroy, feeling sure of the support of the sheikhs, who had assisted him to his present position, only sought to temporise. He soon received the further support of the Mamluk beys of Bardisi's party, who forgot their personal grievances in the desire to be revenged upon the common foe; at the same time, twenty-five French Mamluks, urged thereto by M. Drovetti, deserted the ranks of Elfi's adherents and joined Mehemet Ali.

The Pasha of Egypt possessed a zealous partisan in the French ambassador at Constantinople. The latter, perceiving that the secession of the Mamluks made the regaining of their former power an absolute impossibility, pleaded the cause of Mehemet Ali with the Porte, and obtained a firman re-establishing his viceroyalty, on condition of his payment of an annual tribute of about $1,000,000.

The power of Mehemet Ali was beginning to be more firmly established, and the almost simultaneous deaths of Osman-Bardisi and Muhammed el-Elfi (November, 1806, and January, 1807) seemed to promise a peaceful future, when, on March 17th, the English, displeased at his reconciliation with the Porte, arrived in Egypt. Their forces numbered some seven or eight thousand men, and it was the intention to stir up the Mamluks and render them every assistance. A detachment of the English forces, led by General Fraser, took possession of Alexandria, which the English occupied for six months without being able to attempt any other enterprise. The remainder of the troops were cut to pieces at Rosetta by a small contingent of Albanians: thus ended the expedition. The viceroy, who at the beginning of the campaign had displayed really Oriental cruelty, and sent more than a thousand heads of English soldiers to Cairo to decorate Rumlieh, finished his operations by an act of European generosity, and delivered up his prisoners without demanding ransom. The plan of defence adopted by the pasha was the work of Drovetti, to whom, consequently, is due some of the glory of this rapid triumph.

Mehemet Ali, having nothing further to fear from the English, who evacuated Egypt in September, 1807, began to give scope to his ambitious schemes, when the easily disturbed policy of the Porte saw fit to send the wily pasha against the Wahabis, who threatened to invade the Holy Places. Before obeying these injunctions, the viceroy deemed it wise, previous to engaging in a campaign so perilous, to ensure Egypt against the dangers with which, in the absence of the forces, she would be menaced.

But Egypt had no more powerful enemies than the Mamluks, who, since 1808, had kept the country in a con-

MOSQUE OF MEHEMET ALI IN THE CITADEL.

stant state of agitation. Mehemet Ali therefore determined to put an end to this civil war, root and branch, and to exterminate completely this formidable adversary. He did not hesitate in the choice of means. War would not have succeeded; murder, therefore, was the only alternative, and the viceroy adopted this horrible means of accomplishing his designs. He invited the entire Mamluk corps to a banquet, which he proposed to give in the Citadel Palace in honour of the departure of Tussun Pasha for Mecca. This palace is built upon a rock, and is reached by perpendicular paths. On May 1st, the day fixed upon for the festivity, Mehemet Ali received his guests in great splendour and with a cordiality calculated to dispel any suspicions the Mamluks might have entertained. At the conclusion of the banquet, as they were returning home, they were fired upon in the narrow pass, where retreat and resistance were perfectly impossible. Thus, after having defeated the bravest troops in the world, they died obscurely, ingloriously, and unable to defend themselves. Hassan Bey, brother of the celebrated Elfi, spurred his horse to a gallop, rode over the parapets, and fell, bruised and bleeding, at the foot of the walls, where some Arabs saved him from certain death by aiding his flight. The few who escaped massacre took refuge in Syria or Dongola.

Whilst this horrible drama was being enacted in Cairo, similar scenes were taking place in those provinces whose governors had received stringent commands to butcher every remaining Mamluk in Egypt. Thus nearly all perished, and that famous corps was destroyed for ever.

Although Mehemet Ali had no doubt whatever as to the intentions which had prompted the Porte to organise the expedition against the Wahabis, he hastened to prepare for this lengthy war. Mehemet himself was in command of an army in the Hedjaz when Latif Pasha arrived, bearing a firman of investiture to the pashalic of Egypt. Luckily, Mehemet Ali on his departure had left behind him, as vekyl, a trustworthy man devoted to his interests, namely, Mehemet Bey. This faithful minister pretended to favour the claims of Latif Pasha, and then arrested him, and had him publicly executed.

From this moment the real reign of Mehemet Ali begins. Possessed of a fertile country, he promptly began to consider the ways and means of improving the deplorable state of its finances, and to grasp all the resources which agriculture and commerce could yield for the realisation of his ambitious schemes. Nothing must be neglected in the government of a country for so many years the scene of incessant warfare; the labourer must be made to return to the field he had deserted during the time of trouble; political and civil order must be re-established so as to reassure the inhabitants, and secure the resumption of long abandoned industries.

The most important matter was to restrain the depredations of the Bedouins, and, to assure the obedience of these hitherto unsubdued tribes, he kept their sheikhs as hostages: at the same time he checked the delinquencies of the Kopts, in whose hands the government of the territories had been from time immemorial. A sure and certain peace thus having been ensured to the interior of the country, the pasha turned his attention to another enterprise, the accomplishment of which is always somewhat difficult after a lengthy crisis. He wished to encourage and regulate the payment of taxes without hindering the financial operations of private individuals. To this end, he re-established the custom of receiving tribute in kind, and to support the payment of this tribute he organised the export trade. A thousand vessels built at his own expense ploughed the waters of the Nile in all directions, and conveyed Egyptian produce to the shores of the Mediterranean, where huge warehouses stored the goods destined for foreign countries.

Mehemet Ali preserved a continual intercourse with foreign merchants, and the country owed many fortunate innovations to these relations: agriculture was enriched by several productions hitherto unknown. A Frenchman, M. Jumel, introduced improvements in the production of cotton, whilst M. Drovetti, the pasha's tried friend, helped to further the establishment of manufactories by his advice and great experience of men and things. Before long, cotton mills were built, cloth factories, a sugar refinery, rum distillery, and saltpetre works erected. The foreign trade despatched as much as seven million *ardebs* of cereals every year, and more than six hundred thousand bales of cotton. In return, European gold flowed into the treasury of this industrious pasha, and the revenues of Egypt, which hitherto had never exceeded $150,000,000, were more than doubled in 1816.

The very slight success which Mehemet Ali had obtained when commanding the irregular forces during the expedition against the Wahabis decided him to put a long-cherished idea into execution, namely, to organise an army on European lines. Henceforth this became the sole occupation of the enterprising pasha and the exclusive goal of his perseverance. The Nizam-Jedyd was proclaimed in the month of July, 1815, and all the troops were ordered to model themselves after the pattern of the French army.

This large undertaking, which in 1807 had cost Selim III. his life, proved almost as fatal to Mehemet Ali. A terrible insurrection broke out amongst the alien soldiers, who principally composed the army; the infuriated troops rose against the tyrant and the unbeliever, the palace was pillaged, and the pasha had scarcely time to seek the shelter of his citadel. His only means of saving his life and recovering his authority was solemnly to promise to abandon his plan. Mehemet Ali therefore deferred his military schemes and awaited the opportunity to test its success upon the natives, who would be far more easily managed than the excitable strangers, brought up as they were on the old traditions of the Okaz and the Mamluks. The war which still raged in Arabia gave him the means of ridding himself of the most indomitable men, whom he despatched to Hedjaz under the command of Ibrahim Pasha, his eldest son.

Now came success to console Mehemet Ali for the failure of his reformatory plans. After a long series of disasters, Ibrahim succeeded, in the year 1818, in taking Abd Allah Ibn-Sonud, the chief of the Wahabis, prisoner. He sent him to the Great Pasha, a name often applied to Mehemet Ali in Egypt, at Cairo, bearing a portion of the jewels taken from the temple at Mecca. The unfortunate man was then taken to Constantinople, where his punishment bore testimony to the victory rather than the clemency of his conquerors.

In reward for his services, the sultan sent Ibrahim a mantle of honour and named him Pasha of Egypt, which title conferred on him the highest rank among the viziers and pashas, and even placed him above his own father in the hierarchy of the dignitaries of the Turkish Empire. At the same time Mehemet Ali was raised to the dignity of khan, an attribute of the Ottomans, and the greatest distinction ob-

THE COTTON PLANT.

tainable for a pasha, inasmuch as it was formerly exclusively reserved for the sovereigns of the Crimea.

After destroying Daryeh, the capital of Nedj, Mehemet Ali conceived the idea of extending his possessions in the interior of Africa, and of subduing the country of the negroes, where he hoped to find much treasure. He accordingly sent his son, Ishmail Pasha, with five thousand men, upon this expedition, which ended most disastrously with the murder of Ishmail and his guard by Melek Nemr, and the destruction of the remainder of his forces.

In the year 1824, Sultan Mahmud, realising the impossibility of putting down the Greek insurrection by his own unaided forces, bent his pride sufficiently to ask help of his vassal Mehemet Ali. Mehemet was now in possession of a well-drilled army and a well-equipped fleet, which were placed at the service of the sultan, who promised him in return the sovereignty of Crete, the pashalic of Syria, and possibly the reversion of Morea for his son Ibrahim. The Greeks, deceived by their easy successes over the undisciplined Turkish hosts, failed to realise the greatness of the danger which threatened them. The Egyptian fleet managed, without serious opposition, to enter the Archipelago, and, in December, 1824, Ibrahim, to whom Mehemet Ali had entrusted the supreme command of the expedition, established his base in Crete, within striking distance of the Greek mainland. The following February he landed with four thousand regular infantry and five hundred cavalry at Modon, in the south of Morea.

The Greeks were utterly unable to hold their own against the well-disciplined fellaheen of Ibrahim Bey, and, before the end of the year, the whole of the Peloponnesus, with the exception of a few strongholds, was at the mercy of the invader, and the report was spread that Ibrahim intended to deport the Greek population and re-people the country with Moslem negroes and Arabs.

The only barrier opposed to the entire extinction of the Greek population was their single stronghold of Missolonghi, which was now besieged by Rashid Pasha and the Turks. If Ibrahim had joined his forces with the besieging army of the Turks, Missolonghi could hardly have resisted their combined attack, and the Greek race would have been in danger of suffering annihilation.

Meanwhile the Great Powers of Europe were seriously concerned with this threatened destruction of the Greeks. England proposed a joint intervention in defence of Greece on the part of the Powers, but Russia desired to act alone. A huge army was gradually concentrated upon the Turkish frontier. The Greek leaders now offered to place Greece under British protection, and the Duke of Wellington was sent to St. Petersburg to arrange the terms of the proposed joint intervention. A protocol was signed at St. Petersburg April 4, 1826, whereby England and Russia pledged themselves to co-operate in preventing any further Turco-Egyptian agression. A more definite agreement was reached in September, aiming at the cutting off of Ibrahim in Morea by a united European fleet, thus forcing the Turks and Egyptians to terms. On July 6, 1827, a treaty was signed at London, between England, France, and Russia, which empowered the French and English admirals at Smyrna to part the combatants — by peaceful means if possible, and if not, by force.

Admiral Codrington at once sailed to Nauplia. The Greeks were willing to accept an armistice, but the Turks scorned the offer. At about this time an Egyptian fleet of ninety-two vessels sailed from Alexandria and joined the Ottoman fleet in the bay of Navarino (September 7th). Five days later Admiral Codrington arrived and informed the Turkish admiral that any attempt to leave the bay would be resisted by force. French vessels had also arrived, and Ibrahim agreed not to leave the bay without consulting the sultan. A Greek flotilla having destroyed a Turkish flotilla, Ibrahim took this as a breach of the convention and sailed out to sea, but Codrington succeeded in turning him back. Ibrahim now received instructions from the Porte to the effect that he should defy the Powers. A new ultimatum was at once presented and the allied fleet of the European Powers entered the bay of Navarino. The Turco-Egyptian fleet was disposed at the bottom of the bay in the form of a crescent. Without further parleying, as the fleet of the English and their allies approached, the Turks and Egyptians began to fire, and a battle ensued, apparently without plan on either side: the conflict soon became general, and Admiral Codrington in the *Asia* opened a broadside upon the Egyptian admiral, and quickly reduced his vessel to a wreck. Other vessels in rapid succession shared the same fate, and the conflict raged with great fury for four hours. When the smoke cleared off, the Turks and Egyptians had disappeared, and the bay was strewn with fragments of their ships.

Admiral Codrington now made a demonstration before Alexandria, and Mehemet Ali gladly withdrew his forces from co-operating with such a dangerous ally as

the sultan had proved himself to be. Before the French
expedition, bound for the Morea, had arrived, all the
Egyptian forces had been withdrawn from the Pelo-

A DISTINGUISHED EGYPTIAN JEW.

ponnesus, and the French only arrived after the Anglo-
Egyptian treaty had been signed August 9, 1828.

Mehemet Ali's chief ambition had always been to
enlarge the circle of regeneration in the East. In Morea
he had failed through European intervention. He felt

that his nearer neighbour, Syria, which he had long coveted, would be an easier conquest, and he made the punishment of Abdullah Pasha of Acre, against whom he had many grievances, his excuse to the Porte. In reality it was a case of attacking or being attacked. Through a firman of the Divan of Constantinople, which had been published officially to the European Powers, he knew that his secret relations with Mustapha Pasha of Scodra had become known. He knew also that letters had been intercepted in which he offered this pasha money, troops, and ammunition, while engaging himself to march on the capital of the empire, and that these letters were now in the hand of the Sultan Mahmud. He was also informed that the Porte was preparing to send a formidable army to Egypt; and his sound instinct taught him what to do in this position.

Ibrahim Pasha was appointed commander-in-chief of the invading army, which was composed of six regiments of infantry, four of cavalry, forty field-pieces, and many siege-pieces. Provisions, artillery, and ammunition were on board the men-of-war. Thousands of baggage camels and ambulances were being collected ready for departure when cholera broke out. Coming from India, after having touched along the coasts of the Persian Gulf, it had penetrated into the caravan to Mecca, where the heat and dearth of water had given it fresh intensity. It raged in the Holy Town, striking down twenty thousand victims, and touched at Jeddah and Zambo, where its effects were very dire. Passing through Suez, it decimated the population, and in August it reached Cairo and spread to Upper and Lower Egypt. The army did not escape the common scourge, and when about to invade Syria was overtaken by the epidemic. Five thousand out of ninety thousand perished. All preparations for the expedition were abandoned until a more temperate season improved the sanitary conditions.

About the beginning of October, 1831, the viceroy gave orders to his son to prepare for departure, and on November 2d the troops started for El Arish, the general meeting-place of the army. Ibrahim Pasha went to Alexandria, whence he embarked with his staff and some troops for landing. Uniting at El Arish, the army marched on Gaza and took possession of that town, dispersing some soldiers of the Pasha of Acre. Thence it turned to Jaffa, where it met with no resistance, the Turkish garrison having already evacuated the town.

At this time the army which had sailed from Alexandria was cruising about the port of Jaffa, and Ibrahim Pasha landed there and took over the command of the army, which advanced slowly on St. Jean d'Acre, seizing Caiffa to facilitate the anchoring of the fleet, which had landed provisions, artillery, and all kinds of ammunition. After six months' siege and ten hours' fighting, Ibrahim Pasha obtained possession of St. Jean d'Acre, under whose walls fell so many valiant crusaders, and which, since the repulse of Napoleon, had passed for all but impregnable. Abdullah Pasha evinced a desire to be taken to Egypt, and he landed at Alexandria, where he was warmly welcomed by the viceroy, who complimented him on his defence.

Hostile in everything to Mehemet Ali, the Porte seized every opportunity of injuring him. When Sultan Mahmud learned of the victory of the viceroy's troops in Syria, he sent one of his first officers to enquire the reason of this invasion. The viceroy alleged grievances against the Pasha of Acre, to which his Highness replied that he alone had the right to punish his subjects.

The eyes of Europe were now fixed upon the Levant, where a novel struggle was going on between vassal and suzerain. Authority and liberty were again opposing each other. The Powers watched the struggle with intense interest. The viceroy protested against bearing the cost of the war, and demanded the investiture of Syria. Mehemet Ali was then declared a rebel, and a firman was issued against him, in support of which excommunication an army of sixty thousand men advanced across Asia Minor to the Syrian boundaries, while a squadron of twenty-five sail stood in the Dardanelles ready to weigh anchor.

The Porte forbade the ambassadors of the Powers to import ammunition into Egypt, for it feared that the viceroy might find a support whose strength it knew only too well. But the viceroy had no need of this, for his former connections with Europe had put him in a position of independence, whereas the Porte itself was obliged to fall back on this support. Russia, the one of the three Great Powers whose disposition it was to support the authority of the sultan, lent him twenty thousand bayonets, whilst Ibrahim Pasha made his advance to the gates of Constantinople.

Immediately after the taking of St. Jean d'Acre, Ibrahim Pasha, following up his successes, had turned towards Damascus, which town he entered without a

MOSQUE OF MUAD AT CAIRO.

blow being struck, the governor and the leading inhabitants having taken flight. The commander-in-chief established his headquarters under the walls of the conquered country, and then marched in three columns on

Homs. The battle of Homs (July 8, 1832) demonstrated the vast superiority of the Egyptian troops. On both sides there were about thirty thousand regular soldiers, but the Egyptians were the better organised, the better disciplined, and the more practised in the arts of war. When it is remembered that at Homs the Turks lost two thousand men killed, and 2,500 taken prisoners, while the Egyptian casualties were only 102 killed and 162 wounded, one is not astonished at the enthusiasm with which Ibrahim Pasha wrote after the battle: " I do not hesitate to say that two or three hundred thousand of such troops would cause me no anxiety."

It is not surprising that the beaten pashas were so struck with terror that in their flight they abandoned sixteen more pieces of artillery and all the ammunition they had managed to save from their defeat. They fled as if they could not put sufficient distance between themselves and their redoubtable enemy.

This battle foretold the result of the Syrian campaign. The population of Syria seemed to call for the domination of the conqueror; the viceroy protested his submission to the Porte and his desire for peace, and meanwhile Ibrahim Pasha marched forward.

The Porte counted on its fleet to guard the Dardanelles, but it needed an army and a commander to oppose Ibrahim Pasha, who again defeated the Turks at Oulon-Kislak. He then advanced towards the plains of Anatolia, where he met Rashid Pasha.

It was now December, 1830, and the atmosphere was heavy with a thick fog. The armies opened fire on each other on December 21st, with the town of Koniah in the background. The grand vizier was at the head of close on sixty thousand men, while the Egyptian army only comprised thirty thousand, including the Bedouins. The fighting had continued for about six hours when Rashid Pasha was taken prisoner; the news of his capture spread along the Turkish lines and threw them into disorder, and the Egyptians remained masters of the field, with twenty pieces of mounted cannon and some baggage: the Turks had lost only five hundred men, while the Egyptian losses were but two hundred.

The battle of Koniah was the last act in the Syrian drama. The sultan's throne was shaken, and its fall might involve great changes in the politics of the world. Ibrahim Pasha was only three days' journey from the Bosphorus, and the way was open to him, with no Turkish army to fight and the whole population in his favour. In Constantinople itself Mehemet Ali had a powerful party, and, if the West did not interfere, the Ottoman Empire was at an end. However, European diplomacy considered that, in spite of its weakness, it should still weigh in the balance of the nations.

Trembling in the midst of his harem, Sultan Mahmud cried for help, and Russia, his nearest neighbour, heard the call. This was the Power that, either from sympathy or ambition, was the most inclined to come to his aid. The Emperor Nicholas had offered assistance in a letter brought to the sultan by the Russian General Mouravieff, and a Russian squadron appeared in the Bosphorus with eight thousand men for disembarkment. The Russians, however, agreed not to set foot on shore unless Mehemet Ali should refuse the conditions that were being proposed to him. The viceroy refused the conditions, which limited his possessions to the pashalics of Acre, Tripoli, and Seyd, and which seemed to him incompatible with the glory won by his arms.

The sultan did not wish to give up Syria, but that province was no longer his. The sword of Ibrahim had severed the last bonds that fastened it to him, and he was obliged to yield it, as well as the district of Andama. On his side, the viceroy acknowledged himself a vassal of the Porte, and agreed to make an annual payment of the monies he received from the pashas of Syria. This peace was concluded on May 14, 1833, and was called the peace of Kutayeh, after the place where Ibrahim signed it.

It was impossible that the convention of Kutayeh should be more than an armistice. The pasha benefited by it too greatly not to desire further advantages, and the sultan had lost so much that he must needs make some attempt at recovery. Mahmud's annoyance was caused by the fact and nature of the dispossession rather than by its material extent. The descendant of the Osmanlis, ever implacable in his hatreds, who had allowed Syria, the cradle of his race, to be wrested from him, now awaited the hour of vengeance. Mehemet Ali knew himself to be strong enough to carry a sceptre ably, and he realised that there would be no need for his numerous pashalics to pass out of his family. Henceforth his mind was filled with thoughts of independence and the rights of succession.

The viceroy and the sultan continued to strengthen their forces, and a conflict occurred near Nezib on June 24, 1839. The Egyptians completely routed their ad-

A MUHAMMEDAN PRAYING PRIEST.

versaries, despite the strenuous resistance of the Imperial Guard, who, when called upon to surrender, cried in the same words used at Waterloo, "Khasse sultanem

mamatenda darrhi tuffenguini iere Koimas " (" The
guards of the sultan surrender arms only to death ").

Greatly elated, Ibrahim flung himself into the arms
of his companion in glory, Suleiman Pasha. His pre-
diction was verified: " This time we will go to Constantinople, or they shall come to Cairo." They set out for
Constantinople; but the viceroy was again generous.
Through the mediation of Captain Caillé, aide-de-camp
to Marshal Soult, who, in the name of France, demanded
a cessation of hostilities, Mehemet Ali desired his son
not to proceed into Asia Minor; so the general halted
before Aintab, the scene of his victories, as he had done
on a former occasion before Kutayeh.

Consumptive and exhausted with his excesses, Mahmud, whose virtue lay in his ardent love of reforms, died
before his time, but this untimely demise at least spared
him the knowledge of the Nezib disaster and the treason
of his fleet, which passed into the hands of the viceroy.
Hafiz Pasha, routed by Ibrahim, was arraigned on his
return to Constantinople for leading the attack before
receiving the official mandate; but the Turkish general
produced an autograph of his defunct master. The sultan
had been false to the last, and deceived both European
ambassadors and the ministers of the empire, by means
of mysterious correspondence, combined with his protes-
tations for the maintenance of peace.

It was while Mehemet Ali was organising the national
guard of Egypt, and arranging the military training of
the workmen employed in his many factories, that the
unlucky treaty of July 15, 1840, which gave the whole

of Syria to the Sublime Porte, was concluded. Four Western Powers had secretly met in London and agreed to deprive the sovereign of the Nile of his conquests, and fling him again at the foot of the throne, which he had treated as a plaything. Mehemet Ali haughtily protested against the desecration of his rights, and France, his faithful ally, with hand on sword-hilt, threatened to draw it against whosoever should touch Egypt. England and Austria covered the Syrian sea-coast with their sails and guns. Beyrut, Latakia, Tortosa, Tripoli, Saida, Tyre, St. Jean d'Acre were bombarded and fell. This formidable coalition despatched Lord Napier to Alexandria as negotiator. Mehemet Ali accepted the overtures, and a convention guaranteed to him, as Pasha of Egypt, rights of succession unknown to all other pashalics of the empire. The hatti-sherif of January 12, 1841, consolidated this privilege, with, however, certain restrictions which were regarded as inadmissible by France, the viceroy, and the cabinets. A new act of investiture, passed on June 1, 1841, confirmed the viceroy in the possession of Egypt, transmissible to his male heirs, and also in the government of Nubia. Mehemet Ali asked no more, France declared herself satisfied, and, to prove it, became once more a member of the European league by the treaty of July 15, 1841, which, without being directly connected with the European question, dealing as it did with the claims of Turkey upon the Dardanelles, implied, none the less, accordance upon the Eastern situation. As a token of reconciliation, the Ottoman Porte soon raised its former rival, Mehemet Ali, to the rank of sadrazam.

The political history of Mehemet Ali was now at an end. All the results, good or bad, of his career, had reached fulfilment. As a vanquished conqueror he had been able to remain firm in the midst of catastrophe; his fatherly ideas and feelings had been his salvation. Had he been absolutely heroic, he would have considered it a duty, for his courage and his name's sake, to carry the struggle on to the bitter end, and to perish in the whirlpool he had raised. He showed that he desired to act thus, but in his children's interests he refrained, and this was, we believe, the only influence of importance which made him give way. It is true that there was not much difference between a throne crumbling to ruins, or one built thereon; such as it was, however, it seemed firmly secured to his children, and it was for them to strengthen the foundations. The pasha considered this a fitting reward for his labours; as for himself, he was over seventy years of age, and ready to lay down his burdens.

A man without learning and surrounded by barbarian soldiers, Mehemet Ali appears before the world as nature made him. Dissimulation, diplomacy, and deceit, coupled with capability, great courage, genius, and much perseverance, brought him to the head of the government of Egypt. To gain his ends he flattered the powerful Ulemas who were the nation's representatives to the sultan, but, once having obtained his object, he dismissed them.

Though a clever politician, he was a bad administrator. Being alternately blindly confident and extremely

EGYPTIAN HAREM.

suspicious, he did not choose well the men he employed as his auxiliaries, and, being a Turk and a devout Mussulman, Mehemet Ali wished to give back to the Turks the power they had lost. He only took account of the results of any undertaking, without paying any attention to the difficulties surmounted in its execution, and this characteristic made him commit many injustices. It was his habit to treat men as levers, which he put aside when he had no further use for them. He was quick of apprehension, and of very superior intelligence, and his whole character was a mixture of generosity and meanness, of greatness and littleness.

Mehemet Ali was an affable, an easy business man, and dominated by a desire to talk. He enjoyed relating the incidents of his past life, and, when not preoccupied by affairs of importance, his conversation was full of charm. The foreigners who visited him were always much impressed with his superiority, while his lively humour, his freedom, and that air of good nature he knew so well how to adopt, all captivated his visitors. The expression of his face was exceedingly mobile, and quickly communicated itself to the men who surrounded him, who were in constant observation of his moods, so that one could judge of the state of mind of the viceroy by the calm or disturbed appearance of his servants.

When Mehemet Ali was anxious, his look became fierce, his forehead wrinkled, and his eyes shone with anger, while his speech was broken and his manner brusque and imperious. As regards those in his service, Mehemet Ali was by turns severe or gentle, tolerant or impatient, irascible, and surprisingly forbearing. He was jealous of the glory of others, and desired all honours for himself. He was an enemy of all that was slow. He liked to do everything, to decide everything, and worked night and day. All letters, notices, and memoranda that referred to his government, he read himself or had them read to him. Picked men translated French and English political newspapers into Turkish, and he encouraged discussion on all subjects of high interest, although generally imposing his own opinion. He did not always keep strictly to his word. He was a stoic, and great pain could not destroy his habitual gaiety, and when very ill he would still speak affably to those around him; but illnesses with him were rare, for his health was, as a rule, excellent. He was very careful about his appearance, and was fond of women without being their slave; in his youth his life had been dissolute. He was above the prejudices of his nation, and prayed very often, although a fatalist.

At the age of forty-five he learned to read, and he held European learning in great esteem, confessing it superior to that of Turkey; but he continued to regard European scientists and artists only as salaried foreigners, whom he hastened to replace by natives as soon as he considered the latter sufficiently enlightened. Mehemet Ali made one great mistake, with which his nearest servants reproach him, and that is with not having introduced into his family learned men from Europe, picked men devoted to his cause, and well versed in the special things of which his country was in need.

Had they been brought into a close contact with the viceroy, and admitted unreservedly to all the privileges the Turks enjoyed, these men would have adopted Egypt as their country. They would have spoken the language and have become the sentinels and safeguards necessary for the maintenance of useful institutions which the Turks either refused or did not understand.

During the administration of Mehemet Ali, public hygiene was not neglected, and a sanitary council watched over the health of the country. Measures were taken to increase the cleanliness and sanitation of the towns; military hospitals were built, and a lazarette was established at Alexandria, whilst vaccine was widely used. In the country the planting of many trees helped the atmosphere, and Egypt, which Europeans had hitherto regarded as the seat of a permanent plague epidemic, became more and more a healthy and pleasurable resort. Mehemet, whose aims were always for the furthering of Egyptian prosperity, profited by the leisure of peace to look after the industrial works. Two great projects that occupied his attention were the Nile dams and the construction of a railway from Suez to Cairo.

The actual condition of the canalisation of Egypt, while vastly improved by the viceroy, was still far from complete. Canals, partial dams, and embankments were attempted; fifty thousand draw-wells carried the water up to a considerable height, but the system of irrigation was insufficient.

The railway from Cairo to Suez was an easier, though not less important, work. The road crossed neither mountain, river, nor forest, while a series of little plains afforded a firm foundation, requiring very few earth-works. Its two iron arms stretched out into the desert, and steam-engines could traverse the distance from the Nile to the Red Sea in three hours.

Suez would thus become a suburb of Cairo, and thus, being brought closer to Egypt, would regain her trade. This enterprise, just as the former one, gave promise of bringing to Egypt the two sources of national wealth and prosperity: agriculture and trade.

The agricultural unity which Mehemet Ali consti-tuted enabled him to bring about improvements which with private proprietorship would have been impossible. The fellah, careless of to-morrow, did not sow for future reaping, and made no progress, but when Mehemet Ali undertook the control of agricultural labour in Egypt, the general aspect of the country changed, though, in truth, the individual condition of the fellah was not improved. Besides the work of irrigation by means of canals, dykes, and banks, and the introduction of the cultivation of indigo, cotton, opium, and silk, the viceroy had also planted thousands of trees of various kinds, including 100,000 walnut-trees; he ordered the maimours, or prefects, to open up the roads between the villages, and to plant trees. He wished the villages, towns, and hamlets to be ornamented, as in Europe, with large trees, under whose shelter the tired traveller could rest.

In the various districts were vast tracts of land which for a long time the plough had not touched. Con-cessions of these lands were made to Franks, Turks,

HARBOUR OF BULAK.

Greeks, and Armenians, which concessions were free, and for a term of seven or eight years, while the guarantees were exempt from taxes.

During the closing years of his life, between 1841 and 1849, Mehemet occupied himself with improvements in Egypt. He continued to prosecute his commercial speculations, and manufacturing, educational, and other schemes. The barrage of the Nile, which has only been finished during the British occupation, was begun under his direction. In 1847 he visited Constantinople, and was received with the rank of a vizier. In the year 1848 symptoms of imbecility appeared, and his son Ibrahim was declared his successor. After a reign of only two months he died. Mehemet Ali's death occurred on the 3rd of August, 1849. His direct successor was his grandson, Abbas Pasha, who held the sceptre of Egypt as the direct heir of Ibrahim Pasha. This prince took but little interest in the welfare of his country. He had in him no spark of the noble ambition of his predecessor, and no trace of his genius, and he showed no desire for progress or reforms. He was a real prince of the ancient East, suspicious, sombre, and careless of the destiny of the country entrusted to his care. He liked to withdraw to the privacy of his palace, and, isolated in the midst of his guards, to live that life of the distrustful and voluptuous despots of the East. The palace of Bar-el-Beda, which he had built on the road to Suez in the open desert, a palace without water, lifting its head in the solitude like a silent witness of a useless life and tragic death, impresses the traveller with astonishment and fear.

Abbas Pasha was weak in his negotiations with the European Powers, and this was well for Egypt, as their representative was able to hold in check his silent hostility to Western civilisation. Such guardianship is useful when exercised over a prince like Abbas Pasha, but it tends to become troublesome and baneful when it attempts to interfere with the government of an active and enlightened sovereign animated by just and generous intentions.

Muhammed Said, the successor of Abbas Pasha, was born in 1822, nine years later than his nephew Abbas. He was brought up in Europe by French professors, and M. Kornig, a distinguished Orientalist, remained with his pupil and became his secretary. He not only instructed him in all branches of knowledge becoming to his rank, but also developed in him a love of European civilisation and noble sentiments, of which he gave proof from the moment of his accession. He was imbued with liberal principles, which in an Eastern potentate give proof of great moral superiority, and in this respect Muhammed Said was second to no prince in Europe. He worked for the emancipation of his subjects and the civilisation of Egypt, and was not content to produce that superficial civilisation which consists in transplanting institutions that the mass of the people could not understand. Said Pasha endeavoured to pursue his father's policy and to carry out his high aims. He had not, however, the strength of character nor the health necessary to meet the serious difficulties involved in such a task, and he will be chiefly remembered by his abolition of the more grinding government monopolies, and for the concession of the Suez Canal.

After his death Said Pasha was succeeded in the viceroyalty by his nephew, Ismail Pasha, who was proclaimed viceroy without opposition early in the year 1863. Ismail, the first who accepted the title of khedive from the sultan, was born on December 31, 1830, being the second of the three sons of Ibrahim, and grandson of Mehemet Ali. He had been educated at the Ecole d'Etat Major at Paris, and when Ahmed, the eldest son of Ibrahim, died in 1858, Ismail became the heir to his uncle Said. He had been employed, after his return to Egypt, on missions to the sovereign pontiff; the emperor, Napoleon III.; and the Sultan of Turkey. In the year 1861 he was despatched with an army of 18,000 men to quell an insurrection in the Sudan, which undertaking he brought to a successful conclusion. On ascending the throne he was much gratified to find that, on account of the scarcity of cotton, resulting from the Civil War in America, the revenues had very considerably increased from the export of the Egyptian cotton. At this date the cotton crop was worth $125,000,000, instead of $25,000,000, which was the normal value of the Egyptian output. It was a very serious misfortune to Egypt that during his sojourn abroad Ismail had learned many luxurious ways, and had also discovered that European nations were accustomed to make free use of their credit in raising sums of money for their immediate advantage. From this moment Ismail started upon a career which gave to Egypt, in the eyes of the world, a fictitious grandeur, and which

made him one of the most talked-of rulers among the
cabinets and peoples of the European countries. He
began by transferring his own private debts to the state,
and thereafter looked upon Egypt merely as his private
estate, and himself as the sovereign landholder. Without
any sense of his responsibility to the Egyptians themselves, he increased his own fame throughout Europe
in the sumptuous fashion of a spendthrift millionaire.
He deemed it necessary for his fame that Egypt should
possess institutions modelled upon those of European
countries, and he applied himself with energy to achieve
this, and without any stint of expense. By burdening
posterity for centuries to come, Ismail, during the two
decades subsequent to his accession, always had a supply
of ready money with which to dazzle European guests.
During his entire reign Egypt swarmed with financiers
and schemers of every description, to whom the compla-
cent Ismail lent an only too willing ear.

In the year 1866, in return for an increase of tribute,
he obtained from the sultan a firman giving him the title
of khedive (Turkish, *khidewi*, a king), and changing the
law of succession to that of direct descent from father
to son; and in 1873 he obtained a new firman, purchased
again at an immense cost to his subjects, which rendered
him practically independent of the sultan. Ismail projected vast schemes of internal reform. He remodelled
the system of customs and the post-office, stimulated commercial progress, and created the Egyptian sugar indus-
try. He introduced European improvements into Cairo
and Alexandria; he built vast palaces, entertained vis-

itors with lavish generosity, and maintained an opera and
a theatre.   By his order the distinguished composer,
Verdi, produced the famous opera " Aïda " for the enter-
tainment of his illustrious guests on the occasion of their
visit to Egypt during the festivities connected with the
opening of the Suez Canal.   On this occasion Mariette
Bey ransacked the tombs of the ancient Egyptian kings

A FELLAH PLOWING.

in order to reproduce in a lifelike manner the costumes
and scenery appropriate for the occasion.

The opening of this canal gave Ismail much prominence in the courts of Europe. He was made a Grand
Commander of the Bath, and the same year visited Paris
and London, where he was received by Queen Victoria
and welcomed by the lord mayor. In 1869 he again
visited London. By his great power of fascination and

lavish expenditure he was ever able to make a striking impression upon the foreign courts. During the opening of the canal, when Ismail gave and received royal honours, treating monarchs as equals, and being treated by them in like manner, the jealousy of the sultan was aroused. Ismail, however, contrived judiciously to appease the suspicions of his overlord, Abdul Aziz.

In the year 1876 the old system of consular jurisdiction for foreigners was abolished, and the system of mixed courts was introduced, by which European and native judges sat together to try all civil cases, without respect to nationality.

In the year 1874 Darfur, a province in the Sudan west of Kordofan, was annexed by Ismail. He also engaged in a disastrous war against the Abyssinians, who had ever shown themselves capable of resisting the inroads of Egyptians, Muhammedans, Arabs, and even of European invaders, as was proven by the annihilation of a large Italian army of invasion, and the abandonment of the campaign against Abyssinia by the Italians in the closing years of the nineteenth century.

It was true that Ismail had attempted to carry out the great schemes of his grandfather for the regeneration of the Orient, and it is possible that, if the jealousy of European Powers had not prevented the army of Ibrahim Bey from controlling immense territories in Syria and Anatolia, which they had won by conquest, that the regeneration of the Orient might have been accomplished at least a century earlier. No people would have benefited more by the success of Mehemet Ali's policy than the

ARABS AT A DESERT SPRING.

Christian people who to-day are under the rule of the barbarous Turks. With the regeneration of the Orient, the trade of European nations in the East would have been very largely increased.

The policy of regeneration, wisely begun by Mehemet Ali, was resumed within Egypt itself in a spendthrift manner by his grandson Ismail. Every act of his reign, with its ephemeral and hollow magnificence, moved towards the one inevitable result of foreign intervention. The price of all the transient splendour was the surrender by slow degrees of the sovereignty and independence of Egypt itself. The European Powers of late have withdrawn their interest in the betterment of the native populations in the Asiatic dominions of the sultan, and have concerned themselves exclusively with the immediate interests of commerce and the enforcement of debts contracted to European bondholders. All progress in the later history of Egypt has originated in the desire of the European Powers to see Egypt in a position capable of meeting her indebtedness to foreign bondholders.

In so far as the cry raised of " Egypt for the Egyptians " was a protest against forcing the Egyptians to pay for an assumed indebtedness which was at least four times greater than anything they had actually received, no movement was ever more just and righteous than the protest of the fellaheen against foreign control, a movement which has been chiefly associated with the name of Arabi Pasha. The issue of Ismail's financial troubles was most ignominious and disastrous to Egypt, after nearly a hundred years of heroic struggles to keep

pace with the progress of modern Europe. Had Ismail
modelled his career upon that of his illustrious grandfather, rather than that of Napoleon III., with which it
shows many striking parallels, it is probable that the
advantage secured to Egypt through the British occupation might have resulted in political and financial independence. When the crash came, and the order for his
deposition was sent by the sultan, Ismail resigned the
khedivate in complete submission; and, taking away with
him a large private fortune and a portion of the royal
harem, he spent the remainder of his life in retirement at
Naples and Constantinople, and was buried with solemn
pomp in the royal cemetery at Cairo.

PART OF CAIRO, SHOWING THE MULQUFS ON THE HOUSES
OF MODERN EGYPT.

TOMBS OF BENI HASAN.

CHAPTER IV

THE BRITISH INFLUENCE IN EGYPT

Ismail deposed : Tewfik Pasha : Revolt of Arabi Pasha : Lord Wolseley and
the Battle of Tel-el-Kebir : The Mahdist Rising : General Gordon in the
Sudan : Death of Gordon : The Sudan abandoned and re-conquered :
Battle of Omdurman : Khartum College : Financial Stability : Abbas II. :
Education, Law, and the improved condition of the Fellaheen : The
Caisse de la Dette.

HE official deposition of Ismail Pasha by
the sultan of Turkey, Abdul Hamid, oc-
curred on June 26, in the year 1879, and
his son Tewfik assumed the khedivate,
becoming practically the protégé of England and Egypt. To understand how this came to pass,
it is necessary to review the account of the financial
embarrassments of Ismail. In twelve years he had ex-
tracted more than $400,000,000 from the fellaheen in
taxes. He had borrowed another $400,000,000 from
Europe at the same time, of which nominal sum he

probably received $250,000,000 in cash. The loans were ostensibly contracted for public works. Possibly ten per cent. of the borrowed money was profitably laid out. The railways were extended; Upper Egypt was studded with sugar factories,—most of them doomed to failure,—and certain roads and gardens were made about the city of Cairo.

The remainder of this enormous sum of money was spent in purchasing a change in the law of succession, and the new title of khedive; in disastrous Abyssinian campaigns; in multiplying shoddy palaces, and in personal extravagance, which combined Oriental profusion with the worst taste of the Second Empire. Useless works engaged the corvée; the fellaheen were evicted from vast tracts, which became ill-managed estates; and their crops, cattle, and even seed were taken from them by the tax-gatherers, so that they died by hundreds when a low Nile afflicted the land. The only persons who flourished in Ismail's time were foreign speculators and adventurers of the lowest type. As these conditions became more serious, the khedive attempted to find some means of protection against the concession-monger. He adopted a suggestion of the wise Nubar Pasha, and instituted the mixed tribunals for adjudging civil cases between natives and foreigners.

The Powers agreed to the establishment of these tribunals, and intended to enforce the decisions of the courts, even in case that Ismail himself were the delinquent. When later the khedive repudiated the mixed tribunals, this action precipitated his fall.

It became increasingly difficult for the khedive to meet his accumulated obligations. The price of cotton had fallen after the close of the American war, and there was less response from the impoverished people to the Courbash, which in 1868 was still more strictly enforced; and soon this enforcement by the mixed tribunal of debts due to foreigners by an agricultural population, who lived by borrowing, and were accustomed to settle their debts by haggling, aggravated the misery of the fellaheen, and led to that universal despair which was to give strength and significance to the Arabist revolt. It was no uncommon procedure for the Levantine money-lender to accompany the tax-gatherer into the provinces with a chest of money. He paid the taxes of the assembled and destitute fellaheen, who in return were obliged to give mortgages on their crops or holdings.

The desperate state of Egyptian finance, which led to the sale of the precious Suez Canal shares, at last opened the eyes of the bondholders. Mr. G. T. Goschen (Viscount Goschen) and M. Joubert were deputed to Egypt on behalf of the foreign creditors. The accounts were found to be in a state of wild confusion, with little or no chance of learning the actual facts controlling the financial situation. The minister of finance, or " Mufettish," Ismail Pasha Sadeck, was now arrested and banished to Dongola.

There was an immediate prospect of a dual control by England and France. Commissioners were appointed to constitute a caisse, or court, for receiving the interest due to the bondholders. The great mass of the debt was then unified, but the Goschen and Joubert arrangement was found to be too severe for the impoverished country. A low Nile and a famine resulted in a demand for an investigation into the administration, and the following year Ismail was obliged to authorise a commission of inquiry. The waste, extravagance, and wholesale extortion from the peasantry revealed by this report made a deep impression upon Europe, and Ismail was forced to disgorge the estates which he had received from the fellaheen.

In the meantime, the khedive was not inactive in taking measures to prevent the advent of a confirmed foreign control. He created a constitutional ministry, upon whom the responsibility rested for the different branches of the administration. He likewise fomented an outburst of feeling among the Moslems against the foreign element in the constitutional ministry. This was intended to strengthen the pro-Egyptian element in the government, and Ismail thus hoped to demonstrate to the European Powers the uselessness of attempting to subordinate the Egyptians to foreign methods of finance and control. Ismail subsequently dismissed the ministry, and soon afterwards the controllers themselves. Knowing well the jealousy which existed between England and France, he believed that there was a chance that he might successfully play off one Power against the other. If the Moslems had not been so severely oppressed by taxation, and Ismail had acted with courage and firmness, it is probable that he might have held his own, and Egypt might have refused to again accept the dual control.

Bismarck now intervened, and hinted to the sultan that he would receive the support of the Powers, and Abdul Hamid immediately sent a telegram to the Egyptian government that Ismail Pasha was deposed from the khedivate. At this moment his courage gave way, and Ismail surrendered his throne to his son Tewfik.

THE KHEDIVE TEWFIK.

Tewfik had the misfortune to enter upon a doleful heritage of an empty treasury, a starving people, and an army ready to mutiny. There were now two parties in Egypt. The military movement was of the least importance. The superior posts in the army had been occupied by Circassians since the days of Mehemet Ali.

Slave boys were bought and trained as officers. The number and quality of the Circassians had deteriorated, but they still held the most important posts. The fellaheen officers, under Arabi, who had been brought to protest against reductions in the military establishment, now claimed that the Circassians should make way for the Egyptians. Together with this military dissatisfaction was also a strong civil movement towards national reform, which included a number of serious and sensible administrative reforms, which have since been carried out. Arabi Pasha was the leader of the National Party, and had hopes of convincing fair-minded people of the justice of their cause; but many influences, some good and some bad, were at work simultaneously to divert him from constitutional methods towards making his appeal to the violent and fanatical element.

Just at this time a divergence between English and French views in dealing with the situation had manifested itself, having its root in earlier history. France, now as in 1840, was aiming at the policy of detaching Egypt from the control of the unprogressive Turks; England aimed at the maintenance of the much talked of integrity of the Ottoman Empire. The French premier, Gambetta, was determined that there should be no intervention on the part of the Turks. He drafted the "Identic Note" in January, 1881, and induced Lord Granville, the English Foreign Secretary, to give his assent. This note contained the first distinct threat of foreign intervention. The result was a genuine and spontaneous outburst of Moslem feeling. All parties united to protest against foreign intervention, joined by the fellaheen, who now saw an opportunity of freeing themselves from foreign usurers, to whom they had become so unjustly indebted. Riots broke out in Alexandria in 1881. Gambetta was replaced by the hesitating Freycinet, who looked upon the intervention with alarm, and upon Germany with suspicion. England was thus at the last moment left to act alone. Past experience had taught her that the destiny of Egypt lay in the hands of the dominant sea-power of the Mediterranean, and that Egypt must not be neglected by the masters of India.

After a vain attempt to bring about mediation through Dervish Pasha, the special commissioner of the Porte, it was discovered that the Nationalist Party was too little under control to be utilised in any further negotiations. Ahmed Arabi Pasha had greatly increased his influence, and had finally been appointed Minister of War. On the 11th of June there was serious rioting, in which many Greeks and Maltese, four Englishmen, and six Frenchmen were slain. Arabi now stepped forward to preserve order, being at this moment practically the dictator of Egypt. While endeavouring to maintain order, he also threw up earthworks to protect the harbour of Alexandria, and trained the guns upon the British fleet. The admiral in charge, Sir Beauchamp Seymour, who was waiting for the arrival of the Channel Squadron, sent word to the Egyptians to cease the construction of fortifications. The request was not fully assented to, although it was reinforced by an order from the Porte. An ultimatum was presented on July 10, commanding

Arabi to surrender the forts. The terms were refused, and eight ships and five gunboats prepared for action on the following day. At the same time the French fleet retired upon Port Said.

The first shot was fired on July 11th, at seven o'clock in the morning, by the Alexandrians, and in reply an iron hail rained upon the forts of the Egyptians from the guns of the British fleet. Arabi's troops fought well and aimed correctly, but their missiles were incapable of penetrating the armour of the ironclads. One fort after another was silenced. Lord Charles Beresford, in command of the gunboat *Condor*, led a brilliant attack upon Fort Marabout. The firing re-opened on the next day, and a flag of truce was soon displayed. After some unsatisfactory parleying the bombardment was resumed, and when a second flag of truce was unfurled it was discovered that Arabi Pasha had retreated to Kefr-el-Dowar, fourteen miles away from Alexandria. On his departure the city was given over to plunder and destruction. The convicts escaped from the prison, and, joining forces with the Arabs, looted and burned the European quarters. Two thousand persons, mostly Greeks and Levantines, were slain, and an enormous quantity of property destroyed. Admiral Seymour then sent a body of sailors on land, who patrolled the streets and shot down the looters, and order was thus finally restored in Alexandria. The khedive, who was forced to fly for his life to an English steamer, was reinstated in the Ras-el-Tin Palace, under an escort of seven hundred marines. The British admiral was afterwards severely criticised for not having put a stop to the rioting before it assumed such serious proportions.

Arabi's army of 6,000 was now increased by recruits flocking in from every port in Egypt. After considerable pressure had been brought to bear upon the khedive, Tewfik issued a proclamation dismissing Arabi from his service. To enforce the submission of the Arabists, an English army of 33,000 men was gradually landed in Egypt, under the command of Sir Garnet Wolseley, with an efficient staff, including Sir John Adye, Sir Archibald Alison, Sir Evelyn Wood, and General Hamley. An Indian contingent also arrived under General Macpherson.

Sir Garnet, after making a feint to land near Alexandria, steamed to Port Said and disembarked, moving up the Suez Canal in order to join forces with the Indian contingent, who were advancing from Suez. Fighting took place over the control of the canal at the Mahsameh and Kassassin Locks, and at the latter place the British cavalry won an important victory over the Egyptian advance-guard. Arabi's stronghold was at Tel-el-Kebir, and the English were very anxious to win a decisive victory before the troops which the sultan was sending from Constantinople under Dervish and Baker Pasha should arrive. On September 12, 1882, preparations had been completed for an advance, and the army of 11,000 infantry and 2,000 cavalry, with sixty pieces of artillery, moved forward during the night to within a mile of Arabi's lines. The Egyptians had 20,000 regulars, of which number 2,500 were cavalry, with seventy guns, and they were also aided by 6,000 Bedouins. Though well situated, the army of Arabi was taken by surprise, and the following day, in response to the various flanking movements of the British, directed by Wolseley, and the direct charge of the Highlanders, they made but a very indifferent defence. In a brief space of time the Egyptians were in full retreat, Arabi fleeing to Cairo. The Indian contingent occupied Zagazig, and General Drury-Lowe rode with his cavalry for thirty-nine miles, and entered Cairo on the evening of the 14th. Arabi made a dignified surrender, and with him 10,000 men also gave themselves up.

The Nationalist movement was now at an end, the various garrisons surrendering one after another, and the greater part of the British army left Egypt, 12,000 men remaining behind to maintain order. The Egyptian government wished to try Arabi as a rebel in a secret tribunal. It was generally believed that this would have meant a death sentence. Mr. Wilfrid Blunt, a distinguished British Liberal and a friend of Arabi, who had often expressed his sympathy with the cause of the Nationalists in their endeavour to free Egypt from the slavery of the foreign bondholder, now raised a vigorous protest in favour of an open trial. He personally contributed to the defence of Arabi, and his efforts led to the commutation of the sentence of death to that of perpetual exile in Ceylon — a sentence which was subsequently very much modified. Arabi Pasha returned to Egypt in the year 1902, after an exile which had lasted about nine years.

The difficult task of readjusting the government of
Egypt was then undertaken. Proposals were made to
France for a modification of the dual control, in which
France was offered the presidency of the Debt Commission. France, however, refused to accept the compromise, and the British government finally determined
upon independent action. In place of the officials through

PALACE OF THE KHEDIVE AT ALEXANDRIA.

whom the two governments had hitherto exercised the
control, a single financial adviser was appointed, who
was not allowed to take part in the direct administration
of the country. The outline of this adjustment was given
in a circular note addressed by Lord Granville to the
Powers. He declared that an army would remain in
Egypt as long as it was required; representative institutions were to be created; the Egyptian army and gendarmery were to be placed in the hands of Englishmen;

the Diara estates were to be economically managed; foreigners were to be placed upon the same footing as natives in regard to taxation. The other Powers, including Turkey but excluding France, accepted the agreement. The office of financial adviser was given to Sir Edgar Vincent.

The important work of the reconstruction of Egypt now began in earnest. Sir Benson Maxwell set about establishing an effective means for the impartial administration of justice, and Colonel Moncrieff undertook the responsibility for the work of irrigation. Mr. Clifford Lloyd created a police system, reorganised the prisons and hospitals, and set free the untried prisoners. Baker Pasha formed a provincial gendarmery, and Sir Evelyn Wood organised an army of six thousand men.

In the year 1883, while this work of reconstruction was proceeding, a religious insurrection, which had originated two years previously, was forced upon the notice of the government. It has already been related that the Ismailian sect of the Muhammedans had introduced the doctrine of a coming Messiah, or Mahdi, who was to be the last of the imans, and the incarnation of the universal soul.[1]

Not a few impostors had exploited this doctrine to their own advantage, and some of the Arabian tribes were firmly convinced that the Mahdi had come, and that the Mahdis who had appeared to their kinsmen elsewhere were merely clever charlatans. In the year 1881 Muhammed Ahmet, a religious leader among the Moslem Arabs in the Central African provinces of Kordofan and

[1] See Volume XI., page 375.

Darfur, proclaimed himself as the Mahdi, and called upon the Muhammedans to initiate a holy war.

The Mahdi's continued advances were rendered possible by the precarious state of affairs in Egypt. After a settlement was effected in 1883, Hicks Pasha, an officer of courage and ability, who had retired from the Indian army, gathered 11,000 men at Omdurman to quell the Mahdist insurrection. With this force he started up the Nile and struck across the desert to El-Obeid, where his troops were decoyed into a ravine, and after three days' fighting his whole army was annihilated by the Mahdist army numbering about 300,000 men. The entire Sudan then revolted against Egypt. The redoubtable Osman Digna appeared with the Hadendowa Arabs off the coast of the Red Sea, and harassed the Egyptian garrison. Osman defeated Captain Moncrieff and an army of 3,000 Bashi-Bazouks led by Baker Pasha. Egypt, under the advisement of the British government, then attempted to withdraw from the Sudan. It was decided that the western provinces of Kordofan and Dafur should be abandoned, but that important centres like Khartum on the Nile should be preserved, at least for a time. Here all the Egyptian colonists were to congregate. If the revolting Arab tribes, called by the general name of Dervishes, would not come to friendly terms with the settlers, then, in time, it was decided that Khartum itself, and every other locality in the Sudan, should be entirely relinquished, except the ports of the Red Sea.

General Gordon was sent to Khartum to make terms with the Mahdi and prepare for eventualities. The evacuation of this place was almost immediately decided upon by the British Cabinet, and Gordon arrived on February 18, 1884, but, being unsupported by European troops, he found the position an exceedingly difficult one to maintain. The Mahdi scorned his overtures, and Osman Digna was daily closing in upon the Egyptian port of Suakin. The British then determined to act with vigour. Sinkitat had fallen on February 8th, and to protect Tokar and Suakin they landed four thousand men and fought a fierce battle with nine thousand Hadendowas at El-Teb February 28, 1884. The Egyptian garrison of Tokar, when the British army arrived, was found to have compromised with the Mahdists. Later on was fought the battle of Tamai against Osman Digna, during which a body of Arabs rushed the British guns and broke up the formation of their square. The British were on the point of defeat, but they managed to recover the lost guns, and scatter the Hadendowas.

OSMAN DIGNA.

General Gordon's situation was now extremely critical. It was hoped that an army might advance from Suakin across the desert to Berber, and then ascend the

Nile to Khartum. In the meantime, Gordon urgently called for help, and, after interminable delays, in the autumn of 1884, an English army under Lord Wolseley started up the Nile to relieve him. The troops of Wolseley were aided by a camel corps of one thousand men, who were organised to make a rush across the desert. On the 16th of January, 1885, the camel troops came up with the enemy and fought the decisive battle of Matammeh. The Mahdist troops were mown down by rifles and Gatling-guns as soon as they were within short range. Immediately after the battle, Sir Charles Wilson determined to use the Egyptian flotilla to make an immediate advance. The steamers were protected, and a small relief force started on January 24th. They came in sight of Khartum on the 28th, but were fired upon from every side. At this moment, a native called from the bank that the city had fallen, and that the heroic Gordon had been killed.

A history of Egypt would be incomplete without some account of that leader whose bravery, humanitarian views, and understanding of the Oriental character have made him famous among the pioneers of Christian civilisation in Asia and Africa. Fresh from his laurels won in the service of the Chinese government in suppressing the Tai-peng rebellion, Gordon returned to England in 1871. In 1874 he accepted a position from Egypt, with the consent of the British government. He journeyed to Cairo and up the Nile to take up the command as governor of the Equatorial Provinces in succession to Sir Samuel Baker. There he laboured with incessant energy to put down the slave-trade and to secure the welfare of the natives. He established a series of Egyptian outposts along the Abyssinian frontier and made a survey of Lake Albert Nyanza. Returning to Cairo in 1874, after some delay, he was appointed by Ismail Pasha as governor-general of the whole of the Egyptian Sudan. A war followed with Abyssinia, and, after the army, led by Egyptian officers, had been beaten twice, Gordon went to Massowah to negotiate with the Abyssinian monarch, Atti Johannes. He next proceeded to Khartum, and vigorously undertook the suppression of the slave-trade.

Gordon's death at Khartum, in 1884, is one of the greatest tragedies of modern history. Supported neither by Egypt nor by the English army, of a different religion from all his followers, pressed on all sides by the Mahdist forces, Gordon gallantly kept his few faithful followers at his side, and, with incessant activity and heroism, protected the remaining Egyptian colonists of the cities along the Nile, over which he still held control. He had called upon the British government to send aid across the desert from Suakin via Berber, but this request had been denied him. Berber then fell, and he was cut off to the north by many hundred miles of territory occupied by Mahdists. On January the 1st, nearly a month before the long-delayed succour approached the beleaguered city, the provisions had given out. He had written on December 14th that, with two hundred men, he could have successfully kept up the defence. As his army had been starving since the 5th of January, it is

MOSQUE OF THE HOLY IBRAHIM AT DESUK.

difficult to understand how he managed to hold out till January the 26th. On this date, two days before the relief expedition approached, the Mahdi's troops attacked Khartum, and, finding Gordon's men too weak to fight, the defences were cut down, and the heroic Gordon was killed by a shot at the head of the steps of the palace.

Upon learning of the death of Gordon, the relief expedition retreated, finding that the object of their advance had proved to be a hopeless one. A general evacuation was begun, and Dongola and the whole country south of Wady Halfa surrendered. The Mahdi, soon after winning Khartum, died, and was succeeded by the Califa Abdulla at Taashi. This change facilitated the Anglo-Egyptian retreat. About the same time Slatin Bey surrendered in Darfur and embraced Muhammedanism, and Lupton Bey, following his example, also adopted the religion of Islam, and yielded in Bahr-el-Ghazel. Emin Pasha alone retained his authority, derived originally from Egypt, in the province of Equatoria. Sir H. M. Stanley afterwards made his famous journey " Through Darkest Africa " and rescued this famous pasha. This noted explorer died May 9, 1904.

In the autumn of 1885, the dervish Emir of Dongola, Muhammed el-Kheir, advanced upon the Egyptian frontier. On December 30th he was met by the Egyptian troops under Sir Frederick Stephenson. The Egyptian troops, unaided by Europeans, attacked the dervishes at Ginnis and totally defeated them, winning two guns and twenty banners. It was a source of much gratification that the Egyptian fellaheen had proved themselves so courageous and well disciplined in the encounter with the fierce hosts of the desert.

In October, 1886, Wad en Nejumi, the victor of El-Obeid, was sent by the califa to invade Egypt. The

LORD KITCHENER OF KHARTUM.

advance of this army was delayed by trouble within the Sudan; but the califa, having at length beaten his ene-mies, in the year 1889 sent large reinforcements north-wards to carry on the campaign against Egypt with vigour. The Egyptian troops, with one squadron of hussars, fought a decisive engagement with Wad en Nejumi on August 3rd of the same year. The dervish leader, many of his emirs, and twelve hundred Arab warriors were slain; four thousand more were taken prisoners, and 147 dervish standards were captured.

The ever-increasing progress of Egypt during the next ten years, together with the accounts received from escaped prisoners of the reign of terror and inhumanity which obtained in the Sudan, brought the question of the reconquest of the lost provinces once more into prominence. The Italians had met with a fearful disaster in fighting against the Abyssinians at the battle of Adowa on March 1, 1896. They were holding Kassala within the ex-Egyptian territory by invitation from England, and a reason was presented for attacking the dervishes elsewhere in order to draw off their army from Kassala. With the appointment of Sir Henry Kitchener, on March 11, 1896, as sirdar of the Egyptian army, the final period of hostilities was entered upon between Egypt and the independent Arabs of the Central African Provinces.

General Kitchener was ordered to build a railroad up the Nile, and to push forward with a well-organised Egyptian army, whose chief officers were Englishmen. The whole scheme of the invasion was planned with consummate forethought and deliberation, the officials and advisers in charge of the enterprise being chosen from the most tried and able experts in their several provinces. Lieut.-Col. E. P. C. Girouard, a brilliant young Canadian, undertook the work of railroad reconstruction. Col. L. Rundle was chief of the staff, and Major R. Wingate head of the Intelligence Department, ably assisted by the ex-prisoner of the califa, Slatin Bey. The army consisted in the beginning almost entirely of Egyptian and Sudanese troops, together with one battalion of the North Staffordshire Regiment. There were eight battalions of artillery, eight camel corps, and sixty-three gunboats which steamed up the Nile.

After some sharp skirmishing, the advance was made to Dongola, when the English battalion was sent home disabled, and in time was replaced by a strong English brigade under General Gatacre. Early in 1897, a railroad had been thrown across the desert from Wady Halfa towards Abu Hamed, obviating the need of making an immense detour around the bend of the Nile near Dongola. The califa had, by this time, organised his defence. The Jaalin tribe had revolted against him at Metammeh, and had sought for help from the Egyptians, but before the supply of rifles arrived, the dervishes under the Emir Mahmud stormed Metammeh and annihilated the whole tribe of the Jaalin Arabs.

The van of the army of invasion, both the flying corps and the flotilla of gunboats, advanced upon Abu Hamed towards the end of August. Major-General Hunter carried the place by storm. Berber was found to be deserted, and was occupied on September 5th. Hunter burned Adarama and reconnoitred on the Atbara. The gunboats bombarded Metammeh and reduced the place to ruins. The sirdar, General Kitchener, then went on a mission to Kassala, where he found the Italians anxious to evacuate. He thereupon made an agreement whereby the Egyptians should occupy the place, which was accordingly accomplished under Colonel Parsons on Christmas Day, 1897. Disagreements among the dervishes prevented them from making any concerted defence, and early in 1896 Kitchener renewed the advance and captured the dervish stores at Shendy on March 27th. The zeriba or camp of Mahmud was attacked and stormed with great loss to the dervishes on the 5th of April.

On the date scheduled beforehand by Lord Kitchener, just after the annual rains had refreshed the country, the Anglo-Egyptian army made its final advance upon Khartum. There were ten thousand British troops and fifteen thousand Egyptians. The forces were concentrated at Wady Hamed, sixty miles above Omdurman, from which point they bombarded the city with shells filled with deadly lyddite, and the mosque and tomb of the late Mahdi were destroyed. At length the entire army advanced to within four miles of Khartum. On September 2nd the cavalry and a horse battery reached Kasar Shanbal. From this point they saw the whole army of the califa, consisting of from forty to fifty thousand men, advancing to confront them from behind the hills. The Anglo-Egyptians advanced to meet the dervishes disposed in the form of a horseshoe, with either end resting upon the banks of the river. At intervals along the whole line of the army were field-pieces and Maxims, and the gunboats were within reach to aid in shelling the enemy. The British soldiers then built a square sand rampart called a zarilea, and their Egyptian allies dug defensive trenches.

On the front and left the dervishes came on in great strength, but, when the Maxims, the field-guns, and the repeating rifles opened fire upon them, at a comparatively close range, a frightful havoc was the result. All who remained to fight were immediately shot down, and the whole field was cleared in fifteen minutes. The dervishes retreated behind the hills, and were joined by fresh forces. General MacDonald, in making a detour with a body of Lancers, was suddenly beset by two thousand dervish riflemen, who fiercely charged him on three sides. Quickly forming a square, he succeeded by desperate efforts in repelling the enemy, until he was reinforced by Kitchener, who perceived his desperate situation.

The califa then attacked the extreme left wing of the army, but was again driven off. The Anglo-Egyptians were now in a position to deliver the main attack upon the dervish defences. The troops of the califa fought with heroic bravery, fearlessly advancing within range of the Anglo-Egyptian fire, but each time they were mown down by the cross fire of the Maxims and rifles. Vast numbers were slain, and some divisions of the dervishes suffered complete annihilation. They left ten thousand dead upon the field, and ten thousand wounded. The rest fled in all directions, a scattered and straggling force, with the califa himself. The Anglo-Egyptians lost but two thousand men. Few prisoners were taken, for, in almost every instance, the dervishes refused to surrender, and even when wounded used their swords and spears against the rescuers of the ambulance corps. All the fighting was over by midday, and in the afternoon

General Kitchener entered Omdurman, and the army encamped in the vicinity. Slatin Bey was duly installed as governor in the name of the Egyptian khedive. The European prisoners of the califa were now released, and on Sunday, the 4th of September, the sirdar and all his army held a solemn service in memory of General Gordon near the spot where he was killed.

Bodies of men were now sent out on all sides to pacify the country, and the sirdar, who had been elevated to the peerage as Lord Kitchener of Khartum, started on an expedition up the Nile in a gunboat, in order to settle the difficult question arising from the occupation of Fashoda by a French corps under Major Marchand. The ability and strategy of this French commander were of a very high order. The general plan of the expedition had been in accord with French military traditions, based upon former attempts in India and America to separate the British colonial dominions, or to block the way to their extension by establishing a series of military out-posts or forts at certain strategic points chosen for this purpose. Had the French designs under Desaix in India, or of the army of occupation in the Mississippi Valley in the eighteenth century, been supported by a powerful fleet, there is no doubt that British colonisation would have suffered a severe setback. If Major Marchand remained in Fashoda, the route to all the upper regions of the Nile would be cut off from any English or Egyptian enterprise. Accordingly, Lord Kitchener ran the risk of grave international complications by advancing upon Fashoda to meet Major Marchand. Fortunately, a temporary agreement was entered upon that the home governments should decide the question at issue, and Lord Kitchener then hoisted the Anglo-Egyptian flag south of the French settlement, and the officers fraternised over glasses of champagne.

It is now believed that Russia would have aided France if it had come to a war, but the French government thought the affair not of sufficient importance to warrant an international struggle over the retention of Fashoda, and the respective spheres of influence of France and Great Britain were finally agreed upon early in the following year by the Niger Convention, which left the whole of the ex-Egyptian provinces under British protection, as far south as the Equatorial Lakes, and as far west as the border line between Darfur and Wadai.

The califa was subsequently pursued from place to place in the desert, and was at length overtaken by Colonel Wingate at Om Dubreikat. The dervish leader fought a desperate fight; and, refusing to fly, was slain with all his personal followers on November 26, 1899.

The total cost of these campaigns had been incredibly small, not amounting in all to the total of $12,000,000, and the railroad, the cost of which is here included in the expenditure, is of permanent value to Egypt.

After the re-occupation of Khartum, it was again, as in Gordon's time, made the seat of government, the dervish capital having been located across the Nile at Omdurman. For a memorial to Gordon, $500,000 was enthusiastically raised in England. The memorial took the practical form of an educational establishment for the natives of the Sudan, the foundation-stone of which was laid by Lord Cromer in January, 1900. The school is intended to be exclusively for Muhammedans, and only the Moslem religion is to be taught within its walls.

Though the Mahdism, of which the late califa had been the leading spirit, had degenerated into a struggle of slave-traders versus civilisation, the califa at least showed conspicuous courage in the manner in which he faced his death. For the last twenty years, during which the revolts of the dervishes had troubled the outlying provinces of the Egyptian dominions, trade had been almost at a standstill; large numbers of blacks had been enslaved; an equal number probably had been slaughtered, and whole regions depopulated. The total population was cut down during these years to one-half of what it previously had been, and it was of vital importance to Egypt to reconquer all the lost provinces which lay upon the banks of the river Nile. If the prosperity of Egypt is to rest upon a sound basis, and not be subjected to periodic overthrow at the hands of the hostile inhabitants of the south, it is essential that the Upper Nile should be under the control of those who are responsible for the welfare of the country. Egypt is the gift of the Nile, and the entire population of Egypt is dependent upon this river. To secure prosperity for the country and to develop Egyptian resources to the fullest extent, the rulers of Egypt must also be the rulers of the Nile. When the Anglo-Egyptian expedition under Kitchener set out to reconquer the Sudan, the development of Egypt had been progressing in all directions at a rapid rate. Having greater interests to defend, less indebtedness to meet, and greater facilities for meeting the taxes due the home government, no less than the foreign bondholders, the time was ripe in which to take that great step towards securing the prosperity of Egypt in the future by finally destroying the community of slaveholders, which, under the sanction of Mahdism,

SLAVE BOATS ON THE NILE.

brutally tyrannised over the non-Muhammedan population.

From the beginning of the British occupation, the English have been engaged in persevering efforts at reform in every branch of the administration. The reforms which they instituted in the different departments of the army, finance, public works, and the police system were not at first popular. The native officials found out that they could not use methods of extortion; the upper classes, the pashas, and the wealthy landowners also discovered that they were not at liberty to do as they pleased, and that the English inspectors of irrigation strictly regulated the water-supply. It has since been fully demonstrated that the curtailing of their privilege to make use of the water when and how they chose is more than compensated by improved conditions.

During the fifteen years previous to 1898, the population of Egypt had increased by about three million, or forty-three per cent. It was then ten million; it is now nearly eleven million. Within the boundaries of the irrigated land Egypt has always been a very populous country. By the effort to expand this area of irrigation, the way was prepared for a considerable increase in the total population. There are sections of this land where the density of the population averages from seven to eight hundred or even a thousand persons to the square mile. In early times, the population was still greater, as the irrigation area was increased by the great reservoir of Lake Mœris. When Omar made a census (A. D. 640), there were to be found six million Kopts, exclusive of the aged, the young, and the women, and three hundred thousand Greeks: this would imply, even at that decadent period, a total population of fifteen million.

The increased prosperity shown by the railroads is most satisfactory. Two hundred and twelve miles of new railroad have been constructed, and an enormous development of the railroad and telegraph business has resulted. Since the year 1897 railroad development has been very rapid, and, with the line to the Sudan, amounted in 1904 to some two thousand miles. From the Sudan railway it is intended ultimately to extend a railroad system through the heart of Africa, from Cairo to Capetown.

Great progress has been made in all departments of public works. Hundreds of agricultural roads have been built, and the mileage of canals and drains has been largely increased to the very great benefit of the Egyptian peasant.

The quantity of salt sold was doubled between 1881 and 1897, while the price has been reduced nearly forty per cent. The tonnage of the port of Alexandria increased from 1,250,000 pounds to 2,549,739 between 1881 and 1901. This increase was paralleled by a like increase in Alexandria's great rival, Port Said.

Sir Evelyn Baring (Viscount Cromer) was appointed consul-general and financial adviser to Egypt in January, 1884, succeeding in this position Sir Edward Malet. Sir Evelyn was nominally the financial adviser, but practically the master of Egypt. The khedive never ventured to oppose the carrying out of his wishes, since the British army of occupation was ever at his beck and call to lend its weight to the commands which he issued to the government under the appearance of friendly advice.

The most serious obstacle to the progress of Egypt has been the authority of the mixed administrations, the chief of which is the Caisse de la Dette. The main object of these administrations is to secure for European bondholders payment of the debts incurred by Egypt chiefly under the incredibly profligate government of Ismail Pasha. The Caisse de la Dette has commissions

from six of the Powers. It receives from the tax-gatherer all the taxes apportioned to the payment of the
interest for foreign indebtedness. Its influence, however, extends much farther, and the Caisse exercises the
right of prohibiting expenditure on the part of the Egyptian government until its own demands for current interest have been complied with. It further has the right
to veto any loan which the Egyptian government might
be willing to raise, however urgent the necessity might
be, unless it can be demonstrated that there is not the
least likelihood that payment of the shareholders whom
the Caisse represents will be in the least degree affected.
If all that the Caisse claimed as belonging to its jurisdiction were really allowed to it by the Anglo-Egyptian
government, the Caisse or International Court might
exercise an arbitrary control over Egyptian affairs. It
has many times seriously attempted to block the progress of Egypt with the sole aim of considering the pockets
of the foreign shareholders, and in entire disregard to
the welfare of the people.

Added to this tribunal is the Railway Board and the
Commissions of the Daira and Domains. The Railway
Board administers the railroads, telegraphs, and the port
of Alexandria. The Daira and Domains Commissions
administer the large estates, mortgaged to the holders
of the loans raised by Ismail Pasha under these two respective names. The Daira Estate yielded a surplus over
and above the amount of interest on the debt paid, for
the first time, in 1890. The Domain Estate had to face
a deficit until the year 1900. Until these respective dates

the Egyptian government itself was obliged to pay the deficit due to the bondholders.

In the year 1884, the Convention of London was signed by the European Powers, which was, however, for the most part, oppressive and unjust to the Egyptians. The amount of money raised by taxation, which was allowed to be spent in one year, was limited to the definite sum of $25,927,890. Fortunately for Egypt, the London Convention had one clause by which $44,760,000 could be utilised for the development of the country. With this sum the indemnities of Alexandria were paid, defects in the payment of interest were made good, and a small sum was left wherewith to increase irrigation and other useful works. The criminal folly of the former lavish expenditure was now demonstrated by a brilliant object-lesson. This small sum, when kept out of the hands of the rapacious bondholders, and applied to the development of the rich soil of Egypt, was found to work wonders. From the moment when the finances of Egypt were for the first time used to develop what is naturally the richest soil in the world, progress towards betterment grew rapidly into the remarkable prosperity of to-day. For a time, however, the government was obliged to use extreme parsimony in order to keep the country from further falling under the control of the irresponsible bondholders. Finally, in the year 1888, Sir Evelyn Baring wrote to the home government that the situation was so far improved that in his judgment " it would take a series of untoward events seriously to endanger the stability of Egyptian finance and the solvency of the

Egyptian government.'' The corner had been turned, and progressive financial relief was at length afforded the long-suffering Egyptian people in the year 1890. After several years of financial betterment, it was de-

VISCOUNT CROMER (SIR EVELYN BARING).

cided to devote future surpluses to remunerative objects, such as works of irrigation, railway extension, the construction of hospitals, prisons, and other public buildings, and in the improvement of the system of education. Great difficulty was experienced in making use of this surplus, on account of technical hindrances which were persistently placed in the way of the Egyptian government by the Caisse de la Dette. These difficulties are now almost entirely removed.

In 1896 it was decided, as has been narrated, to be for the interest of Egypt to start a campaign against the dervishes. Appeal was made to the Caisse de la Dette to raise additional funds for the necessary expenses of the projected campaign. The Caisse, following its universal precedent, immediately vetoed the project. England then made special grants-in-aid to Egypt, which both aided the Egyptian government and greatly strengthened her hold upon Egypt. By means of this timely assistance, Egypt was enabled successfully to pass through the period of increased expenditure incurred by the reconquest of the Sudan.

During the lifetime of Khedive Tewfik, who owed his throne to the British occupation, there had been little or no disagreement between the British and Egyptian authorities. In the year 1887 Sir Henry Drummond Wolff prepared a convention, in accordance with which England promised to leave Egypt within three years from that date. At the last moment the sultan, urged by France and Russia, refused to sign it, and the occupation which these two Powers would not agree to legalise even for a period of three years was now less likely than ever to terminate. The following year Tewfik dismissed Nubar Pasha, who had, by the advice of the foreign Powers, stood in the way of reforms planned by the English officials.

Tewfik died in 1892, and was succeeded by Abbas
Hilmi Pasha, called officially Abbas II. He was born in
1874, and was barely of age according to Turkish law,
which fixes magistracy at eighteen years of age in the
case of the succession to the throne. He came directly
from the college at Vienna to Cairo, where his accession
was celebrated with great pomp; and the firman, con-
firming him in all the powers, privileges, and territorial
rights which his father had enjoyed, was read from the
steps of the palace in Abdin Square. For some time the
new khedive did not coöperate with cordiality with Great
Britain. He was young and eager to exercise his power.
His throne had not been saved for him by the British,
as his father's had been, and he was surrounded by in-
triguers, who were scheming always for their own
advantage. He at first appeared almost as unprogressive
as his great-uncle, Abbas I., but he later learned to understand the importance of British counsels. During his
visit to England in 1899 he frankly acknowledged the
great good which England had done in Egypt, and declared himself ready to coöperate with the officials ad-
ministering British affairs. This friendliness was a great
change from the disposition which he had shown in previous years, during the long-drawn-out dispute between
himself and Sir Evelyn Baring regarding the appointment of Egyptian officials. The controversy at one time
indicated a grave crisis, and it is reported that on one
occasion the British agent ordered the army to make
a demonstration before the palace, and pointed out to
the young ruler the folly of forcing events which would

inevitably lead to his dethronement. The tension was gradually relaxed, and compromises brought about which resulted in harmony between the khedive and the British policy of administration, and no one rejoiced more than Abbas Hilmi over the victory of Omdurman.

Agricultural interests are dearer to the heart of the khedive than statecraft. He rides well, drives well, rises early, and is of abstemious habits. Turkish is his mother tongue, but he talks Arabic with fluency and speaks English, French, and German very well.

An agreement between England and Egypt had been entered upon January 19, 1899, in regard to the administration of the Sudan. According to this agreement, the British and Egyptian flags were to be used together, and the supreme military and civil command was vested in the governor-general, who is appointed by the khedive on the recommendation of the British government, and who cannot be removed without the latter's consent. This has proved so successful that the governor-general, Sir Reginald Wingate, reported in 1901:

" I record my appreciation of the manner in which the officers, non-commissioned officers, soldiers, and officials,—British, Egyptian, and Sudanese,—without distinction, have laboured during the past year to push on the work of regenerating the country. Nor can I pass over without mention the loyal and valuable assistance I have received from many of the loyal ulemas, sheiks, and notables, who have displayed a most genuine desire to see their country once more advancing in the path of progress, material success, and novel development."

BAZAR IN ASWAN.

In 1898 there were in all about 10,000 schools, with 17,000 teachers and 228,000 pupils. Seven-eighths of these schools were elementary, the education being confined to reading, writing, and the rudiments of arithmetic. The government has under its immediate direction eighty-seven schools of the lowest grade, called kuttabs, and thirty-five of the higher grades, three secondary, two girls' schools, and ten schools for higher or professional education,—the school of law, the school of medicine, with its pharmaceutical school and its school for nursing and obstetrics, polytechnic schools for civil engineers, two training-schools for schoolmasters, a school of agriculture, two technical schools, one training-school for female teachers, and the military school. In addition to the schools belonging to the Ministry of Public Instruction, there were under the inspection of that department in 1901 twenty-three primary schools of the higher grade, with an attendance of 3,585, and 845 schools of the lowest grade, with 1,364 teachers and an attendance of 26,831 pupils. There are 187 schools attached to various Protestant and Catholic missions, and forty-three European private schools.

The Koptic community supports one thousand schools for elementary education, twenty-seven primary boys' and girls' schools, and one college. The teaching of the Koptic language in the schools is now compulsory; the subjects taught, and the methods of teaching them, are the same as in vogue in other countries. Fifty per cent. of the Koptic male population can read and write well. The indigenous tribunals of the country are called

Mehkemmehs, and are presided over by cadis. At the present time they retain jurisdiction in matters of personal law relating to marriage succession, guardianship, etc. Beyond this sphere they also fulfil certain functions connected with the registration of title of land. In matters of personal law, however, the native Christians are subject to their own patriarchs or other religious leaders.

In other matters, natives are justiciable before the so-called native tribunals, established during the period of the British occupation. These consist of forty-six summary tribunals, each presided over by a single judge, who is empowered to exercise jurisdiction in matters up to $500 in value, and criminal jurisdiction in offences punishable by fine or by imprisonment of three years or less. Associated with these are seven central tribunals, each chamber consisting of three judges. There is also a court of appeal in Cairo, one-half of its members being Europeans. In criminal matters there is always a right to appeal, sometimes to the court of appeal, sometimes to a central tribunal. In civil matters an appeal lies from a summary tribunal to a central tribunal in matters exceeding $500 in value, and from the judgment of a central tribunal in the first instance to the court of appeal in all cases. The prosecution in criminal matters is entrusted to the parquet, which is directed by a procurer-general; the investigation of crime is ordinarily conducted by the parquet, or by the police under its direction. Offences against irrigation laws, which were once of such frequent occurrence and the occasion of injustice and lawlessness, are now tried by special and summary administration tribunals.

The capitulations or agreements concerning justice entered into by all the Great Powers of Europe and the Ottoman Empire, relative to the trial and judgment of Europeans, include Egypt as an integral part of the Turkish Empire. Foreigners for this reason have the privilege of being tried by European courts. But if one party in a case is European and another Egyptian, there are special mixed tribunals, established in 1876, consisting partly of native and partly of foreign judges. These tribunals settle civil and also some criminal cases between Egyptians and Europeans, and in 1900 penal jurisdiction was conferred upon them in connection with offences against the bankruptcy laws.

There are three mixed tribunals of the first class, with a court of appeal, sitting at Alexandria. Civil cases between foreigners of the same nationality are tried before their own consular courts, which also try criminal cases not within the jurisdiction of the mixed tribunals, in which the accused are foreigners. By this well organised administration of justice, crime has steadily decreased throughout Egypt, and the people have learned to enjoy the benefit of receiving impartial justice, from which they had been shut off for many centuries.

About sixty per cent. of the inhabitants of modern Egypt belong to the agricultural class—the fellaheen. The peasantry are primitive and thrifty in their habits, and hold tenaciously to their ancient traditions. They are a healthy race, good-tempered and tractable, and fairly

intelligent, but, like all Southern nations breathing a
balmy atmosphere, they are unprogressive. Centuries of
oppression have not, however, crushed their cheerfulness.
There is none of that abject misery of poverty among the

MOSQUE OF EL GHURI AT CAIRO.

Egyptians which is to be seen in cold countries. There is
no starvation amongst them. Food is cheap, and a
peasant can live well on a piastre (five cents) a day.
A single cotton garment is enough for clothing, and the

merest hut affords sufficient protection. The wants of
the Egyptians are few. Their condition, now freed from
forced labour, called the " Courbash," as also from injustice, crushing taxation, and usury, which character-
ised former administrations, compares favourably with
the peasantry of many countries in Europe, and is equal,
if not superior, to that of the peasantry of England itself.

Under the British protection there has been a renewal of the Koptic Christian race. They are easily to
be distinguished from their Muhammedan countrymen,
being lighter in colour, and resembling the portraits on
the ancient monuments. They are a strong community
in Upper Egypt, whither they fled from the Arab invaders, and they there hold a large portion of the land.
They live mostly in the towns, are better educated than
other Egyptians, and are employed frequently in the
government service as clerks and accountants.

Koptic is still studied for church purposes by the
Kopts, who both by their physiognomy and by their retention of the old Egyptian institution of monasticism
are the only true descendants having the social and phys-
ical heredity of the ancient Egyptians. Four of the
oldest monasteries in the world still survive in the Natron
Valley. In spite of their distinguished social ancestry,
the Kopts are by no means a superior class morally to
the fellaheen, who are in part the descendants of those
ancient Egyptians who renounced the Christian religion,
the language and institutions of the Egyptian Christians,
and accepted Muhammedanism and the Arabic language
and institutions.

The creed of the Kopts is Jacobite. They have three metropolitans and twelve bishops in Egypt, one metropolitan and two bishops in Abyssinia, and one bishop in Khartum. There are also arch-priests, priests, deacons, and monks. Priests must be married before ordination, but celibacy is imposed upon monks and high dignitaries. The Abyssinian Church is ruled by a metropolitan, and bishops are chosen from amongst the Egyptian-Koptic ecclesiastics, nor can the coronation of the King of Abyssinia take place until he has been anointed by the metropolitan, and this only after the authorisation by the Patriarch of Alexandria.

CROCODILES AND A HIPPOPOTAMUS IN THE NILE.

CHAPTER V

THE WATER WAYS OF EGYPT

The White and Blue Niles : The Barrage ; Clearing the Sudd : The Suez Canal : Ancient and modern irrigation : The Dam at Aswan : The modern exploration of the Nile.

ETWEEN the Sudan and the Mediterranean the only perennial stream is the Nile, a word probably derived from the Semitic root nahal, meaning a valley or a river-valley, and subsequently a "river," in a pre-eminent and exclusive sense. The ancient Egyptians called it the Ar or Aur (Koptic, Iaro), or "black"; hence the Greek word μέλας in allusion to the colour, not of the water, but of the sediment which it precipitated during the floods. In contrast to the yellow sands of the surrounding desert, the Nile mud is black enough to have given the land itself its oldest name, Kem, or Kemi, which has the same meaning of "black." At Khartum, where the White Nile joins the Blue Nile, the main branch has a fall from its upper level in the region of the tropical lakes, four

235

thousand feet above the sea, to twelve hundred feet, while traversing a distance of twenty-three hundred miles. From Khartum to the sea the distance through which the waters of the Nile wend their way is about eighteen hundred and forty miles. During the greater part of this course the flow is level, the average descent being about eight inches per mile. If it were not, therefore, for the obstruction met with in the Nubian section, the course of the Nile would be everywhere navigable. Although no perennial affluents enter the main stream lower down than Khartum, the volume of the Nile remains with little diminution throughout the entire distance to the Mediterranean. During the period of low water the amount of water in different localities is still uniform, notwithstanding all the irrigation, infiltration, and evaporation constantly taking place. The only explanation which has been given to this phenomenon is that there are hidden wells in the bed of the Nile, and from their flow the waste is ever renewed.

As the earth revolves from west to east, the waters of the Nile tend to be driven upon the right bank on the west, where the current is constantly eating away the sandstone and limestone cliffs. For this reason the left side of the river is far more fertile and well cultivated than the right bank. Below Ombos the valley is narrowly constructed, being but thirteen hundred yards in width, the cliffs overhanging the river on either side, but at Thebes it broadens out to nine or ten miles, and farther up, in the Keneh district, the valley is twelve or fifteen miles in width. The river here approaches within sixty miles of the Red Sea, and it is believed that a branch of the Nile once flowed out into the sea in this direction.

Seventy miles below Keneh the Nile throws from its left bank the Bahr Yusef branch, a small current of 350 feet in breadth, which flows for hundreds of miles through the broader strip of alluvial land between the

THE PLAIN OF THEBES.

main stream and the Libyan escarpments. In the Beni-Suef district this stream again bifurcates, the chief branch continuing to wind along the Nile Valley to a point above the Delta, where it joins the main stream. The left branch penetrates westward through a gap in the Libyan escarpments into the Fayum depression, ramifying into a thousand irrigating rills, and pouring its overflow into the Birket-el-Qarûm, or "Lake of

Horns," which still floods the lowest cavity and is a remnant of the famous ancient Lake Mœris. The Fayum, which is the territory reclaimed from the former lake, is now an exceedingly productive district, a sort of inland delta, fed like the marine delta by the fertilising floodwaters of the Nile.

The traveller Junker wrote of this district in 1875: " I found myself surrounded by a garden tract of unsurpassed fertility, where there was scarcely room for a path amid the exuberant growths; where pedestrians, riders, and animals had to move about along the embankments of countless canals. Now a land of roses, of the vine, olive, sugar-cane, and cotton, where the orange and lemon plants attain the size of our apple-trees, it was in primeval times an arid depression of the stony and sandy Libyan waste." [1]

North of the Fayum the Nile flows on to Cairo, where the narrow water way allowed to its course by the two lines of cliffs widens, and the cliffs recede to the right and left. There is thus space for the waters to spread and ramify over the alluvial plain. Nearly all this portion of Egypt has been covered by the sediment of the Nile, and from the earliest times there have been numerous distinct branches or channels of the river running out by separate openings into the sea. As several of these branches have been tapped to a great extent for irrigation, all except two have ceased to be true outlets of the Nile. In the Greek period there were seven mouths and several $\Psi\epsilon\upsilon\delta\sigma\sigma\tau\acute{o}\mu\alpha\tau\alpha$, or " false mouths." The two

---

[1] Dr. Wilhelm Junker's "Travels in Africa."

remaining mouths are those of Rosetta and Damietta, and these were always the most important of the number. They branched off formerly close to the present spot where Cairo stands, a little below Memphis; but during two thousand years the fork has gradually shifted to about thirteen miles lower down.

The triangular space enclosed by these two branches and the sea-coast was called by the Greeks the delta, on account of the likeness in shape to the Greek letter of that name Δ. At the head, or apex, of the triangle stands the famous barrage, or dam, begun in 1847 by Mehemet Ali, for the twofold purpose of reclaiming many thousand acres of waste land, and of regulating the discharge and the navigation through the Delta. The idea was originated by a Frenchman in his service named Linant Bey. This engineer desired to alter the course of the river and build a weir at a point farther to the north, where the contour of land seemed to favour the design more than that of the present locality. Mehemet Ali thought his plans too costly, and accepted in preference those of Mougel Bey. Unexpected difficulties were encountered from the very beginning. Mehemet was exceedingly anxious to hurry the work, and Mougel Bey had only made a beginning, when an exceptionally high Nile carried away all the lime in the concrete base. Mehemet Ali did not live to see the completion of this work. The object, could it have been realised, was to hold up the waters of the Nile during the eight months of the ebb, and thus keep them on a level with the soil, and at the same time to supply Lower Egypt with an amount of water equal to that which came down during flood-time. It was hoped to cover the very large expenditure by the additional land which it was expected would come under irrigation, and by doing away with the primitive *shadoofs* and setting free for productive enterprise the numerous army of the agricultural labourers who spent the greater part of their time in slowly raising up buckets of water from the Nile and pouring them into the irrigating channels.

The barrage is a double bridge, or weir, the eastern part spanning the Damietta branch of the Nile, the western part the Rosetta branch. The appearance of the structure is so light and graceful that the spectator finds it hard to conceive of the difficulty and the greatness of the work itself. Architecturally, the barrage is very beautiful, with a noble front and a grand effect, produced by a line of castellated turrets, which mark the site of the sluice gates. There are two lofty crenellated towers, corresponding with the towers over the gateway of a mediæval baronial castle. The sluices are formed of double cones of hollow iron, in a semicircular form, worked on a radii of rods fixed to a central axis at each side of the sluice-gate. They are slowly raised or let down by the labour of two men, the gates being inflected as they descend in the direction of the bed of that part of the river whose waters are retained. The working of the barrage was never what it was intended to be. After the year 1867 it ceased to be of any practical utility, and was merely an impediment to navigation. Between the years 1885—90, however, during the

Harbour at Suez

British occupation, Sir Colon Scott-Moncrieff successfully completed the barrage at a cost of $2,500,000, and
now the desired depth of eight feet of water on the lower
part of the Nile can always be maintained. It proved
to be of the greatest advantage in saving labour worth
hundreds of thousands of dollars a year, and in the irrigation and navigation facilities that had been contem-
plated as among the benefits which would naturally
accrue from its successful completion.

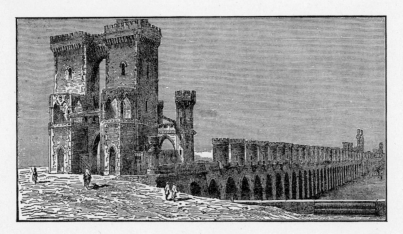

THE NILE BARRAGE.

Compared with the advance of the land seaward at
the estuary of the Mississippi and the Ganges, the advance of the Nile seaward is very slow. This is accounted for by the geological theory that the Delta of
the Nile is gradually sinking. If this is so, the tendency
of the periodical deposit to raise the level of the Delta
will be counteracted by the annual subsidence. These
phenomena account for the gradual burial of Egyptian
monuments under the sand, although the actual level

of the sea above what it formerly was is quite unappreciable.

The periodical rise in the Nile, recurring as regularly as the revolutions of the heavenly bodies, necessarily remained an unsolved mystery to the ancients, for until the discovery of the tropical regions, with their mountainous lakes and deluging rains, it was impossible to learn the occasion of this increase. It is now known that the Blue Nile, flowing out of the mountainous parts of Abyssinia, is the sole cause of the periodic overflow of the Nile. Without the tropical rains of the Ethiopian tablelands, there would be no great rise nor any fertilising deposits. Without the White Nile, which runs steadily from the perennial reservoirs of the great Central African lakes, the Lower Nile would assume the character of an intermittent wady, such as the neighbouring Khor Baraka, periodically flushed by the discharge of the torrential downpours from Abyssinia. Though there is a periodical increase in the flow of the upper waters of the White Nile, yet the effect of this, lower down, is minimised by the dense quantities of vegetable drift, which, combining with the forest of aquatic growth, forms those vast barriers, known by the name of *sudd*, which not only arrest navigation but are able to dam up large bodies of water.

The sudd, it is supposed, stopped the advance of the Roman centurions who were sent up the Nile in the days of Nero. Sir Samuel Baker was the one who first pointed out the great disadvantage of allowing the vegetable matter to accumulate, both to merchants and to those who were employed to suppress the slave-trade. In the year 1863 the two branches of the White Nile were blocked above their junction at Lake No. Once blocked, the accumulation rapidly increased from the stoppage of outlet, forming the innumerable floating islands which at this part of the Nile customarily float down-stream. A marsh of vast extent had been formed, and to all appearance, as Baker narrates, the White Nile had disappeared. Baker cut through fifty miles of the sudd, and urged the khedive to reopen the Nile. The work was successfully undertaken by Ishmail Ayub Pasha, and the White Nile became clear for large vessels when Gordon reached Khartum in 1874. It is practically impossible to keep the central provinces of the Nile open to civilisation unless the course of the Nile is free. Yet in 1878 the obstruction had been renewed, and during the occupation of these provinces by the rebel dervishes under the Mahdi and the califa the Nile was completely blocked, as formerly, at Lake No. The alarming failure of the Nile flood in 1899—1900 was generally attributed to this blockade, and in 1899 fifty thousand dollars was placed at the disposal of the governor-general for reopening the White Nile by removing the vast accumulation of sudd which blocked the Bahr-el-Jebel from Lake No almost as far as Shambeh. The work was started under the direction of Sir William Garstin in 1899. In 1900 the greater part of the sudd had been removed by the strenuous labours of Major Peake, and the Nile again became navigable from Khartum to Rejaf. The sudd was found to be piled up and of almost as close a structure as peat. It was sawn out in blocks ten feet square and carried away by gunboats. In the years 1901—02 further progress was made, and twenty thousand dollars appropriated for the work; and by means of constant patrolling the sudd is now practically absent from the whole course of the White Nile.

The discharge of the flood waters from the Upper Nile begins to make itself felt in Lower Nubia and Egypt in the month of June, at first slightly, and after the middle of July much more rapidly, the river continuing to rise steadily till the first week in October, when it reaches high-water mark, nearly fifty-four or fifty-five feet at the Egyptian frontier, and twenty-five or twenty-six feet at Cairo. A subsidence then sets in, and continues till low-water level is again reached, usually about the end of May. The floods are then much higher and confined to a narrower space in the Nubian section of the Nile, while they gradually die out in the region of the Delta, where the excess seawards is discharged by the Rosetta and Damietta branches. In place of the old Nilometers, the amount of the rise of the Nile is now reported by telegraph from meteorological stations.

It is popularly supposed that at every rise the plains of the Delta are inundated, but this is not the case. The actual overflow of the banks of the river and canals is the exception, and when it happens is most disastrous. The irrigation of fields and plantations is effected by slow infiltration through the retaining dykes, which are prevented from bursting by the process of slow absorption. The first lands to be affected are not those which

are nearest to the dyke, but those which are of the lowest
level, because the waters, in percolating through under
the ground, reach the surface of these parts first.   In
Manitoba during a dry season sometimes the roots of
the wheat strike down deep enough to reach the reservoir of moisture under ground.   In Egypt this underground moisture is what is counted upon, but it is
fed by a special and prepared system, and is thus
brought to the roots of the plants artificially.   An
analysis of the Nile alluvium, which has
accumulated in the course of ages to a
thickness of from three to four feet above
the old river-bed, shows that it contains a
considerable percentage of such fertilising
substances as carbonate of lime and mag-
nesia, silicates of aluminum, carbon, and
several oxides.   Where the water has to
be raised to higher levels, two processes
are used.   The primitive shadoof of native
origin figured on a monument as far back
as 3,300 years ago, and the more modern
sakieh was apparently introduced in later
times from Syria and Persia.   The shadoof
is used on small farms, and the sakieh is
more often used for larger farms and
plantations.   These contrivances line the whole course
of the Nile from Lower Egypt to above Khartum.   The
shadoof will raise six hundred gallons ten feet in an
hour, and consists of a pole weighted at one end, with a
bucket at the other; when the water is raised the weight

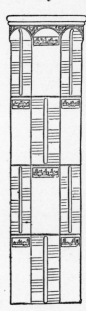

SCALE OF THE
NILOMETER.

counterbalances the weight of the full bucket. The sakieh, which will raise twelve hundred gallons twenty or twenty-four feet in an hour, is a modified form of a Persian wheel, made to revolve by a beast of burden; it draws an endless series of buckets up from the water, and automatically empties them into a trough or other receptacle. In former times these appliances were heavily taxed and made the instruments of oppression, but these abuses have been reformed since Egypt came under a more humane form of government.

Another interesting feature of the water ways of Egypt is the intermittent watercourses. The largest of these is the Khor Baraka (Barka), which flows out towards Tapan, south of Suakin. It presents some analogy to the Nile, and in part was undoubtedly a perennial stream 250 miles long, and draining seven or eight thousand square miles. At present its flat sandy bed, winding between well-wooded banks, is dry for a great part of the year. This route is extensively used for the caravan trade between Suakin and Kassala. During September the water begins to flow, but is spasmodic. After the first flood the natives plant their crops, but sometimes the second flow, being too great, cannot be confined to the limits prepared for it, and the crops are carried away and the sowing must of necessity be started again.

The canals of Egypt are of great aid in extending the beneficial influence of the inundations of the Nile. In Lower Egypt is the Mahmudiyeh Canal, connecting Alexandria with the Rosetta branch, and following the same direction as an ancient canal which preceded it.

A MODERN SAKIEH.

Mehemet Ali constructed this canal, which is about fifty miles long and one hundred feet broad. It is believed that twelve thousand labourers perished during its construction. Between the Rosetta and the Damietta branches of the Nile there are other canals, such as the Manuf, which connects the two branches of the river at a point not far from the Delta. East of the Damietta branch are other canals, occupying the ancient river-beds of the Tanitic and Pelusiac branches of the Nile. One of these is called the canal of the El-Muiz, from the first Fatimite caliph who ruled in Egypt, and who ordered it to be constructed. Another is named the canal of Abul-Munegga, from the name of the Jew who executed this work under the caliph El-'Amir, in order to bring water into the province of Sharkiyah. This last canal is connected with the remains of the one which in ancient times joined the Nile with the Red Sea. After falling into neglect it has again in part been restored and much increased in length as the Sweet Water Canal.

Further mention may also be made of the great canal called the Bahr-Yusef, or River Joseph, which is important enough to be classed as a ramification of the Nile itself. As has been mentioned, this water way runs parallel with the Nile on the west side below Cairo for about 350 miles to Farshut, and is the most important irrigation canal in Egypt. It is a series of canals rather than one canal. Tradition states that this canal was repaired by the celebrated Saladin. Another tradition, relating that the canal existed in the time of the Pharaohs, has recently been proved to be correct.

Egypt possesses not only the greatest natural water way in the world, but also the greatest artificial water way—the Suez Canal. Before the opening of this canal there were in the past other canals which afforded communication between the Red Sea and the Mediterranean. These ancient canals differed in one respect from the Suez Canal, since they were all fed by the fresh waters of the Nile. One of these still remains in use, and is called the Fresh Water Canal. According to Aristotle, Strabo, and Pliny, Sesostris was the first to conceive and carry out the idea of a water connection between the two seas, by means of the Pelusiac branch of the Nile from Avaris to Bubastis, and by rendering navigable the irrigation canal which already existed between Bubastis and Heroopolis. It is believed by some that the fragment bearing the oval of Ramses II. found near the course of the present canal affords confirmation of this assertion.

The first authentic account of the carrying out of the conception of an inter-sea water way is to be found in the time of Pharaoh Necho II., about the year 610 B. C. Herodotus records of Necho that he was " the first to attempt the construction of the canal to the Red Sea." This canal tapped the Nile at Bubastis, near Zagazig, and followed closely the line of modern Wady Canal to Heröopolis, the site of which lies in the neighbourhood of Toussun and Serapeum, between the Bitter Lakes and Lake Tinseh. At that date the Red Sea reached much farther inland than it does now, and was called in the upper portion the Heröopolite Gulf. The expanse of brackish water, now known as the Bitter Lakes, was

then, in all probability, directly connected with the Red
Sea. The length of this canal, according to Pliny, was
sixty-two miles, or about fifty-seven English miles. This
length, allowing for the sinuosity of the valley traversed,
agrees with the distance between the site of old Bubastis
and the present head of the Bitter Lakes. The length
given by Herodotus of more than one thousand stadia
(114 miles) must be understood to include the whole
distance between the two seas, both by the Nile and

HIEROGLYPHIC RECORD OF AN ANCIENT CANAL.

by the canal. Herodotus relates that it cost the lives
of 120,000 men to cut the canal. He says that the undertaking was abandoned because of a warning from an
oracle that the barbarians alone, meaning the Persians,
would benefit by the success of the enterprise. The true
reason for relinquishing the plan probably was that the
Egyptians believed the Red Sea to have been higher in
altitude than the Nile. They feared that if the canal
were opened between the Nile and the Red Sea the salt
water would flow in and make the waters of the Nile

brackish. This explanation would indicate a lack of knowledge of locks and sluices on the part of the Egyptians.

The work of Necho was continued by Darius, the son of Hystaspes (520 B. C.). The natural channel of communication between the Heröopolite Gulf and the Red Sea had begun to fill up with silt even in the time of Necho, and a hundred years later, in the time of Darius, was completely blocked, so that it had to be entirely cleaned out to render it navigable. The traces of this canal can still be plainly seen in the neighbourhood of Shaluf, near the south end of the Bitter Lakes. The present fresh-water canal was also made to follow its course for some distance between that point and Suez. Persian monuments have been found by Lepsius in the neighbourhood, commemorating the work of Darius. On one of these the name of Darius is written in the Persian cuneiform characters, and on a cartouche in the Egyptian form. Until this date it therefore appears that ships sailed up the Pelusiac branch of the Nile to Bubastis, and thence along the canal to Heröopolis, where the cargoes were transhipped to the Red Sea. This inconvenient transfer of cargoes was remedied by the next Egyptian sovereign, who bestowed much care on the water connection between the two seas.

Ptolemy Philadelphus (285 B. C.), in addition to cleaning out and thoroughly restoring the two canals, joined the fresh-water canal with the Heröopolite Gulf by means of a lock and sluices, which permitted the passage of vessels, and were effective in preventing the salt water from mingling with the fresh water. At the point where the canal joined the Heröopolite Gulf to the Red Sea, Ptolemy founded the town of Arsinoë, a little to the north of the modern Suez.

The line of communication between the two seas was impassable during the reign of Cleopatra (31 B. C.). It is believed by some that it was restored during the reign of the Roman emperor Trajan (98—117). During this period the Pelusiac branch of the Nile was very low, the water having almost completely deserted this formerly well-filled course. If Trajan, therefore, undertook to reopen the water way, he must have tapped the Nile much higher up, in order to reach a plentiful supply of water. The old canal near Cairo, which elsewhere joined the line of the former canal on the way to the Bitter Lakes, was once called " Amnis Trajanus," and from this it has been inferred that Trajan was really the builder, and that during his reign this canal was cleaned and rendered navigable. As there is no further evidence than the name to prove that Trajan undertook so important an enterprise, the " Amnis Trajanus " was probably constructed during the Arabic period.

When Amr had conquered Egypt, according to another account, the caliph Omar ordered him to ship rich supplies of grain to Mecca and Medina, because during the pilgrimages these cities and often the whole of Hedjaz suffered severely from famine. As it was extremely difficult to send large quantities of provisions across the desert on the backs of camels, it is supposed that to facilitate this transportation Omar ordered the construction of the canal from a point near Cairo to the head of the Red Sea. On account of his forethought in thus providing for the pilgrims to the Hedjaz, Omar received the title of " Prince of the Faithful " (Emir el-Momenéen), which thenceforth was adopted by his successors in the caliphate. One hundred and thirty-four years after this time, El-Mansur, the second caliph of the Abbasid dynasty, is said to have closed the canal to prevent supplies from being shipped to one of the descendants of Ali who had revolted at Medina. Since that time it is probable that it has never been reopened, although there is a report that the Sultan Hakim rendered it available for the passage of boats in the year A. D. 1000, after which it was neglected and became choked with sand. While not thereafter used for navigation, there were parts which during the time of the annual inundation of the Nile were filled with water, until Mehemet Ali prevented this. The parts filled during the inundation extended as far as Sheykh Hanaydik, near Toussun and the Bitter Lakes.

The old canal which left the Nile at Cairo had long ceased to flow beyond the outskirts of the city, and the still more ancient canal from the neighbourhood of Bubastis, now known as the Wady Canal, extended only a few miles in the direction of the isthmus as far as Kassassin. During the construction of the Suez Canal the need of supplying the labourers with fresh water was imperative. The company, therefore, determined in 1861 to prolong the canal from Kassassin to the centre of the isthmus, and in the year 1863 they brought the fresh-

REMAINS OF THE CANAL OF OMAR.

water canal as far as Suez. In one or two places the bed of the old canal was cleared out and made to serve the new canal. The level of the fresh-water canal is about twenty feet above that of the Suez Canal, which it joins at Ismailia by means of two locks. The difference of level between it and the Red Sea is remedied by four locks constructed between Nefeesh and its terminus at Suez. Its average depth of water at high Nile is six feet, and at low Nile three feet.

A canal from Bulak, near Cairo, passing by Heliopolis and Belbeys, and joining the Wady Canal a few miles east of Zagazig, restores the line of water communication between the Nile and the Red Sea as it existed perhaps in the time of Trajan, and certainly as it was in the time of the Caliph Omar. The improvement of this canal as a means of transit is local and external only.

Napoleon Bonaparte was the first in modern times to take up the subject of a water connection between the two seas. In 1798 he examined the traces of the old canal of Necho and his successors, and ordered Monsieur Lepère to survey the isthmus and prepare a project for uniting the two seas by a direct canal. The result of this French engineer's labours was to discover a supposed difference of thirty feet between the Red Sea at high tide and the Mediterranean at low tide. As this inequality of level seemed to preclude the idea of a direct maritime canal, a compromise was recommended.

Owing to the exertions of Lieutenant Waghorn, the route through Egypt for the transmission of the mails between England and India was determined upon in

1839. The Peninsular and Oriental Company established
a service of steamers between England and Alexandria,
and between Suez and India. In spite of this endeavour
nothing was actually accomplished with regard to a canal
until 1846, when a mixed commission was appointed to
enquire into the subject. This commission entirely exploded the error into which Lepère had fallen in report-
ing a difference of level between the two seas.

A plan was projected in 1855 by M. Linant Bey and
M. Mougel Bey, under the superintendence of M. de Lesseps, who had already received a firman of concession
from Said Pasha. This plan recommended a direct canal
between Suez and Pelusium, which should pass through
the Bitter Lakes, Lake Tinseh, Ballah, and Menzaleh,
and connecting with the sea at each end by means of a
lock. A fresh-water canal from Bulak to the centre of
the isthmus and thence through Suez, with a conduit for
conveying water to Pelusium, was also proposed. This
project was in 1856 submitted to an international commission company composed of representatives from England, France, Italy, the Netherlands, Austria, Prussia,
and Spain, and the following modification was suggested:
that the line of the canal to the north should be slightly
altered and brought to a point seventeen and a half miles
west of Pelusium, this change being determined upon
from the fact that the water at this point was from
twenty-five to thirty feet deep at a distance of two miles
from the coast, whereas at Pelusium this depth of water
was only to be found at a distance of five miles from the
coast. It was suggested that the plan for locks be abol-

ished, and the length of the jetties at Suez and Port Said be diminished. Various other details of a minor character were determined, and this project was finally accepted and carried through by the Suez Canal Company.

In 1854 M. Ferdinand de Lesseps, whose father was the first representative of France in Egypt after the

FERDINAND DE LESSEPS.

occupation, and who was chosen consul at Cairo (1831—1838), obtained a preliminary concession from Said Pasha, authorising him to form a company for the purpose of excavating a canal between the two seas, and laying down the connections on which the concession was granted. This was followed by the drawing up and revision of the project mentioned above, and by the renewal in 1856 of the first concession with certain modifications and additions. Meanwhile the British government, under the influence of Lord Palmerston, then foreign secretary, endeavoured for various political reasons to place obstacles in the way of the enterprise, and so far succeeded in this unworthy attempt as to prevent the sultan from giving his assent to the concessions made by the viceroy of Egypt. Nothing, however, could daunt the intrepid promoter, M. de Lesseps. He declared his motto to be " Pour principe de commencer par avoir de la confiance." Undeterred by intrigues, and finding that his project met with a favourable reception throughout the Continent of Europe, he determined, in 1858, to open a subscription which would secure funds for the undertaking. The capital, according to the statistics of the company, approved in the firman of the concession, was to consist of forty million dollars in shares of one hundred dollars each. More than half of this amount was subscribed for, and eventually, in 1860, Said Pasha consented to take up the remaining unallotted shares, amounting to more than twelve million dollars. Disregarding the opposition of the English government, and ignoring the Sublime Porte, which was influenced by England, M. de Lesseps began his work in 1859, and on the 25th of April of that year the work was formally commenced, in the presence of M. de Lesseps and four directors of the company, by the digging of a small trench along the projected line of the canal, on the narrow strip of land between Lake Menzaleh and the Mediterranean. This was followed by the establishment of working encampments in different parts of the isthmus.

Although the first steps were thus taken, incredible difficulties prevented de Lesseps from pushing forward with his work. Towards the close of 1862 the actual results were only a narrow " rigole " cut from the Mediterranean to Lake Tinseh, and the extension of the fresh-water canal from Rasel-Wady to the same point. The principal work done in 1863 was the continuation of the fresh-water canal to Suez. At this point a fresh obstacle arose which threatened to stop the work altogether. Among the articles of the concession of 1856 was one providing that four-fifths of the workmen on the canal should be Egyptians. Said Pasha consented to furnish these workmen by conscription from different parts of Egypt, and the company agreed to pay them at a rate equal to about two-thirds less than was given for similar work in Europe, and one-third more than they received in their own country, and to provide them with food, dwellings, etc. In principle this was the *corvée*, or forced labour. The fellaheen were taken away from their homes and set to work at the canal, though there is no doubt that they were as well treated and better paid than at home. The injustice and impolicy of this clause had always been insisted upon to the sultan by the English government, and when Ismail Pasha became viceroy, in the year 1863, he saw that the constant drain upon the working population required to keep twenty thousand fresh labourers monthly for the canal was a loss to the country for which nothing could compensate. In the early part of 1864 he refused to continue to send the monthly contingent, and the work was almost stopped.

By the consent of all the parties, the subjects in dispute were submitted to the arbitrage of the French Emperor Napoleon III., who decided that the two concessions of 1854 and 1856, being in the nature of a contract and binding on both parties, the Egyptian government should pay an indemnity equal to the fellah labour and $6,000,000 for the resumption of the lands originally granted, two hundred metres only being retained on each side of the canal for the erection of workshops, the deposit of soil, etc., and $3,200,000 for the fresh-water canal, and the right of levying tolls on it. The Egyptian government undertook to keep it in repair and navigable, and to allow the company free use of it for any purpose. The sum total of these payments amounted to $16,800,000, and was to be paid in sixteen instalments from 1864 to 1879.

The company now proceeded to replace by machinery the manual labour, and, thanks to the energy and ingenuity of the principal contractors, Messrs. Borel and Lavalley, that which seemed first of all to threaten destruction to the enterprise now led to its ultimate success. Without the machinery thus called into action, it is probable that the canal would never have been completed when it was. The ingenuity displayed in the invention of this machinery, and its application to this vast undertaking, constituted one of the chief glories in the enterprise of M. de Lesseps.

The work now proceeded without interruption of any kind; but at the end of the year 1867 it became evident that more money would be needed, and a subscription was opened for the purpose of obtaining $20,000,000 by means of one hundred dollar shares, issued at $600 a share, and bearing interest at the rate of five dollars a share. When more money was needed in 1869, the government agreed to renounce the interest on the shares held by it for twenty-five years, and more bonds were issued.

By help of these subventions and loans the work was pushed onward with great vigour. The sceptical were

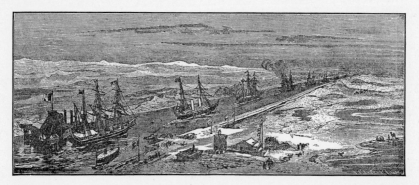

THE OPENING OF THE SUEZ CANAL.

gradually losing their scepticism, and all the world was awakening to see what an immense advantage to civilisation the triumph of de Lesseps' engineering enterprise would be. The great Frenchman had shown consummate skill as an organiser, but still more perhaps as an astute diplomatist, who knew how to upset the machinations of his numerous and powerful opponents by judicious counter-strokes of policy. By the beginning of 1869, the great labours of the company had very nearly reached their completion. The waters, flowing from the Mediterranean, first entered into the Bitter Lakes on March

18, 1869. Ismail Pasha was present to watch the initial success of the grand undertaking, and predicted that in a very short space of time the canal would be open to the ships of all the world. The first steamer which made the passage was one which carried M. de Lesseps on board, and which steamed the whole length of the canal September, 1869, in an interval of fifteen hours. This was a great triumph for the intrepid and persevering engineer, whose enterprise had been scoffed at by many men of the greatest European fame, and the completion of which had been delayed by incredible obstacles arising from jealousy or want of funds. By this time the unworthy tactics of the former Palmerston ministry of Great Britain in opposition to a scheme of such universal helpfulness to commerce had been succeeded by an official interest in the success of the enterprise which grew from sentiment, in the first instance, to a willingness later to buy up all the shares held by the Egyptian government.

M. de Lesseps gave formal notice early in September that the canal would be opened for navigation on November 17, 1869. The khedive made costly preparations in order that the event might become an international celebration. Invitations were sent to all the sovereigns of Europe. The sultan refused to be present, but the Empress Eugenie accepted the invitation in the name of the French people. The Austrian emperor, the Prussian crown prince, and Prince Amadeus of Italy also took part in the festivity. The initial ceremony was on November 15th, at Port Said. Emperor Francis Joseph landed at midday, and was received with pomp and mag-

nificence by the Khedive Ismail. There were splendid
decorations in the streets and triumphal arches were
raised. Meanwhile salutes were exchanged between the
batteries and the ships of war in the harbour. At night
there were gorgeous illuminations and fireworks. The
khedive gave a grand ball on his own yacht, at which the
Emperor of Austria and all the distinguished guests were
in attendance. The French empress then arrived in
Alexandria, and was received by Ismail and Francis
Joseph with salutes of guns and the acclamations of the
people. The next day the French imperial yacht *Aigle*,
with the empress on board, proceeded to steam up the
canal, being followed by forty vessels. They reached
Ismailia after eight hours and a half, and were there met
by vessels coming from the south end at Suez. On
November 19th the fleet of steamers, led by the French
imperial yacht, set out for Suez. They anchored overnight at the Bitter Lakes, and on November 21st the
whole fleet of forty-five steamers arrived at Suez and
entered the Red Sea. The empress, accompanied by the
visiting fleet, returned on November 22nd, and reached
the Mediterranean on the 23rd.

England, the country which more than any other had
opposed the progress of the canal, derived more benefit
than any other country from its completion. In 1875
the British government bought 176,600 shares from the
khedive for a sum of nearly $20,000,000; and at the pres-
ent time the value of these shares has risen more than
fourfold. By this acquisition the British government
became the largest shareholder. Of the shipping which

avails itself of this route to the East, which is shorter by six thousand miles than any other, about eighty per cent. is British. In 1891, of 4,207 ships, with a grain tonnage of 12,218,000, as many as 3,217 of 9,484,000 tons were British.

Extensive works were undertaken in 1894 for the widening of the canal. Illuminated buoys and electric lights have been introduced to facilitate the night traffic, so that, proceeding continuously, instead of stopping overnight, ships can now pass through in less than twenty hours in place of the thirty-five or forty hours which were formerly taken to effect the passage. These greater facilities postponed the need of discussing the project for running a parallel canal to the East which some time ago was thought to be an impending necessity on account of the blockage of the canal by the number of vessels passing through its course.

By the Anglo-French Convention of 1888, the canal had acquired an international character. Both the water way itself and the isthmus for three miles on either side were declared neutral territory, exempt from blockade, fortification, or military occupation of any kind. The passage is to remain open for all time to ships of all nations, whether they are war-ships or merchantmen or liners, or whether the country to which they belong is engaged in war or enjoying peace. Within this convention was included the fresh-water canal which supplies drinking water to Ismailia and Port Said, and all the floating population about the banks of the Suez Canal. On April 8, 1904, by the terms of a new Anglo-French

Colonial Treaty, it has been jointly agreed that the provisions of the Convention of 1888 shall remain in force for the next thirty years.

Egypt was the scene of the earliest of all advances in engineering science. The system of irrigation, which originated in the days of the oldest Egyptian dynasties, has remained practically the same through all the intervening centuries until very recent times. During every period of vigorous government the rulers of Egypt paid special attention to irrigation canals and sluices, through which the flood waters could be brought to some hitherto uncultivated area. The famous barrage, projected early in the nineteenth century and only rendered efficient for what it was intended since the British occupation, made very little alteration in the actual supply of water during the seasons of low water in the Nile. The most serious problem is how to ward off the periodical famine years, of which there has been record from the earliest ages, and of which the Book of Genesis has left an account in the history of Joseph and the seven years of plenty and seven years of famine. Without creating such a vast reservoir in the upper waters of the Nile, that the storage there retained can be available in years of low water to fill the river to its accustomed level, it is impossible to prevent the calamity occasioned by leaving many districts of Egypt without cultivation for one or more seasons. With the desire of accomplishing this, Sir Benjamin Baker, the leading authority on engineering works in Egypt, prepared a scheme for reserving a vast storage of water in Upper Egypt at Aswan. It was also decided to follow up the enterprise with another to be undertaken at Assiut.

On February 20, 1898, the khedive approved of a contract with Messrs. John Aird and Company, which settled the much-debated question of the Nile reservoir and the scheme for the great dam at Aswan. The government was able to start the undertaking without any preliminary outlay. It was agreed that the company should receive the sum of $800,000 a year for a period of thirty years. Aswan, six hundred miles south of Cairo, was selected as an advantageous site because the Nile at that place flows over a granite bed, and is shut in on either side by granite rocks, which, when the course of the river is barred, would form the shores of the artificial irrigation lake.

Before this work started, there had been a long controversy as to the effect produced by the rising waters upon the renowned temple on the Isle of Philæ. Lord Leighton, the president of the Royal Academy, had vigorously protested against allowing the destruction of this famous ancient ruin. In the modification of the plans caused by this protest, it was hoped that no serious harm would result to this well-preserved relic of ancient Egyptian religion and art.

The enterprise was put through with great rapidity, the project fully realising the designs of its inaugurators. By aid of this great structure, 2,500 square miles have been added to the area of the 10,500 miles hitherto subject to cultivation. Its value to the country is at the least worth $100,000,000. The dam extends for one and a quarter miles, and possesses 180 openings, each of which is twenty-three feet high, and will altogether allow the outpour of fifteen thousand tons of water per second. Navigation up and down the Nile has not been impeded, since, by a chain of four locks, vessels are able to pass up and down the river. Each lock is 260 feet long and thirty-two feet wide. During flood-time the gates of the

APPROACH TO PHILÆ.

dam are open; while the flood is subsiding the gates are gradually closed, and thus, in a long season of low water, the reservoir is gradually filled up for use through a system of canals, whereby the waters can be drawn off for irrigation and the main flow of the Nile can be increased. The lake thus formed is nearly three times the superficial area of Lake Geneva in Switzerland, and the waters are held back for a distance of 140 miles up the course of the river. The reservoir is filled during the months of January and February, and from April to the end of August the water is let out for irrigation purposes from the bottom of the reservoir, thus enabling the sediment, which is of such value, to be carried out through the sluices. Four or five waterings are allowed to percolate from it to the various regions which are thus brought under cultivation, and besides this the main supply of the river itself is artificially increased at the same time.

The dam has been constructed of granite ashlar taken from quarries near Aswan. These quarries are the very same from which the ancient obelisks were hewn. The amount of rock used was about one million tons in weight. In building the dam it was found to be very difficult to lay the foundation, since the bottom of the river proved to be unsound, although in the preliminary reports it had been declared to be of solid granite. In some instances it was found necessary to dig down for forty feet, in order to lay a perfectly secure foundation on which the heavy wall could be superimposed. This required much additional labour, and great risk and damage was encountered during the progress of the work at the date of the impending rise of the waters of the Nile. Rubble dams were raised to ward off the waters from the point where it was necessary to excavate. The holes were gradually filled with solid blocks of granite; then the base of the structure, one hundred feet in width, was laid, and the massive piers, capable of resisting the immense pressure of the water during the height of the floods, were raised, and the whole edifice was at length completed with great rapidity by the aid of many thousand workmen, just before the rise in the Nile occurred. The official opening of the dam took place on the 10th of December, 1902.

The dam at Aswan is the greatest irrigation project ever yet undertaken, but is by no means the last one likely to be executed in relation to the waters of the Nile. A smaller dam is to be constructed at Assiut, in order to supply a system of irrigation in the neighbourhood of that city, and also to carry water across to thousands of acres between this region and Cairo. This project is planned somewhat after the design of the barrage which is below Cairo.

It is impossible to forecast what engineering skill may have in store for the future of Egypt. One may hope, at least, that the most prosperous days of the Pharaohs, the Ptolemies, and the Romans will be reproduced once more for the modern Egyptians, as an outcome of the wise administration which has originated through the occupation of the country by the English, as an international trust held for civilisation. By aid of British initiative, Egypt now controls a vast empire in equatorial Africa and the Sudan, and the great water ways of this immense territory are being gradually brought under such control that the maximum advantage to all the population will be the necessary result. The whole Nile is now opened to commerce. The British have guaranteed equal rights, and what has been called the policy of the " open door," for the commerce of all nations.

The history of the modern exploration of the Nile is closely associated with the history of Egypt in modern times. The men who first visited Egypt and ascended the Nile valley were in almost every case Indo-Europeans. The early Egyptians were familiar perhaps with the Nile as far as Khartum, and with the Blue Nile up to its source in Lake Tsana, but they showed little or no interest in exploring the White Nile. In 457 B. C., Herodotus entered Egypt, and ascended the Nile as far as the First Cataract. He then learned many things about its upper waters, and made enquiries about the territories which lay beyond. He heard that the source was unknown; that there was a centre of civilisation in a city of the Ethiopians, in the bend of the Nile at Meroë (Merawi of to-day), but about the regions beyond he was unable to learn anything. Eratosthenes, the earliest geographer of whom we have record, was born in 276 B. C. at Cyrene, North Africa. From the information he gathered and edited, he sketched a nearly correct route of the Nile to Khartum. He also inserted the two Abyssinian affluents, and suggested that lakes were the source of the river.

When Rome extended her domains over Egypt, in 30 B. C., the interest of the Romans was aroused in the solution of the problem of the discovery of the source of the Nile. Strabo set out with Ælius Gallus, the Roman Governor of Egypt, on a journey of exploration up the Nile as far as Philæ, at the First Cataract. About 30 B. C. Greek explorers by the names of Bion, Dalion, and Simondes were engaged in active exploration of the Nile above the First Cataract and perhaps south of Khartum, according to the account of Pliny the Elder, writing in 50 A. D. The Emperor Nero, in A. D. 66, sent an expedition up the Nile, and its members journeyed as far as the modern Fashoda and perhaps even beyond the White Nile. Their advance was impeded by the sudd, and, after writing discouraging reports, their attempt was abandoned. Among the Greek merchants who traded on the East African coast was one named Diogenes, who had been informed by an Arab that by a twenty-five days' journey one could gain access to a chain of great lakes, two of which were the headwaters of the White Nile. They also said that there was a mountain range, named from its brilliant appearance the Mountains of the Moon. He was informed that the Nile formed from the two head streams, flowed through marshes until it united with the Blue Nile, and then it flowed on until it entered into well-known regions. Diogenes reported this to a Syrian geographer named Marinus of Tyre, who wrote of it in his *Geography* during the first century of the Christian era.

The writings of Marinus disappeared, it is supposed, when the Alexandrian Library was scattered, but luckily Gladius Ptolemy quoted them, and thus they have been preserved for us. Ptolemy wrote, in 150 A. D., the first clearly intelligible account of the origin of the White Nile, the two lakes, Victoria and Albert Nyanza, and the Mountains of the Moon. But no less than 1,740 years elapsed before justice could be done to this ancient geographer, and his account verified. It was Sir Henry M. Stanley who discovered the Ruwanzori mountain range, corresponding to the classical Mountains of the Moon, and who thus justified Ptolemy's view of the topography of Africa. For many years after Ptolemy, the work of exploring the sources of the Nile was entirely discontinued, and the solution of the problem was still wrapped in impenetrable mystery.

The first modern explorer of any consequence who came from Great Britain was a Scotchman named Bruce. In 1763 he travelled through many ports of Northern Africa and visited the Levant, and subsequently Syria and Palestine. Wherever he went he drew sketches of antiquities, which are now preserved in the British Museum. Landing in Africa in 1786, he went up the Nile as far as Aswan. From there he travelled to the Red Sea and reached Jiddah, the port of Hajas. He then returned to Africa, stopping at Massawa, and from there penetrated into the heart of Abyssinia. The emperor received him with favour and suffered him to reach the Blue Nile, which to the mind of Bruce had always been considered as the main stream of the Nile. Having determined the latitude and longitude, he went down the Blue Nile as far as the site of Khartum, where the waters of the White Nile join with those of the Blue Nile. He next proceeded to Berber, and crossed the desert to Korosko, returning, after a three years' journey, in the year 1773. In journeying through France many learned men took a great interest in the story of his explorations, but he was bitterly disappointed to hear that he had not been the first to reach the sources of the Blue Nile. Partly for this reason he delayed publishing his travels for seventeen years after his return. Bruce was a truthful and accurate writer, but nevertheless his book was received on all sides with incredulity. Although received at the British court, he was not given any special honours or decorations. He first pointed out the great importance to England of controlling the Egyptian route to India, and he also secured for English merchants a concession on the Red Sea.

In 1812, John Ludwig Burckhardt, of Swiss nationality, the first among Europeans, made a pilgrimage to Mecca and then travelled up the Nile to Korosko, after which he crossed the desert to Berber and Shendy. His death occurred after his return to Cairo, and he left a valuable collection of Oriental manuscripts to the University of Cambridge, England, which were published after his death.

In 1827, a Belgian, named Adolphe Lisiant, ascended the White Nile to within 150 miles of Khartum. The expedition which he led was aided by an English society, called the "African Association," which became afterwards a part of the Royal Geographical Society. Many explorers visited the White Nile between 1827 and 1845. In 1845, John Pethrick, a Welshman, explored the Nile for coal and precious metals in the interest of Mehemet Ali. After the death of this pasha, Pethrick visited El-Obeid in Kordofan as a trader, and remained there for five years. In 1853 he ventured upon an enterprise relating to the ivory trade. For this purpose he travelled backwards and forwards upon the White Nile and the Bahr-el-Ghazal for a period of six years, reaching some of the important affluents of the Bahr-el-Ghazal, the Jur and the Jalo, or the Rol. Returning to England, he was commissioned to undertake a relief expedition to help Captains Speke and Grant, who had set out upon their journey of exploration, and in the year 1861 he returned to Central Africa. Interest in the slave-trade deterred him from following the directions under which he had been sent out, namely, to bring relief to Speke and Grant. Sir Samuel Baker anticipated him in relieving the expedition, and this so angered Speke that he attempted to have Pethrick deprived of his consular position. Pethrick died in 1882.

When Lieutenant Richard Francis Burton had completed his famous journey through Hedjaz to the sacred city of Mecca, he called at the port of Aden at the southwest extremity of Arabia. While there, he made friends with the authorities, and persuaded them to allow him to penetrate Africa through Somaliland, which is situated to the southwest of Abyssinia. He hoped by an overland journey westbound to strike the Nile at its headwaters. John H. Speke accompanied Burton on his journey, and thus gained his first experience of African exploration. Unfortunately this expedition was not a success, for the Somali were so suspicious of the object of the travellers that they forced them to return to the coast.

Once more, in 1856, the same party started farther south from Zanzibar. Hearing of a great inland lake, they pressed forwards to make an exploration, but were prevented by the Masai tribes. Burton was now laid

THE MAIN STREAM OF THE NILE.

up with fever, and Speke formed a large party and crossed the Unyamivezi and Usukuma. On July 30, 1858, they were fortunate enough to cross one of the bays of the southern half of Lake Victoria Nyanza. They struck northwards, and, on August 3rd, gained sight of the open waters of the great lake. Speke did not realise the vast area of the lake at this time, and put down its width at about one hundred miles. As he had promised Burton to return at a certain pre-arranged date, he went back to the coast. Burton, however, was unreasonable enough to be displeased with Speke's discovery, and the two fell into strained relations. On arriving at the coast, Speke at once went back to England, and there raised funds to make a longer and more complete exploration. He was naturally anxious to learn more about the great lake in the middle of the continent, and, besides this, he thought that he could demonstrate to the satisfaction of the scientific world that this vast basin of water was the source of the White Nile. Captain James A. Grant asked leave to accompany Speke, and became his efficient lieutenant. Grant was a good shot, a matter of importance, for it was almost certain that the party would have to confront the danger of being surrounded by wild beasts and hostile natives. He was also a good geologist and painted well in water-colours, and proved himself to be a capable lieutenant to the leader of the party. The Indian government sent the expedition a quantity of ammunition and surveying instruments.

The party started from Zanzibar for the interior in October, 1860. At Usugara they were detained by the

illness of Captain Grant and some of the Hottentot re-
tainers. A number of the instruments were now sent
back in order to lighten the burdens, and among other
things was returned the cumbrous photographic apparatus, which was the only kind in use in the sixties. At
Ugogo serious trouble arose with the native chiefs, who
demanded tolls from the party. Many of the remaining
porters here deserted, and others were frightened by the
hostility of the local tribes. When at length they reached
the Unyamivezi most of the beasts of burden had died,
and half of the stores they had intended to bring with
them were found to have been stolen by the natives. The
Arabs here told Speke that there was another lake besides the Victoria, whose waters, according to some, were
reported to be salty.

Fierce internecine wars were now being waged between the tribes of the locality, which made any
thought of progress, so long as they lasted, an impossibility. Speke, having successfully endeavoured to negotiate a peace between the chief Mouwa and the Arabs of
the region, resolved upon the bold enterprise of pushing
on without Grant and the supplies towards Buzina, the
nearest country ruled by Bahima chiefs. The venture,
however, was a fruitless one, and he bravely struggled
to reach Usui. In this he succeeded, remaining there
till October, 1861, when he went through the region of
the Suwaroras, who demanded excessive tolls for permission to pass through their territory. Proceeding into
the wilderness, they were met by envoys from Rumanika,
a king whose court they intended to visit, and who had

heard in advance of their impending journey. The messengers of the king received them well and brought them to the court. Rumanika now desired them to remain at his capital until he had sent word before them that the party intended to go to Uganda. Grant, about this time, was laid up with an ulcerated leg; and, when the time came for moving forward, Speke was obliged to set out for Uganda alone, which place he entered on January 16, 1862. He became a close friend of the royal family and the chief men, and his beard was a constant source of admiration and conversation.

The illness of Grant prevented him from joining the party at Uganda till the end of May, and on July 7th of the same year, after many delays, they obtained leave from the king to leave Uganda. By July the 28th, Speke had reached the Ripon Falls, where the Victoria Nyanza branch of the Nile flows out of the great lake at the head of Napoleon Gulf. These falls were called after the Marquis of Ripon, who was then the president of the Royal Geographical Society. At this time, Grant, still convalescent, was moving by a more direct route towards Ungaro. Speke met him again on the way thither, and they finished their journey together. After suffering vexatious impositions from the monarch, Speke asked leave to go and visit a new lake which the natives called Lutanzige, but was refused permission. He then sent Bombay, his servant and interlocutor, along the course of the Nile towards the outposts of Pethrick. The messenger returned with hopeful news that there was a clear course open to them in that direction. The whole party then journeyed down the Kafu River to the point where it enters the Nile. On the way thither, they came to the Karuma Falls, and were obliged to march across swampy ground. Finally they met a Sudanese black named Muhammed Wad-el-Mek, who was dressed like an Egyptian and who spoke Arabic. Muhammed first of all told them that he had come from Pethrick, but it was later discovered that he was in the employment of Doctor Bono, a trader from Malta. The Sudanese was not anxious that the party should proceed, and told them stories about the impossibility of ascending the river at that time, during the month of December. It was difficult to dissuade Speke, however, and on January 12, 1863, he set out for a place which is now called Affudu. There the party paused for awhile in order to kill enough game to feed the native servants. On the 1st of February, having forced some of the natives into their service as porters, they descended the Nile to its confluence with the Asua River. They next crossed this river, and proceeded onwards to the Nile Rapids, and from thence skirted the borders of the Bari country. On February 15, 1863, they made an entrance into Gondokoro, where the whole party was filled with joy to meet Sir Samuel Baker, who had arrived there on the way out to relieve them. They all advanced together to Khartum, after which Speke and Grant returned to England, in the spring of 1863. Thus was the task of the discovery of the sources of the Nile, which had baffled the seekers for many centuries, at length completed. Speke was received by the Prince of Wales (King Edward VII.),

but the satisfaction of being allowed to place an additional motto on his coat-of-arms was the only recognition which he received for his services.

As a result of Speke's discoveries, the Victoria
Nyanza took its place on the maps of Africa, and a fair
conception had been obtained of the size and shape of
Lake Albert Nyanza. The whole course of the White

THE FERRY AT OLD CAIRO.

Nile was also revealed with more or less accuracy, and
all the mysterious surmises as to the great flow of the
Nile from some unknown headwaters of enormous extent
were now solved. It was only necessary to fill in the
details of the map in regard to the great lakes and the
rivers which flowed into them, and further to investigate
the extensive territory between the lakes and the Egyptian settlements to the north. Sir Samuel Baker was the
man who more than any other helped to supply the de-

tails of the work already accomplished. From Cairo he
started on a journey up the course of the Nile. When
he had reached Berber, he chose the course of the Atbara, or Blue Nile, the branch which receives the floods
of water from the Abyssinian table-lands. He travelled
up the western frontier of Abyssinia, proceeding as far
as the river Rahad, a river flowing into the Blue Nile
from the Egyptian side. From this point Baker turned
backwards towards Khartum, which he reached in June,
1862, where he made a stay of some duration. He now
made up his mind to search for Speke, and went up the
White Nile as far as Gondokoro, where the meeting with
Speke took place. Baker left this place March 26, 1863,
but met with almost insuperable obstacles in trying to
make further advance. The porters deserted, the camels
died, and the ammunition and the presents intended to
ease the way through the territory of native princes had
to be all abandoned. Thus disencumbered, his party
ascended the White Nile until they reached the Victoria
affluent. The Bauyno tribes now prevented his intended
advance to the Albert Nyanza. Baker, however, had the
good fortune to be well received by the chieftain Kamu-
rasi, and, as he was at this moment suffering from a
severe attack of fever, the friendliness of this Central
African chieftain was probably the means of saving his
life. The king graciously received Baker's present of a
double-barrelled gun, and then sent him onward with two
guides and three hundred men. The party now managed
to push their way to the shores of the Albert Nyanza.
They first arrived at a place called Mbakovia, situated

near the south-east coast, and on March 16, 1864, they
saw for the first time the great lake itself, which they
now named the Albert Nyanza. After a short stay at
Mbakovia, they proceeded along the coast of the lake
until they reached Magungo, where the Victoria branch
of the Nile flows into the Albert Nyanza. Continuing the
journey up the source of the Victoria Nile, they discovered the Murchison Falls. When they set out for the
Karuma Falls the porters deserted, and after many desperate adventures they at length returned to Khartum
in May, 1865. Baker then went on to Berber, and crossed
the desert to Suakin on the Red Sea. He returned to
England late in the year 1865, and was received with
honour and decorated by the queen with a well-earned
knighthood.

In the year 1869 Baker entered the service of the
Egyptian government, and was commissioned by the
viceroy to subdue the regions of Equatorial Africa, and
annex them to the Egyptian Empire. To succeed in this
enterprise he waged many a war with African tribes like
the Boni. On several occasions these conflicts had been
forced upon him; on other occasions Baker Pasha was
the aggressor, owing to his fixed determination to extend
on all sides the limits of the Egyptian Sudan. With all
the rulers, however, who treated him well, he remained
on terms of loyalty and friendship; and, in time, he
inspired them with respect for his fairness and liberality.
Baker Pasha scattered the slave-traders on all sides, and,
for the time being, effectually broke up their power. The
slave-traders of the Sudan were of Arab nationality, and

were in the habit of advancing farther, year by year, upon the villages of the defenceless Africans, and spreading their ravages into the heart of Africa. They always attacked the less warlike tribes, and, upon breaking into a negro settlement, would carry off the whole population, except the aged or sick. The slaves were herded together in vast numbers by help of logs of wood sawn in two, with holes cut large enough to enclose the neck of a slave, and the two sides of the log afterwards securely fastened again, thereby yoking together a row of these unfortunate beings. Every year, out of five hundred thousand or more slaves, at least half the number perished. The markets for the slaves were the cities of the Muhammedans all through North Africa, Syria, Turkey, and Persia. The death-dealing hardships to the slaves were for the most part endured on the long journey to Cairo, or, when the trade was suppressed there, to points north of the Sudan, such as Tripoli, or certain ports on the Red Sea. Those who were hardy enough to reach the slave-markets were usually well treated by their Muhammedan masters. During the time of Baker Pasha's administration, while he was pursuing the slave-traders and establishing Egyptian outposts, the whole course of the Nile from the Great Lakes became well known to the civilised world, though after this period Baker Pasha did not make any further voyages of discovery into unknown parts.

During the years of 1859 and 1860, an adventurous Dutch lady of fortune, Miss Alexandrine Tinné, journeyed up the Nile as far as Gondokoro, and in 1861 she commenced to organise a daring expedition to find the source of the Bahr-el-Ghazel, and explore the territory between the Nile basin and Lake Chad. She started from Khartum, and ascended the Bahr-el-Ghazel as far as the affluent Bahr-el-Hamad. She then crossed overland as far as the Jur and Kosango Rivers, and reached the mountains on the outlying districts of the Nyam-Nyam country. Here the members of the expedition suffered from black-water fever, and only with the greatest difficulty were they able to return to Khartum, where they arrived in July, 1864. In 1868 Miss Tinné, nothing daunted, started for Lake Chad from Tripoli, with the intention of closing in upon the Nile from the eastern sources of the affluents of the Bahr-el-Ghazel. On reaching Wadi-Aberjong, however, this brave-hearted woman was waylaid by the fierce Tuaregs, and was beheaded August 1, 1868.

In the sixties, Georg Schweinfurth, a native of Riga, in the Baltic provinces of Russia, set out to explore Nubia, Upper Egypt, and Abyssinia for botanical purposes. Subsequently the Royal Academy of Science in Berlin equipped him for an expedition to explore the region of the Bahr-el-Ghazel. He entered the Sudan by Suakin on the Red Sea, and crossed the desert to Berber, reaching Khartum on November 1, 1868. The following January he set out along the course of the White Nile, passed Getina, and examined the vegetation (sudd) which had drifted down from all the affluents of the White Nile. He prolonged his stay for three years on the Bahr-el-Ghazel, solely absorbed in scientific studies, and, unlike his predecessors, he was unconcerned with reforms and attempts to suppress the slave-trade.

Schweinfurth penetrated so far into the heart of Africa that he reached the Congo basin and explored the upper waters of the Welle River, and on his return to Europe he published a work, in 1873, called " The Heart of Africa." In this book he tried to demonstrate that the area of the Victoria Nyanza was taken up by a chain of five lakes.

About this time, in the same year, the famous Henry Morton Stanley returned to London from his adventurous discovery and relief of Dr. David Livingstone. The distinguished missionary and explorer died not long afterwards, and the fame of his brilliant discoveries and heroic life aroused great sympathy and interest in African exploration. The great river which Livingstone had explored was believed by him to have been the Nile, but was more correctly thought by others to have been the Congo River. On account of the interest aroused in Livingstone, the *New York Herald* and the *Daily Telegraph* of London decided to send Stanley on a fully equipped expedition to solve the many problems relating to the heart of Africa about which the civilised world was still in the dark.

Stanley chose the route of Zanzibar, and, landing there, he went up the course of the river and crossed the country to the Victoria Nyanza by the way of Unyamwezi. He reached the lake by the end of February, 1875. On March the 8th he set out to explore the shores of the lake, and mapped the whole region, including its bays, islands, and archipelagoes, with a considerable amount of accuracy. He also examined Napoleon Gulf, and reached as far as Ripon Falls, at which point the waters of the lake flow towards the Albert Nyanza. He then verified the accuracy of Speke's supposition that the Victoria Nyanza really was the main source of the White Nile. Stanley set out from Uganda at the end of the year 1875, and travelled across the country to the Congo. About the same time three English surveyors, Colonels Purdy, Colston, and Sidney Enser, made several topographical reports on much of the territory between the Bahr-el-Ghazel, the Shari, and the Nile. Later on, in 1876, General Gordon sent Romolo Gesei, an Italian in the service of the khedive, to navigate and to explore Lake Albert Nyanza. In the following year Colonel Mason, an American, surveyed the lake, of which he made an accurate topographical chart.

In the year 1880, Mr. E. G. Ravenstein, an eminent geographer, made some valuable surveys of eastern equatorial Africa, which had the effect of inciting the Royal Geographical Society to send out, in 1882, an expedition under Joseph Thomson, a brilliant young African explorer, in order to find out a direct route to the Victoria Nyanza. Thomson set out from Momhasa early in the year 1883, but he never succeeded in realising the purpose of his mission.

Emin Pasha, as we have seen, was the governor appointed by the khedive to rule the Egyptian equatorial provinces. He made a few discoveries, such as the Semliki River, which was called by him Divern. Whilst he was engaged in travelling through the Bahr-el-Ghazel district, the revolt of the Mahdi occurred, and Emin Pasha was isolated from the outer world. In the year 1886 Doctor Junker returned to Europe from Emin, and roused great interest by his account of the adventures of the pasha, whom most people had believed to have died, but whom they now learned had set up an independent sovereignty in the heart of Africa, awaiting anxiously the advent of a relief expedition. Then Henry M. Stanley volunteered to go out on a relief expedition to bring Emin Pasha home.

Stanley avoided the route through the German colony on the East, and started upon his ever memorable relief expedition by the Congo route. The veteran adventurer succeeded in relieving Emin Pasha, and, furthermore, he discovered the Mountains of the Moon, called by the natives Ruwenjori, on May 24, 1888. He also traced to its sources the Semliki River, and explored Lake Albert Edward and a gulf of the Victoria to the south-west. The remainder of this famous journey, for the success of which he was knighted as Sir Henry M. Stanley, was outside the basin of the Nile, and is recorded in his book, " Through Darkest Africa."

In 1900, Dr. Donaldson Smith, an American, made an important journey through the countries between the north end of Lake Rudolf and the Mountain Nile.

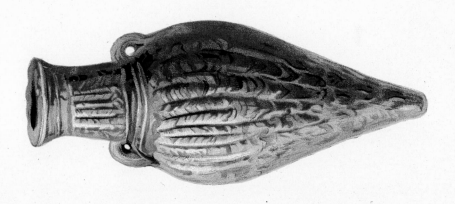

ARCHITRAVE INSCRIPTION OF PAPI II.

CHAPTER VI

THE DECIPHERMENT OF THE HIEROGLYPHS[1]

The Rosetta Stone : The Discoveries of Dr. Thomas Young : The Classification of the Egyptian Alphabet by Champollion : Egyptian Love-songs and the Book of the Dead.

CONSPICUOUSLY placed in the great hall of Egyptian antiquities, in the British Museum, is a wonderful piece of sculpture known as the Rosetta Stone. A glance at its graven surface suffices to show that three sets of inscriptions are recorded there. The upper one, occupying about one-fourth of the surface, is a pictured scroll, made up of chains of those strange outlines of serpents, hawks, lions, and so on, which are recognised, even by the least initiated, as hieroglyphics. The middle inscription, made up of lines, angles, and half-pictures, one might suppose to be a sort of abbreviated or shorthand hieroglyphic. The third, or lower, inscription, is manifestly Greek, obviously a thing of

---

[1] The early portion of this chapter is selected, by kind permission of Dr. Henry Smith Williams, from his " History of the Art of Writing," Copyright, 1902 and 1903.

291

words. If the screeds above be also made of words, only the elect have any way of proving the fact.

Fortunately, however, even the least scholarly observer is left in no doubt as to the real import of the thing he sees, for an obliging English label tells us that these three inscriptions are renderings of the same message, and that this message is a " decree of the Priests of Memphis conferring divine honours on Ptolemy V., Epiphanes, King of Egypt, B. c. 195." The label goes on to state that the upper transcription (of which, unfortunately, only parts of the last dozen lines or so remain, the slab being broken) is in " the Egyptian language, in hieroglyphics, or writing of the priests "; the second inscription in the same language, " in demotic, or the writing of the people "; and the third " in the Greek language and character."

Then comes a brief biography of the Rosetta Stone itself, as follows: " This stone was found by the French in 1798 among the ruins of Fort St. Julian, near the Rosetta mouth of the Nile. It passed into the hands of the British by the treaty of Alexandria, and was deposited in the British Museum in the year 1801." There is a whole volume of history in that brief inscription, and a bitter sting thrown in, if the reader chance to be a Frenchman. Yet the facts involved could scarcely be suggested more modestly. They are recorded much more bluntly in a graven inscription on the side of the stone, which runs: " Captured in Egypt by the British Army, 1801." No Frenchman could read those words without a sinking of the heart.

The value of the Rosetta Stone depended on the fact that it gave promise, even when originally inspected, of furnishing a key to the centuries-old mystery of the hieroglyphics. For two thousand years the secret of these strange markings had been forgotten. Nowhere in the world—quite as little in Egypt as elsewhere—had any man the slightest clue to their meaning; there were even those who doubted whether these droll picturings really had any specific meaning, questioning whether they were not merely vague symbols of esoteric religious import and nothing more. And it was the Rosetta Stone that gave the answer to these doubters, and restored to the world a lost language and a forgotten literature.

The trustees of the British Museum recognised that the problem of the Rosetta Stone was one on which the scientists of the world might well exhaust their ingenuity, and they promptly published a carefully litho-graphed copy of the entire inscription, so that foreign scholarship had equal opportunity with British to try to solve the riddle. How difficult a riddle it was, even with this key in hand, is illustrated by the fact that, though scholars of all nations brought their ingenuity to bear upon it, nothing more was accomplished for a dozen years than to give authority to three or four guesses regarding the nature of the upper inscriptions, which, as it afterwards proved, were quite incorrect and altogether misleading. This in itself is sufficient to show that ordinary scholarship might have studied the Rosetta Stone till the end of time without getting far on the track of its secrets. The key was there, but to apply it required the inspired insight—that is to say, the shrewd guessing power—of genius.

The man who undertook the task had perhaps the keenest scientific imagination and the most versatile profundity of knowledge of his generation—one is tempted to say, of any generation. For he was none other than the extraordinary Dr. Thomas Young, the demonstrator of the vibratory nature of light.

Young had his attention called to the Rosetta Stone by accident, and his usual rapacity for knowledge at once led him to speculate as to the possible aid this tri-lingual inscription might give in the solution of Egyptian problems. Resolving at once to attempt the solution himself, he set to work to learn Koptic, which was rightly believed to represent the nearest existing approach to the ancient Egyptian language. His amazing facility in the acquisition of languages stood him in such good stead that within a year of his first efforts he had mastered Koptic and assured himself that the ancient Egyptian language was really similar to it, and had even made a tentative attempt at the translation of the Egyptian scroll. His results were only tentative, to be sure, yet they constituted the very beginnings of our knowledge regarding the meaning of hieroglyphics. Just how far they carried has been a subject of ardent controversy ever since. Not that there is any doubt about the specific facts; what is questioned is the exact importance of these facts. For it is undeniable that Young did not complete and perfect the discovery, and, as always in such matters, there is opportunity for difference of opinion as to the share of credit due to each of the workers who entered into the discovery.

Young's specific discoveries were these: (1) that many of the pictures of the hieroglyphics stand for the names of the objects actually delineated; (2) that other pictures are sometimes only symbolic; (3) that plural numbers are represented by repetition; (4) that numerals are represented by dashes; (5) that hieroglyphics may read either from the right or from the left, but always from the direction in which the animals and human figures face; (6) that proper names are surrounded by a graven oval ring, making what he called a cartouche; (7) that the cartouches of the preserved portion of the Rosetta Stone stand for the name of Ptolemy alone; (8) that the presence of a female figure after such cartouches, in other inscriptions, always denotes the female sex; (9) that within the cartouches the hieroglyphic symbols have a positively phonetic value, either alphabetic or syllabic; and (10) that several different characters may have the same phonetic value.

Just what these phonetic values are, Doctor Young pointed out in the case of fourteen characters, representing nine sounds, six of which are accepted to-day as correctly representing the letters to which he ascribed them, and the three others as being correct regarding their essential or consonantal element. It is clear, therefore, that he was on the right track thus far, and on the very verge of complete discovery. But, unfortunately, he failed to take the next step, which would have been to realise that the same phonetic values given the alphabetic characters within the cartouches were often ascribed to them also when used in the general text of an inscription; in other words, that the use of an alphabet was not confined to proper names. This was the great secret which Young missed, but which his French successor, Jean François Champollion, working on the

JEAN FRANÇOIS CHAMPOLLION.

foundation that Young had laid, was enabled to ferret out.

Young's initial studies of the Rosetta Stone were made in 1814; his later publications bore date of 1819. Champollion's first announcement of results came in 1822; his second and more important one in 1824. By this time, through study of the cartouches of other inscriptions, he had made out almost the complete alphabet, and the " Riddle of the Sphinx " was practically solved. He proved that the Egyptians had developed a relatively complete alphabet (mostly neglecting the vowels, as early Semitic alphabets did also) centuries before the Phœnicians were heard of in history.

Even this statement, however, must in a measure be modified. These pictures are letters and something more. Some of them are purely alphabetical in character, and some are symbolic in another way. Some characters represent syllables. Others stand sometimes as mere representatives of sounds, and again, in a more extended sense, as representatives of things, such as all hieroglyphics doubtless were in the beginning. In a word, this is an alphabet, but not a perfected alphabet such as modern nations generally use.

The word " hieroglyphic " is applied, as we have seen, to various forms of picture writing; but the original interpretation which the Greeks, who invented it, put upon the word was the " holy writing " of the Egyptians. The earliest Greek travellers who went to Egypt, when that country was finally opened up to the outside world, must have noticed the strange picture scrolls everywhere to be seen there on the temple walls, on obelisks, on statues, and mummy-cases, as well as on papyrus rolls, which were obviously intended to serve the purpose of handing down records of events to future generations.

It is now known that this writing of the Egyptians was of a most extraordinary compound character. Part of its pictures are used as direct representations of the objects presented. Here are some examples:

mat eye.   *maui* eyes.

pau   birds.

Again the picture of an object becomes an ideograph, as in the following instances:

or }--*ba*   soul

net   honey.

pet   to see.

Here the sacred ibis or the sacred bull symbolises the soul. The bee stands for honey, the eyes for the verb " to see." Yet again these pictures may stand neither as pictures of things nor as ideographs, but as having the phonetic value of a syllable:

pa   the   *meh*   to fill.

pet   the sky or heaven.

χu   to protect.   *ta*   male.

pet   the sky.

pet   heaven & earth.

pet   heaven earth & hell.

pet   to see.   *pet* ----{ to open out, to extend.

pet   a kind of unguent.

Such syllabic signs may be used either singly, as above, or in combination, as illustrated below.

But one other stage of evolution is possible, namely, the use of signs with a purely alphabetical significance. The Egyptians made this step also, and their strangely conglomerate writing makes use of the following alphabet:

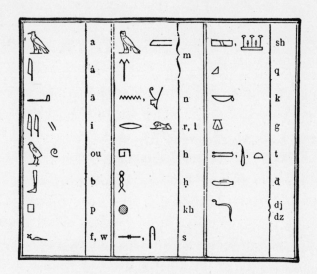

In a word, then, the Egyptian writing has passed through all the stages of development, from the purely pictorial to the alphabetical, but with this strange qualification,—that while advancing to the later stages it retains the use of crude earlier forms. As Canon Taylor has graphically phrased it, the Egyptian writing is a completed structure, but one from which the scaffolding has not been removed.

The next step would have been to remove the now useless scaffolding, leaving a purely alphabetical writing as the completed structure. Looking at the matter from the modern standpoint, it seems almost incredible that so intelligent a people as the Egyptians should have failed to make this advance. Yet the facts stand, that as early as the time of the Pyramid Builders, say four thousand years B. C.,[1] the Egyptians had made the wonderful analysis of sounds, without which the invention of an alphabet would be impossible. They had set aside certain of their hieroglyphic symbols and given them alphabetical significance. They had learned to write their words with the use of this alphabet; and it would seem as if, in the course of a few generations, they must come to see how unnecessary was the cruder form of picture-writing which this alphabet would naturally supplant; but, in point of fact, they never did come to a realisation of this seemingly simple proposition. Generation after generation and century after century, they continued to use their same cumbersome, complex writing, and it remained for an outside nation to prove that an alphabet pure and simple was capable of fulfilling all the conditions of a written language.

Thus in practice there are found in the hieroglyphics the strangest combinations of ideographs, syllabic signs, and alphabetical signs or true letters used together indiscriminately.

It was, for example, not at all unusual, after spelling a word syllabically or alphabetically, to introduce a figure giving the idea of the thing intended, and then even to

[1] The latest word on the subject of the origin of the alphabet takes back some of the primitive phonetic signs to prehistoric times. Among these prehistoric signs are the letters A, E, I, O, U, (V), F and M. Other signs are seen in the diagram on page 309.

supplement this with a so-called determinative sign or figure:

Here *Queften,* monkey, is spelled out in full, but the picture of a monkey is added as a determinative; second, *Qenu,* cavalry, after being spelled, is made unequivocal by the introduction of a picture of a horse; third, *Temati,* wings, though spelled elaborately, has pictures of wings added; and fourth, *Tatu,* quadrupeds, after being spelled, has a picture of a quadruped, and then the picture of a hide, which is the usual determinative of a quadruped, followed by three dashes to indicate the plural number.[1] These determinatives are in themselves so interesting, as illustrations of the association of ideas, that it is worth while to add a few more examples. The word *Pet,* which signifies heaven, and which has also the meaning *up* or *even,* is represented primarily by what may be supposed to be a conventionalised picture of the covering to the earth. But this picture, used as a determinative, is curiously modified in the expression of other ideas, as it symbolises evening when a closed flower is added, and night when a star hangs in the sky, and rain or tempest when

---

[1] Another illustration of the plural number is seen in the sign Pau, on page 298, where the plural is indicated in the same manner.

a series of zigzag lines, which by themselves represent water, are appended.

māśer evening.   *kekiu* darkness.

kerḥ   night.

hai   rain.   *śenār* tempest.

As aids to memory such pictures are obviously of advantage, but this advantage in the modern view is outweighed by the cumbrousness of the system of writing as a whole.

Why was such a complex system retained? Chiefly, no doubt, because the Egyptians, like all other highly developed peoples, were conservatives. They held to their old method after a better one had been invented. But this inherent conservatism was enormously aided, no doubt, by the fact that the Egyptian language, like the Chinese, has many words that have a varied significance, making it seem necessary, or at least highly desirable, either to spell such words with different signs, or, having spelled them in the same way, to introduce the varied determinatives.

Here are some examples of discrimination between words of the same sound by the use of different signs:

pa   the.   *paut*   nine.

pa   house.   *paut* —{ stuff, matter.

paut   company.   *paut*   good.

paut   cycle.

Here, it will be observed, exactly the same expedient is adopted which we still retain when we discriminate between words of the same sound by different spelling, as to, two, too; whole, hole; through, threw, etc.

But the more usual Egyptian method was to resort to the determinatives; the result seems to us most extraordinary. After what has been said, the following examples will explain themselves:

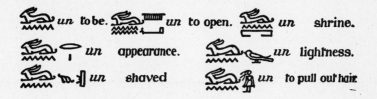

It goes without saying that the great mass of people in Egypt were never able to write at all. Had they been accustomed to do so, the Egyptians would have been a nation of artists. Even as the case stands, a remarkable number of men must have had their artistic sense well developed, for the birds, animals, and human figures constantly presented on their hieroglyphic scrolls are drawn with a fidelity which the average European of to-day would certainly find far beyond his skill.

Until Professor Petrie [1] published his " Medum," and Professor Erman his " Grammar," no important work on Egyptian hieroglyphic writing had appeared in recent years. Professor Petrie's " Medum " is the mainstay

[1] The information as to the modern investigation in hieroglyphics has been obtained from F. L. Griffith's paper in the 6th Memoir of the Archæological Survey on Hieroglyphics from the collections of the Egypt Exploration Fund, London, 1894–95.

of the student in regard to examples of form for the old kingdom; but for all periods detailed and trustworthy drawings and photographs are found among the enormous mass of published texts.[1] There is an important collection of facsimiles at University College, London, made for Professor Petrie by Miss Paget. A large proportion of these are copied from the collections from Beni Hasan and El Bersheh; others are from coffins of later periods, and have only paleographical interest; and others are from earlier coffins in the British Museum. But the flower of the collection consists in exquisite drawings of sculptured hieroglyphics, sometimes with traces of colour, from the tomb of Phtahhotep at Saqqâra, supplemented by a few from other tombs in the same neighbourhood, and from the pyramid of Papi I. These were all copied on the spot in 1895—96.

The only critical list of hieroglyphics with their powers published recently is that of Erman, printed in his " Grammar." The system by which he classifies the values—obscured in the English edition by the substitution of the term of " ideograph " for *Wortzeichen* (word-sign)—displays the author's keen insight into the nature of hieroglyphic writing, and the list itself is highly suggestive.

In the case of an altogether different system of ancient writing that has come down to us,—the old cuneiform syllabary of the Assyrians,—dictionaries, glossaries,

---

[1] To these may now be added the 105 coloured signs in Beni Hasan, Part III., and still more numerous examples in the Memoir of the Egypt Exploration Fund (Archæological Survey), for the season 1895-96.

and other works of a grammatical character have been preserved to the present day. Documents such as these are, of course, of material aid in regard to obscure texts, but in the case of the Egyptian writing the only surviving native word-list is the Sign Papyrus of Tanis,[1] which is, unfortunately, of the Roman Period, when the original meanings of the signs had been well-nigh forgotten. It has its own peculiar interest, but seldom furnishes the smallest hint to the seeker after origins. The famous " Hieroglyphics of Horapollo " occasionally contains a reminiscence of true hieroglyphics, but may well be a composition of the Middle Ages, embodying a tiny modicum of half-genuine tradition that had survived until then.

Scattered throughout Egyptological literature there are, as may be imagined, many attempts at explaining individual signs. But any endeavour to treat Egyptian hieroglyphics critically, to ascertain their origins, the history of their use, the original distinction or the relationship of signs that resemble each other, reveals how little is really known about them. For study, good examples showing detail and colouring at different periods are needed, and the evidence furnished by form and colour must be checked by examination of their powers in writing.

In investigating the powers of the uses of the signs, dictionaries give most important aid to the student. The key-words of the meanings, viz., the names of the objects

[1] Egypt Exploration Fund, Ninth Memoir, 1889-1890. This is an extra volume, now out of print.

or actions depicted, are often exceedingly rare in the
texts. Doctor Brugsch's great Dictionary (1867—82) frequently settles with close accuracy the meanings of the
words considered in it, supplying by quotations the proof
of his conclusions.[1]

In 1872, Brugsch, in his "Grammaire Hieroglyphique," published a useful list of signs with their phonetic and ideographic values, accompanying them with
references to his Dictionary, and distinguishing some of
the specially early and late forms. We may also note the
careful list in Lepsius' "Aegyptische Lesestücke," 1883.

Champollion in his "Grammaire Egyptienne," issued
after the author's death in 1836, gave descriptive names
to large numbers of the signs. In 1848, to the first volume
of Bunsen's "Egypt's Place in Universal History," Birch

---

[1] There has been in preparation since 1897 an exhaustive dictionary, to be
published under the auspices of the German government. The academies
of Berlin, Göttingen, Leipsig and Munich have charge of the work, and they
have nominated as their respective commissioners Professors Erman, Pietsch-
mann, Steindorff, and Ebers (since deceased). This colossal undertaking is the
fitting culmination of the labours of a century in the Egyptian language and
writing. The collection and arrangement of material are estimated to occupy
eleven years; printing may thus be begun about 1908.

Despite its uncritical method of compilation, Levy's bulky Vocabulary
(1887-1804), with its two supplements and long tables of signs, is indispensable
in this branch of research, since it gives a multitude of references to rare words
and forms of words that occur in notable publications of recent date, such as
Maspero's excellent edition of the Pyramid Texts. There are also some important special indices, such as Stern's excellent "Glossary of the Papyrus Ebers,"
Piehl's "Vocabulary of the Harris Papyrus," Erman's "Glossary of the Westcar
Papyrus," and Doctor Budge's "Vocabulary" of the XVIIIth Dynasty "Book
of the Dead." Schack's Index to the Pyramid Texts will prove to be an important work, and the synoptic index of parallel chapters prefixed to the work is of
the greatest value in the search for variant spellings.

contributed a long list of hieroglyphics, with descriptions and statements of their separate phonetic and ideographic values. De Rougé, in his " Catalogue des signes hieroglyphiques de l'imprimerie nationale," 1851, attached to each of many hundreds of signs and varieties of signs a short description, often very correct. He again dealt with the subject in 1867, and published a " Catalogue Raisonné " of the more usual signs in the first *livraison* of his " Chrestomathie Egyptienne." Useful to the student as these first lists were, in the early stages of decipherment, they are now of little value. For, at the time they were made, the fine early forms were mostly unstudied, and the signs were taken without discrimination from texts of all periods; moreover, the outlines of the signs were inaccurately rendered, their colours unnoted, and their phonetic and ideographic powers very imperfectly determined. Thus, whenever doubt was possible as to the object represented by a sign, little external help was forthcoming for correct identification. To a present-day student of the subject, the scholarly understanding of De Rougé and the ingenuity of Birch are apparent, but the aid which they afford him is small.

As a result of recent discoveries, some very interesting researches have been made in Egyptian paleography in what is known as the *signary*.[1] We reach signs which seem to be disconnected from the known hieroglyphs, and we are probably touching on the system of geometrical signs used from prehistoric to Roman times in Egypt, and

[1] The information regarding the alphabet here given is derived from the Eighteenth Memoir of the Egypt Exploration Fund, 1899–1890.

also in other countries around the Mediterranean. How far these signs are originally due to geometrical invention, or how far due to corruption of some picture, we cannot say. But in any case they stood so detached from the hieroglyphic writing and its hieratic and demotic derivations, that they must be treated as a separate system. For the present the best course is to show here the similarity of forms between these marks and those known in Egypt in earlier and later times, adding the similar forms in the Karian and Spanish alphabets. The usage of such forms in the same country from about 6000 B. C. down to 1200 B. C., or later, shows that we have to deal with a definite system. And it seems impossible to separate that used in 1200 B. C. in Egypt from the similar forms found in other lands connected with Egypt from 800 B. C. down to later times: we may find many of these also in the Kretan inscriptions long before 800 B. C. The only conclusion then seems to be that a great body of signs—or a *signary* —was in use around the Mediterranean for several thousand years. Whether these signs were ideographic or syllabic or alphabetic in the early stages we do not know; certainly they were alphabetic in the later stage. And the identity of most of the signs in Asia Minor and Spain shows them to belong to a system with commonly received values in the later times.

What then becomes of the Phœnician legend of the alphabet? Certainly the so-called Phœnician letters were familiar long before the rise of Phœnician influence. What is really due to the Phœnicians seems to have been the selection of a short series (only half the amount of the surviving alphabets) for numerical purposes, as $A = 1$, $E = 5$, $I = 10$, $N = 50$, $P = 100$, $\Phi = 500$, etc. This usage would soon render these signs as invariable in order as our own numbers, and force the use of them on all countries with which the Phœnicians traded. Hence, before long these signs drove out of use all others, except in the less changed civilisations of Asia Minor and Spain. According to our modern authorities this exactly explains the phenomena of the early Greek alphabets; many in variety, and so diverse that each has to be learned separately, and yet entirely uniform in order. Each tribe had its own signs for certain sounds, varying a good deal; yet all had to follow a fixed numerical system. Certainly all did not learn their forms from an independent Phœnician alphabet, unknown to them before it was selected.

EGYPT				KARIA	SPAIN
Prehis.	1st Dyn.	XIIth Dyn.	XVIII D.		

(Comparative table of alphabetic letter-forms for Egypt — Prehistoric, 1st Dynasty, XIIth Dynasty, XVIIIth Dynasty — Karia, and Spain. The Karia column gives the phonetic values: a, ä, e, e, e, ê, ê, a, ai, i, i, i, o, o, u, w, bh, b, g, d, v, z, kh, th, dh, k, l, m, m, n, p, r, s, sh, t, h, vu, re, rd, kh, kh, ki.)

The work of Young and Champollion, says Doctor Williams,[1] gives a new interest to the mass of records, in the form of graven inscriptions, and papyrus rolls, and cases and wrappings, which abound in Egypt, but which hitherto had served no better purpose for centuries than to excite, without satisfying, the curiosity of the traveller. Now these strange records, so long enigmatic, could be read, and within the past fifty years a vast literature of translations of these Egyptian records has been given to the world. It was early discovered that the hieroglyphic character was not reserved solely for sacred inscriptions, as the Greeks had supposed in naming it; indeed, the inscription of the Rosetta Stone sufficiently dispelled that illusion. But no one, perhaps, was prepared for the revelations that were soon made as to the extent of range of these various inscriptions, and the strictly literary character of some of them.

A large proportion of these inscriptions are, to be sure, religious in character, but there are other extensive inscriptions, such as those on the walls of the temple of Karnak, that are strictly historical; telling of the warlike deeds of such mighty kings as Thûtmosis III. and Ramses II. Again, there are documents which belong to the domain of belles-lettres pure and simple. Of these the best known example is the now famous " Tale of Two Brothers "—the prototype of the " modern " short story.

Up to the middle of the nineteenth century, no Egyptologist had discovered that the grave-faced personages who lie in their mummy-cases in our great museums ever

[1] History of the Art of Writing, Portfolio I., plate 8.

read or composed romance. Their literature, as far as recovered, was of an eminently serious nature,—hymns to the divinities, epic poems, writings on magic and science, business letters, etc., but no stories. In 1852, however, an Englishwoman, Mrs. Elizabeth d'Orbiney, sent M. de Rougé, at Paris, a papyrus she had purchased in Italy, and whose contents she was anxious to know. Thus was the tale of the "Two Brothers" brought to light, and for twelve years it remained our sole specimen of a species of literature which is now constantly being added to.

This remarkable papyrus dates from the thirteenth century B. C., and was the work of Anna, one of the most distinguished temple-scribes of his age. Indeed, it is to him that we are indebted for a large portion of the Egyptian literature that has been preserved to us. This particular work was executed for Seti II., son of Meneptah, and grandson of Ramses II. of the nineteenth dynasty, while he was yet crown prince.

The tale itself is clearly formed of two parts. The first, up to the Bata's self-exile to the Valley of the Cedar, gives a really excellent picture of the life and habits of the peasant dwelling on the banks of the Nile. The civilisation and moral conditions it describes are distinctly Egyptian. Were it not for such details as the words spoken by the cows, and the miraculous appearance of the body of water between the two brothers, we might say the ancient Egyptians were strict realists in their theory of fiction. But the second part leads us through marvels enough to satisfy the most vivid of imaginations. It is

possible, therefore, that the tale as we have it was originally two separate stories.

The main theme of the story has occupied a great deal
of attention. Its analogy to the Biblical narrative of
Joseph and Potiphar's wife comes at once into the reader's mind. But there is just as close a similarity in the
Greek tales, where the hero is killed or his life endangered
for having scorned the guilty love of a woman, as in the
stories of Hippolytus, Peleus, Bellerophon, and the son
of Glaucus, not to mention the extraordinary adventure
of Amgiad and Assad, sons of Prince Kamaralzaman, in
the *Thousand and One Nights*.

The religions of Greece and Western Asia likewise
contain myths that can be compared almost point for
point with the tale of the two brothers. In Phrygia, for
example, Atyo scorns the love of the goddess Cybele, as
does Bata the love of Anpu's wife. Like Bata, again,
he mutilates himself, and is transformed into a pine
instead of a persea tree. Are we, therefore, to seek for
the common origin of all the myths and romance in the
tragedy of Anpu and Bata that was current, we know not
how long, before the days of King Seti?

Of one thing we may be sure: of this particular type
the Egyptian tale is by far the oldest that we possess,
and, if we may not look to the valley of the Nile as the
original home of the popular tale, we may justly regard
it as the locality where it was earliest naturalised and
assumed a true literary form.

Analogies to the second part of the tale are even more
numerous and curious. They are to be found everywhere,

in France, Italy, Germany, Hungary, in Russia and all Slavonic countries, Roumania, Peloponnesia, in Asia Minor, Abyssinia, and even India.

Of late years an ever-increasing accumulation of the literature of every age of Egyptian history has either been brought to light or for the first time studied from a wider point of view than was formerly possible. In making a few typical selections from the mass of this new material, none perhaps are more worthy of note than some of the love-songs which have been translated into German from Egyptian in " Die Liebespoesie der Alten Ægypten," by W. Max Muller. This is a very careful edition of the love-songs on the recto (or upper surface) of the Harris Papyrus 500, and of similar lyrics from Turin, Gizeh, and Paris. The introduction contains an account of Egyptian notions of love and marriage, gathered from hieroglyphic and demotic sources, and a chapter is devoted to the forms of Egyptian verse, its rhythm and accent. The interesting " Song of the Harper," which is found on the same Harris Papyrus, is also fully edited and collated with the parallel texts from the Theban tombs, and compared with other writings dealing with death from the agnostic point of view. The following extracts are translated from the German:

LOVE - SICKNESS

I will lie down within doors
  For I am sick with wrongs.
Then my neighbours come in to visit me.
  With them cometh my sister,
She will make fun of the physicians;
  She knoweth mine illness.

THE LUCKY DOORKEEPER

The villa of my sister! —
    Her gates (are) in the midst of the domain —
(So oft as) its portals open,
    (So oft as) the bolt is withdrawn,
Then is my sister angry:

O were I but set as the gatekeeper!
    I should cause her to chide me;
(Then) I should hear her voice in anger,
    A child in fear before her!

THE UNSUCCESSFUL BIRD - CATCHER

The voice of the wild goose crieth,
    (For) she hath taken her bait;
(But) thy love restraineth me,
    I cannot free her (from the snare);

(So) must I take (home) my net.
    What (shall I say) to my mother,
To whom (I am wont) to come daily
    Laden with wild fowl?
I lay not my snare to-day
    (For) thy love hath taken hold upon me.

The most ardent interest that has been manifested in the Egyptian records had its origin in the desire to find evidence corroborative of the Hebrew accounts of the Egyptian captivity of the Jewish people.[1] The Egyptian word-treasury being at last unlocked, it was hoped that much new light would be thrown on Hebrew history. But the hope proved illusive. After ardent researches of hosts of fervid seekers for half a century, scarcely a word of reference to the Hebrews has been found among the

---

[1] The only inscription relating directly to the Israelites will be found described in Chapter VII.

Egyptian records. If depicted at all, the Hebrew captives are simply grouped with other subordinate peoples, not even considered worthy of the dignity of names. Nor is this strange when one reflects on the subordinate position which the Hebrews held in the ancient world. In historical as in other matter, much depends upon the point of view, and a series of events that seemed all-important from the Hebrew standpoint might very well be thought too insignificant for record from the point of view of a great nation like the Egyptians. But the all-powerful pen wrought a conquest for the Hebrews in succeeding generations that their swords never achieved, and, thanks to their literature, succeeding generations have cast historical perspective to the winds in viewing them. Indeed, such are the strange mutations of time that, had any scribe of ancient Egypt seen fit to scrawl a dozen words about the despised Israelite captives, and had this monument been preserved, it would have outweighed in value, in the opinion of nineteenth-century Europe, all the historical records of Thûtmosis, Ramses, and their kin that have come down to us. But seemingly no scribe ever thought it worth his while to make such an effort.

It has just been noted that the hieroglyphic inscriptions are by no means restricted to sacred subjects. Nevertheless, the most widely known book of the Egyptians was, as might be expected, one associated with the funeral rites that played so large a part in the thoughts of the dwellers by the Nile. This is the document known as " The Chapters of the Coming-Forth by Day," or, as it is more commonly interpreted, "The Book of the Dead." It is a veritable book in scope, inasmuch as the closely written papyrus roll on which it is enscrolled measures sometimes seventy feet in length. It is virtually the Bible of the Egyptians, and, as in the case of the sacred books of other nations, its exact origin is obscure. The earliest known copy is to be found, not on a papyrus roll, but upon the walls of the chamber of the pyramid at Saqqâra near Cairo. The discovery of this particular recension of "The Book of the Dead" was made by Lepsius. Its date is 3333 B. C. No one supposes, however, that this date marks the time of the origin of "The Book of the Dead." On the contrary, it is held by competent authority that the earliest chapters, essentially unmodified, had been in existence at least a thousand years before this, and quite possibly for a much longer time. Numerous copies of this work in whole or in part have been preserved either on the walls of temples, on papyrus rolls, or upon the cases of mummies. These copies are of various epochs, from the fourth millennium B. C., as just mentioned, to the late Roman period, about the fourth century A. D.

Throughout this period of about four thousand years the essential character of the book remained unchanged. It is true that no two copies that have been preserved are exactly identical in all their parts. There are various omissions and repetitions that seem to indicate that the book was not written by any one person or in any one epoch, but that it was originally a set of traditions quite possibly handed down for a long period by word of mouth before being put into writing. In this regard, as in many others, this sacred book of the Egyptians is closely comparable to the sacred books of other nations. It differs, however, in one important regard from these others in that it was never authoritatively pronounced upon and crystallised into a fixed, unalterable shape. From first to last, apparently, the individual scribe was at liberty to omit such portions as he chose, and even to modify somewhat the exact form of expression in making a copy of the sacred book. Even in this regard, however, the anomaly is not so great as might at first sight appear, for it must be recalled that even the sacred books of the Hebrews were not given final and authoritative shape until a period almost exactly coeval with that in which the Egyptian " Book of the Dead " ceased to be used at all.

A peculiar feature of " The Book of the Dead," and one that gives it still greater interest, is the fact that from an early day it was the custom to illustrate it with graphic pictures in colour. In fact, taken as a whole, " The Book of the Dead " gives a very fair delineation of the progress of Egyptian art from the fourth millennium B. C. to its climax in the eighteenth dynasty, and throughout the period of its decline; and this applies not merely to the pictures proper, but to the forms of the hieroglyphic letters themselves, for it requires but the most cursory inspection to show that these give opportunity for no small artistic skill.

As to the ideas preserved in " The Book of the Dead," it is sufficient here to note that they deal largely with the condition of the human being after death, implying in the most explicit way a firm and unwavering belief in the immortality of the soul. The Egyptian believed most fully that by his works a man would be known and judged after death. His religion was essentially a religion of deeds, and the code of morals, according to which these deeds were adjudged, has been said by Doctor Budge, the famous translator of " The Book of the Dead," to be " the grandest and most comprehensive of those now known to have existed among the nations of antiquity."

PHŒNICIAN JEWELRY.

HOUSE OF MARIETTE, SAQQARA.

CHAPTER VII

THE DEVELOPMENT OF EGYPTOLOGY

Mariette, Wilkinson, Bunsen, Brugsch, and Ebers : Erman's speech on Egyptology : The Egypt Exploration Fund : Maspero's investigations : The Temple
of Bubästis : Ancient record of " Israel " : American interest in Egyptology.

ACCOMPANYING Napoleon's army of invasion in Egypt was a band of savants representative of every art and science, through
whom the conqueror hoped to make known
the topography and antiquities of Egypt to the European world. The result of their researches was the
famous work called " Description de l'Egypte," published under the direction of the French Academy
in twenty-four volumes of text, and twelve volumes
of plates. Through this magnificent production the
Western world received its first initiation into the

319

mysteries of the wonderful civilisation which had flourished so many centuries ago, on the banks of the Nile.
Egypt has continued to yield an ever-increasing harvest
of antiquities, which, owing to the dry climate and the
sand in which they have been buried, are many of them
in a marvellous state of preservation. From the correla-
tion of these discoveries the new science of Egyptology
has sprung, which has many different branches, relating
either to hieroglyphics, chronology, or archæology proper.

The earliest and most helpful of all the discoveries
was that of the famous Rosetta Stone, found by a French
artillery officer in 1799, while Napoleon's soldiers were
excavating preparatory to erecting fortifications at Fort
St. Julien. The deciphering of its trilingual inscriptions
was the greatest literary feat of modern times, in which
Dr. Thomas Young and J. F. Champollion share almost
equal honours.

Jean François Champollion (1790—1832) is perhaps
the most famous of the early students of Egyptian hieroglyphs. After writing his " De l'écriture hieratique des
anciens égyptiens " at Paris, he produced in 1824 in two
volumes, his " Précis du système hieroglyphique des
anciens égyptiens," on which his fame largely depends,
as he was the first to furnish any practical system of
deciphering the symbolic writing, which was to disclose
to the waiting world Egyptian history, literature, and
civilisation. Champollion wrote many other works relating to Egypt, and may truly be considered the pioneer
of modern Egyptology. While much of his work has
been superseded by more recent investigations, he was

so imbued with the scientific spirit that he was enabled securely to lay the foundation of all the work which followed.

The distinguished French savant, Augustus Mariette, (1821—1881) began his remarkable excavations in Egypt

THE GREAT HALL OF ABYDOS.

in the year 1850. The series of discoveries inaugurated by him lasted until the year 1880. Mariette made an ever-memorable discovery when he unearthed the famous Serapeum which had once been the burial-place of the sacred bulls of Memphis, which the geographer Strabo records had been covered over by the drifting sands of the desert even in the days of Augustus. The Serapeum was in the neighbourhood of the Sphinx, and, on account of its great height, remained in part above the ground, and was visible to all passers-by; while everything else in the neighbourhood except the great Pyramid of Khûfûi was totally buried under the sand. Mariette worked his way along the passage between the Great Sphinx and the other lesser sphinxes which lay concealed in the vicinity, and thus gradu-

PROPYLON AT DENDERAH.

ally came to the opening of the Serapeum. In November, 1850, his labours were crowned with brilliant success. He discovered sixty-four tombs of Apis, dating from the eighteenth dynasty until as late as the reign of Cleopatra. He likewise found here many figures, images, ancient Egyptian ornaments and amulets, and memorial stones erected by the devout worshippers of antiquity. Fortunately for Egyptian archæology and history, nearly all the monuments here discovered were dated, and were thus of the highest value in settling the dates of dynasties and of the reigns of individual monarchs. Mariette afterwards discovered a splendid temple in the same place, which he proved to have been the famous shrine of the god Sokar-Osiris. He was soon appointed by the Egyptian Viceroy, Said Pasha, as director of the new museum of antiquities which was then placed at Bulak, in the vicinity of Cairo, awaiting the completion of a more substantial building at Gizeh. He obtained permission to make researches in every part of Egypt; and with varying success he excavated in as many as thirty-seven localities. In some of the researches undertaken by his direction, it is to be feared that many invaluable relics of antiquity may have been destroyed through the carelessness of the workmen. This is to be accounted for from the fact that Mariette was not always able to be present, and the workmen naturally had no personal interest in preserving every relic and fragment from the past. It is also to be regretted that he left no full account of the work which he undertook, and for this reason much of it had to be gone over again by more modern explorers.

In the Delta excavations were made at Saïs, Bubastis, and elsewhere. Mariette also discovered the temple of Tanis, and many curious human-headed sphinxes, which probably belong to the twelfth dynasty, and represent its kings. He further continued the labours of Lepsius about the necropolis of Memphis and Saqqâra. Here several hundred tombs were discovered with the many inscriptions and figures which these contained. One of the most important of these findings—a superb example of Egyptian art—is the statue called by the Arabs " The Village Chief," which is now in the museum at

Bulak.   Mariette followed out his researches on the site of the sacred city of Abydos.   Here he discovered the temple of Seti I. of the nineteenth dynasty.   On the walls

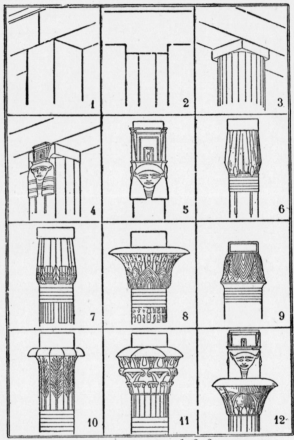

TYPES OF EGYPTIAN COLUMNS: 1, 2, 3, GEOMETRIC; 6–11, BOTANICAL; 4, 5, 12, HATHORIC.

are beautiful sculptures which are exquisite examples of Egyptian art, and a chronological table of the Kings of Abydos.   Here Seti I. and Ramses II., his son, are represented as offering homage to their many ancestors seated upon thrones inscribed with their names and dates.

Mariette discovered eight hundred tombs belonging for the most part to the Middle Kingdom. At Denderah he discovered the famous Ptolemaic temple of Hâthor, the goddess of love, and his accounts of these discoveries make up a large volume. Continuing his labours, he excavated much of the site of ancient Thebes and the temple of Karnak, and, south of Thebes, the temple of Medinet-Habu. At Edfu Mariette found the temple of Horus, built during the time of the Ptolemies, whose roof formed the foundation of an Arab village. After persevering excavations the whole magnificent plan of the temple stood uncovered, with all its columns, inscriptions, and carvings nearly intact.[1]

Owing to Mariette's friendship with the viceroy he was able to guard his right to excavate with strict exclusiveness. He was accustomed to allow other scholars the right to examine localities where he had been the first one to make the researches, but he would not even allow the famous Egyptologist, also his great friend, Heinrich Brugsch, to make excavations in new places. After his death, conditions were somewhat altered, al-

[1] In connection with the architecture of the ancient Egyptian tombs, it is interesting to note that there was a development of architectural style in the formation of Egyptian columns not dissimilar in its evolution to that which is visible in the case of the Greek and Roman columns.

The earliest Egyptian column appears to have been of a strictly geometrical character. This developed into a column resembling the Doric order. A second class of Egyptian column was based upon plant forms, probably derived from the practice of using reeds in the construction of mud huts. The chief botanical form which has come down to us is that of the lotus. A more advanced type of decoration utilised the goddess Hâthor for the support of the superincumbent weight and has its analogy in the decadent caraytides of late Roman times.

though the general directorship of the excavations was still given exclusively to Frenchmen. The successors of Mariette Bey were Gaston Maspero, E. Grébault, J. de Morgan, and Victor Laret. But as time went on, savants of other nationalities were allowed to explore, with certain reservations. Maspero founded an archæological mission in Cairo in 1880, and placed at its head, in successive order, MM. Lebebure, Grébault, and Bouriant. The first of all to translate complete Egyptian books and entire inscriptions was Emanuel de Rougé, who exerted a great influence upon an illustrious galaxy of French savants, who followed more or less closely the example set by him. Among these translators we may enumerate Mariette, Charles Deveria, Pierret, Maspero himself, and Revillout, who has proved himself to be the greatest demotic scholar of France.

England is also represented by scholars of note, among whom may be mentioned Dr. Samuel Birch (1813—85). He was a scholar of recognised profundity and also of remarkable versatility. One of the most important editorial tasks of Doctor Birch was a series known as "The Records of the Past," which consisted of translations from Egyptian and Assyrio-Babylonian records. Doctor Birch himself contributed several volumes to this series. He had also the added distinction of being the first translator of the Egyptian *Book of the Dead.*

Another English authority was Sir J. Gardner Wilkinson, who wrote several important works on the manners and customs of the ancient Egyptians. Wilkinson was born in 1797 and died in 1875. Whoever would know the Egyptian as he was, in manner and custom, should peruse the pages of his Egyptian works. His " Popular Account of the Ancient Egyptians " has been the chief source of information on the subject.

German scholars have done especially valuable work in the translation of texts from the Egyptian temples, and in pointing out the relation between these texts and historical events. Foremost among practical German archæologists is Karl Richard Lepsius, who was born in 1810 at Naumburg, Prussia, and died in 1884 at Berlin. In his maturer years he had a professorship in Berlin. He made excursions to Egypt in an official capacity, and familiarised himself at first hand with the monuments and records that were his life-study. The letters of Lepsius from Egypt and Nubia were more popular than his other writings, and were translated into English and widely read.

Another famous German who was interested in the study of Egyptology was Baron Christian Bunsen (1791—1867). From early youth he showed the instincts of a scholar, but was prevented for many years from leading a scholar's life, owing to his active duties in the diplomatic service for Prussia at Rome and London. During the years 1848—67, Bunsen brought out the famous work called " Egypt's Place in Universal History," which Brugsch deemed to have contributed more than any other work in popularising the subject of Egyptology.

Heinrich Carl Brugsch was born at Berlin in 1827 and died there in 1894. Like Bunsen, he was a diplomatist and a scholar. He entered the service of the Egyptian

government, and merited the titles of bey and subsequently of pasha. He became known as one of the
foremost of Egyptologists, and was the greatest authority
of his day on Egyptian writing. He wrote a work of
standard authority, translated into English under the
title of " The History of Egypt under the Pharaohs."
The chronology of Egypt now in use is still based upon
the system created by Brugsch, which, though confess-
edly artificial, nevertheless is able to meet the difficulties
of the subject better than any other yet devised.

Among distinguished German Egyptologists must be
mentioned Georg Moritz Ebers (1839—96). He is best
known by his far-famed novels, whose subjects are taken
from the history of ancient Egypt, perhaps the most
popular being " An Egyptian Princess." Besides these
popular novels and a valuable description of Egypt, Ebers
also made personal explorations in the country, and discovered at Thebes the great medical papyrus, which is
called the Papyrus Ebers. This remarkable document,
to which he devoted so much labour, is our chief source
of information regarding the practice of medicine as it
existed, and would alone keep the name of Ebers alive
among Egyptologists.

The leading German Egyptologist of to-day is Dr.
Adolf Erman, who was born at Berlin in 1854. He is
the worthy successor to Brugsch in the chair of Egyptology at the University of Berlin, and is director of the
Berlin Egyptian Museum. His writings have had to do
mainly with grammatical and literary investigations.
His editions of the " Romances of Old Egypt " are models

of scholarly interpretation. They give the original hieratic text, with translation into Egyptian hieroglyphics, into Latin and into German. Doctor Erman has not, however, confined his labours to this strictly scholarly type of work, but has also written a distinctly popular book on the life of the ancient Egyptians, which is the most complete work that has appeared since the writings of Wilkinson.

The memorable speech of Erman, delivered on the occasion of his election as a member of the Berlin Academy, sets forth clearly the progress made in the science of Egyptology and present-day tendencies. On that occasion he said:

" Some of our older fellow-specialists complain that we of the younger generation are depriving Egyptology of all its charm, and that, out of a delightful science, abounding in startling discoveries, we have made a philological study, with strange phonetic laws and a wretched syntax. There is doubtless truth in this complaint, but it should be urged against the natural growth of the science, and not against the personal influence of individuals or its development. The state through which Egyptology is now passing is one from which no science escapes. It is a reaction against the enthusiasm and the rapid advance of its early days.

" I can well understand to outsiders it may seem as though we had only retrograded during later years. Where are the good old times when every text could be translated and understood? Alas! a better comprehension of the grammar has revealed on every side difficulties and impediments of which hitherto nothing had been suspected. Moreover, the number of ascertained words in the vocabulary is continually diminishing, while the host of the unknown increases; for we no longer arrive at the meaning by the way of audacious etymologies and still more audacious guesses.

" We have yet to travel for many years on the arduous path of empirical research before we can attain to an adequate dictionary. There is indeed an exceptional reward which beckons us on to the same goal, namely, that we shall then be able to assign to Egyptian its place among the languages of Western Asia and of Africa. At present we do well to let this great question alone. As in the linguistic department of Egyptology, so it is in every other section of the subject. The Egyptian religion seemed intelligently and systematically rounded off when each god was held to be the incarnation of some power of nature. Now we comprehend that we had better reserve our verdict on this matter until we know the facts and the history of the religion; and how far we are from knowing them is proved to us by every text. The texts are full of allusions to the deeds and fortunes of the gods, but only a very small number of these allusions are intelligible to us.

" The time has gone by in which it was thought possible to furnish the chronology of Egyptian history, and in which that history was supposed to be known, because the succession of the most powerful kings had been ascertained. To us the history of Egypt has become something altogether different. It comprises the history of her civilisation, her art, and her administration; and we rejoice in the prospect that one day it may be possible in that land to trace the development of a nation throughout five thousand years by means of its own monuments and records. But we also know that the realisation of this dream must be the work of many generations.

" The so-called ' demotic ' texts, which lead us out of ancient Egypt into the Græco-Roman period, were deciphered with the acumen of genius more than half a century ago by Heinrich Brugsch, but to-day these also appear to us in a new light as being full of unexpected difficulties and in apparent disagreement with both the older and the later forms of the language. In this important department we must not shrink from a revision of past work.

" I will not further illustrate this theme; but the case is the same in every branch of Egyptology. In each, the day of rapid results is at an end, and the monotonous time of special studies has begun. Hence I would beg the Academy not to expect sensational discoveries from their new associate. I can only offer what *labor improbus* brings to light, and that is *small* discoveries; yet in the process of time they will lead us to those very ends which seemed so nearly attainable to our predecessors."

The German school may perhaps be said to have devoted its time especially to labours upon Egyptian grammar and philology, while the French school is better known for its excellent work on the history and archæology of ancient Egypt. On these topics the leading authority among all the scholars of to-day is the eminent

Frenchman, Professor Gaston C. C. Maspero, author of the first nine volumes of the present work. He was born at Paris, June 24, 1846. He is a member of the French Institute, and was formerly Professor of Egyptian Archæology and Ethnology in the Collège de France, and, more recently, Director of the Egyptian Museum at Bulak. His writings cover the entire field of Oriental antiquity. In this field Maspero has no peer among Egyptologists of the present or the past. He possesses an eminent gift of style, and his works afford a rare combination of the qualities of authority, scientific accuracy, and of popular readableness.

Some extraordinary treasures from tombs were discovered in the year 1881. At that date Arabs often hawked about in the streets what purported to be genuine works of antiquity. Many of these were in reality imitations; but Professor Maspero in this year secured from an Arab a funeral papyrus of Phtahhotpû I., and after considerable trouble he was able to locate the tomb in Thebes from which the treasure had been taken. Brugsch now excavated the cave, which was found to be the place where a quantity of valuable treasures had been secreted, probably at the time of the sacking of Thebes by the Assyrians. Six thousand objects were secured, and they included twenty-nine mummies of kings, queens, princes, and high priests, and five papyri, among which was the funeral papyrus of Queen Makeru of the twentieth dynasty. The mummy-cases had been opened by the Arabs, who had taken out the mummies and in some instances replaced the wrong ones. Many mummies of the eighteenth and nineteenth dynasties had been removed to this cave probably for safety, on account of its secrecy. Out of the twenty-nine mummies found here, seven were of kings, nine of queens and princesses, and several more of persons of distinction. The place of concealment was situated at a turn of a cliff southwest of the village of Deîr-el-Baharî.

The explorers managed successfully to identify King Raskamen of the seventeenth dynasty, King Ahmosis I., founder of the eighteenth dynasty, and his queen Ahmosis-Nofrîtari, also Queen Arhotep and Princess Set Ammon, and the king's daughters, and his son Prince Sa Ammon. They also found the mummies of Thûtmosis I., Thûtmosis II. and of Thûtmosis III. (Thûtmosis the Great), together with Ramses I., Seti I., Ramses XII., King Phtahhotpû II., and noted queens and princesses.

In the year 1883 the Egypt Exploration Fund was founded for the purpose of accurate historical investigation in Egypt. The first work undertaken was on a mound called the Tel-el-Mashuta, in the Wadi-et-Tumilat. This place was discovered to be the site of the ancient Pithom, a treasure-city supposed to have been built by the Israelites for Pharaoh. In the Greek and Roman period the same place had been called Heröopolis. M. Naville also discovered Succoth, the first camping-ground of the Israelites while fleeing from their oppressor, and an inscription with the word " Pikeheret," which he judged to be the Pihahiroth of the Book of Exodus. The next season the site of Zoan of the Bible was explored, a village now termed Sân.

Professor W. M. Flinders Petrie started work where a rim of red granite stood up upon one of the many mounds in the neighbourhood. The site of the ancient city had been here, and the granite rim was on the site of a temple. The latter had two enclosure walls, one of which had been built of sun-dried bricks, and was of extreme antiquity; the other was built of bricks of eight times the size and weight of modern bricks, and the wall was of very great strength. Dwelling-houses had been built in the locality, and coins and potsherds discovered. These remains Professor Petrie found to belong to periods between the sixth and twenty-sixth dynasties. Stones were found in the vicinity with the cartouche of King Papi from one of the earliest dynasties. There were also red granite statues of Ahmenemhâît I., and a black granite statue of Kind Usirtasen I. and of King Ahmenemhâît II., and a torso of King Usirtasen II. was found cut from yellow-stained stone, together with a vast number of relics of other monarchs. Parts of a giant statue of King Ramses II. were discovered which must have been ninety-eight feet in height before it was broken, the great toe alone measuring eighteen inches across, and the weight of the statue estimated to be about 1,200 tons. In addition to these relics of ancient monarchs, a large number of antiquities were discovered, with remains of objects for domestic use in ancient Egyptian society.

The explorations conducted at Tanis during 1883—84 brought to light objects mainly of the Ptolemaic period, because a lower level had not at that period been reached, but here many invaluable relics of Ptolemaic arts were unearthed. The results of researches were published at this date bearing upon the Great Pyramid. Accurate measurements had been undertaken by Professor Petrie, who was able to prove that during one epoch systematic but unavailing efforts had been made to destroy these great structures.

Professor Maspero discovered among the hills of Thebes an important tomb of the eleventh dynasty, which threw light upon obscure portions of Egyptian history, and contained texts of the " Book of the Dead." The following year he discovered the necropolis of Khemnis in the neighbourhood of Kekhrneen, a provincial town in Upper Egypt built on the site of the ancient Panopolis. The remains were all in a state of perfect preservation.

In July, 1884, Professor Maspero secured permission from the Egyptian government to buy from the natives the property which they held on the site of the Great Temple at Luxor, and to prevent any further work of destruction. These orders, however, were not carried out till early in 1885, when Maspero began excavating with one hundred and fifty workmen. He first unearthed the sanctuary of Amenhôthes III., with its massive roof. He brought to light the great central colonnade, and discovered a portico of Ramses II., and many colossi, which were either still erect or else had fallen on the ground. The columns of Amenhôthes III. were next explored, which were found to be among the most beautiful of all specimens of Egyptian architecture. It is believed that Luxor will prove to have been a locality of almost as great a beauty as Karnak.

During the season of 1884—85 Professor Petrie started excavations at the modern Nehireh, which he learned was the site of the ancient Naucratis.[1] Here many Greek inscriptions were found. This city was one of great importance and a commercial mart during the reign of Ahmosis, although in the time of the Emperor Commodus it had wholly disappeared. Two temples of Apollo were discovered, one of which was built from limestone in the seventh century B. C.; and the other was of white marble, beautifully decorated, and dating from the fifth century.

Magnificent libation bowls were also discovered here, some of which had been dedicated to Hera, others to Zeus, and others to Aphrodite. The lines of the ancient streets were traced, and a storehouse or granary of the ancient Egyptians was unearthed, also

RUINS AT LUXOR.

[1] The investigations on this site were continued in the season of 1888–89.

many Greek coins. Besides these were discovered vo-
tive deposits, cups of porcelain, alabaster jugs, limestone
mortars; and trowels, chisels, knives, and hoes.

Much light was thrown by these discoveries on the
progress of the ceramic arts, and many links uniting
the Greek pottery with the Egyptian pottery were here
for the first time traced. It was learned that the Greeks
were the pupils of the Egyptians, but that they idealised
the work of their masters and brought into it freer con-
ceptions of beauty and of proportion.

M. Naville was engaged about this time in contro-
versies as to the true site of this ancient Pithom. He
also made, in 1886, a search for the site of Goshen. He
believed he had identified this when he discovered at
Saft an inscription dedicated to the gods of Kes, which
Naville identified with Kesem, the name used in the
Septuagint for Goshen. Others, however, disagree, and
locate the site of Goshen at a place called Fakoos, twelve
miles north of Tel-el-Kebir.

The explorations of 1885—86 started under the direction of Professor W. M. Flinders Petrie, Mr. F. Llewellen Griffith, and Mr. Ernest A. Gardiner. Gardiner set
out in the direction of Naucratis, and Petrie and Griffith
proceeded to explore the site of Tanis. The mound at
which they worked, like many other localities of modern
and ancient Egypt, has been known by a variety of
names. It is called Tel Farum, or the Mound of the
Pharaoh; Tel Bedawi, the Mound of the Bedouins; and
Tel Nebesheh, after the name of the village upon this
site. There are remains here of an ancient cemetery

and of two ancient towns and a temple. The cemetery was found to be unlike those of Memphis, Thebes, or Abydos. It contained many small chambers and groups of chambers irregularly placed about a sandy plain. These were built mostly of brick, but there were other and larger ones built of limestone. A black granite altar of the reign of Ahmenemhâît II. was discovered, and thrones of royal statues of the twelfth dynasty. Here were also found a statue of Harpocrates, a portion of a statue of Phtah, with an inscription of Ramses II., a sphinx and tombs of the twentieth century B. C., containing many small relics of antiquity.

Professor Petrie went on from here to the site of Tell Defenneh, the Tahpanhes of the Bible, called Taphne in the version of the Septuagint. This proved to be the remains of the earliest Greek settlement in Egypt, and contains no remains from a later period than the twenty-sixth dynasty. It was here that Psammeticus I. established a colony of the Carian and Ionian mercenaries, by whose aid this monarch had won the throne; and this Greek city had been built as one out of three fortresses to prevent the incursions of the Arabians and Syrians. The city of Tahpanhes or Taphne is referred to in the book of Jeremiah.

There were found on this site the remains of a vast pile of brick buildings, which could be seen in outline from a great distance across the plains. The Arabs called this " El Kasr el Bin el Yahudi," that is, " The Castle of the Jew's Daughter." This was found to have been a fort, and it contained a stele with a record of the

garrison which had been stationed there; pieces of ancient armour and arms were also found in the neighbourhood. There was likewise a royal hunting-box on this
site, and all the principal parts of the settlement were
found to have been surrounded by a wall fifty feet thick,
which enclosed an area of three thousand feet in length
and one thousand in breadth. The gate on the north
opened towards the Pelusiac canal, and the south looked
out upon the ancient military road which led up from
Egypt to Syria. Pottery, bronze-work, some exquisitely
wrought scale armour, very light but overlapping six
times, were unearthed within this enclosure. There were
also Greek vases and other Greek remains, dating in the
earlier part of the reign of Ahmosis, who had subsequently sent the Greeks away, and prevented them from
trading in Egypt. Since this Greek colony came to an end
in the year 570 B. C., and as the locality was no longer
frequented by Greek soldiers or merchants, it is possible
to set an exact term to the period of Greek art which
these antiquities represent. The Greek pottery here is
so unlike that of Naucratis and of other places that it
seems to be well ascertained that it must have been all
manufactured at Defenneh itself. Outside the buildings
of the Kasr, Petrie discovered a large sun-baked pavement resting upon the sands, and this discovery was of
value in explaining a certain passage of the forty-third
chapter of Jeremiah, translated from the Revised Version as follows: " Then came the word of the Lord to
Jeremiah in Tahpanhes, saying, Take great stones in
thine hand, and hide them in the mortar of the brick-

work which is at the entry of Pharaoh's house in Tahpanhes in the sight of the men of Judah [*i. e.* Johannan and the captains who had gone to Egypt]; and say unto them, Thus saith the Lord of hosts, the God of Israel: Behold I will send and take Nebuchadrezzar the King of Babylon, my servant, and will set his throne upon these stones that I have hid; and he shall spread his royal pavilion over them. And he shall come and smite the land of Egypt." An alternate reading for " brickwork " is the pavement or square. The pavement which Jeremiah described was evidently the one which Petrie discovered, though he was not able at the time to discover the stones which, according to Jeremiah, had been inserted in the mortar. Outside the camp wall was further discovered the remains of a large settlement, strewn on all sides with bits of pottery and jewelry and a great number of weights.

During this season Maspero carried on researches at Luxor, and proceeded to excavate in the neighbourhood of the Great Sphinx. There are many Egyptian pictures which represent the Sphinx in its entirety down to the paws, but the lower parts had for centuries been buried in the accumulations of sand which had covered up all of the ancient site. It had previously been supposed that the Sphinx had been hewn out of a solid mass of rock resembling an immense boulder. Professor Maspero's excavations enabled him not only to verify the accuracy of the old Egyptian paintings of the Sphinx, but also to show that a vast amphitheatre had been hewn out of the rock round the Sphinx, which was not therefore sculptured from a projecting rock. Since the upper rim of this basin was about on the same level with the head of the figure, it became evident that the ancient sculptors had cut the rock away on all sides, and had subsequently left the Sphinx isolated, as it is at the present day. Maspero dug down during this season to a depth of thirty yards in the vicinity.

Professor Maspero's last official act as Director-General of the Excavations and Antiquities of Egypt was his examination of the mummy of Ramses II. found in 1884, in the presence of the khedive and other high dignitaries. The mummy of this great conqueror was well preserved, revealing a giant frame and a face expressive of sovereign majesty, indomitable will, and the pride of the Egyptian king of kings. He then unbandaged the mummy of Nofrîtari, wife of King Ahmosis I. of the eighteenth dynasty, beside which, in the same sarcophagus, had been discovered the mummy of Ramses III. The physiognomy of this monarch is more refined and intellectual than that of his warlike predecessor; nor was his frame built upon the same colossal plan. The height of the body was less, and the shoulders not so wide. In the same season Maspero also discovered an ancient Egyptian romance inscribed on limestone near the tomb of Sinûhît at Thebes. A fragment on papyrus had been preserved at the Berlin Museum, but the whole romance was now decipherable.

Professor Maspero resigned his office of directorship on June 5, 1886, and was succeeded in the superintendency of excavations and Egyptian archæology by

M. Eugene Grébault. In the same month Grébault started upon the work of unbandaging the mummy of the Theban King Sekenenra Ta-aken, of the eighteenth dynasty. It was under this monarch that a revolt against the Hyksôs, or Shepherd Kings, had originated, in the course of which the Asiatics were expelled from Egypt. The history of this king has always been considered legendary, but from the signs of wounds present in the mummy, it is certain that he had died in battle.[1] In the same season the mummy of Seti I. was unbandaged, and also that of an anonymous prince.

The next season the work of clearing away the sand from around the Great Sphinx was vigorously prosecuted by Grébault. In the beginning of the year 1887, the chest, the paws, the altar, and plateau were all made visible. Flights of steps were unearthed, and finally accurate measurements were taken of the great figures. The height from the lowest of the steps was found to be one hundred feet, and the space between the paws was found to be thirty-five feet long and ten feet wide. Here there was formerly an altar; and a stele of Thûtmosis IV. was discovered, recording a dream in which he was ordered to clear away the sand that even then was gathering round the site of the Sphinx.

M. Naville and Mr. F. Llewellen Griffiths explored during the season of 1886—87 the mound of Tel-el-Yehudieh (the mound of the Jew). The site is probably that on which was once built the city that Ptolemy Philadelphus allowed the Jews to construct. The remains of a

[1] See Volume IV., page 110.

statue of the cat-headed goddess Bast, to which there
is a reference in Josephus, was also found here. The
discovery of tablets of definitely Jewish origin make
it clear that the modern name had been given to the place
for some reason connected with the colony thus proved
to have once been settled there.

Naville also made researches at Tel Basta, the site
of the Bubastis of the Greeks, the Pi Beseth of the Bible,
and the Pi Bast of the Egyptians, which was formerly
the centre of worship of the goddess Pasht and her sacred
animal, the cat. The whole plan of the ancient temple
was soon disclosed, the general outline of which bears
much resemblance to that of the great Temple of Sân.
In the division which Naville called the Festival Hall
were numerous black and red statues inscribed with the
name of Ramses II., but many of which were probably
not really erected by this monarch. Here there was also
found a standing statue of the Governor of Ethiopia,
a priest and priestess of the twenty-sixth dynasty, and
many other monuments of the greatest historical interest. The hall itself was built of red granite.

Another hall, which Naville called the " Hypostyle
Hall," possessed a colonnade of such beauty that it would
seem to justify the statement of Herodotus, that the temple of Bubastis was one of the finest in Egypt. The columns were either splendid red granite monoliths, with
lotus-bud or palm-leaf capitals; or, a head of Hâthor
from which fell two long locks. These columns probably
belonged to the twelfth dynasty. In what Naville called
the " Ptolemaic Hall " occurs the name Nephthorheb or

Nectanebo I. of the thirtieth dynasty. The relics of this remarkable temple thus cover a period from the sixth to the thirtieth dynasties, some 3,200 years. During this season Professor Petrie made important discoveries in relation to the obscure Hyksôs dominion in Egypt. Many representations of these Shepherd Kings were found, and, from their physiognomy, it was judged that they were not Semites, but rather Mongols or Tatars, who probably came from the same part of Asia as the Mongul hordes of Genghis Khan.

Early in 1888 excavations were resumed on the site of the great temple of Bubastis by M. Edouard Naville, Mr. F. Ll. Griffiths, and the Count d'Hulst. The investigation again yielded the usual crop of antiquities that was now always expected from the exploration of the famous sites. A third hall was discovered, which had been built in the time of Osorkon I., of red granite inlaid with sculptured slabs. There were also many other monuments and remains of the monarchs, together with much valuable evidence relating to the rule of the Hyksôs.

Petrie brought to London many beautiful Ptolemaic and Roman portraits, which he had discovered in a vast cemetery near the pyramid which bears the name of King Ahmenemhâît III. The portraits are in an excellent state of preservation, and are invaluable as illustrative of the features, manners, and customs of the Greek and Roman periods in Egyptian history.

His researches in the neighbourhood of the Fayum at this time commenced to bear fruit; and many questions were answered regarding the ancient Lake Mœris. It was in this season also that the ever memorable excavations conducted at Tel-el-Amarna were first begun. This place is situated in Upper Egypt on the site of the capital, which had been built by Ahmenhotpû IV. Here were discovered many clay tablets in cuneiform characters containing documents in the Babylonian language. These were found in the tomb of a royal scribe. The list contained a quantity of correspondence from the kings or rulers of Palestine, Syria, Mesopotamia, and Babylonia to Ahmenhotpû III. and IV. There were Egyptian garrisons in those days in Palestine, and they were accustomed to keep their royal masters well informed as to what was going on in the country. Among other cities mentioned are Byblos, Smyrna, Appo or Acre, Megiddo, and Ashpelon. During this season many relics of early Christian art were discovered. In many cases [1] a pagan picture had been in part painted over, and thus given a Christian significance. Two figures of Isis suckling Horus are, with slight alterations, made to represent the Virgin and the Child. A bas-relief of St. George slaying the dragon was discovered, which closely resembled that of Horus slaying Set.

During the following season of 1888—89, Petrie resumed his excavations round the pyramid of Hawara, which was supposed to be the site of the famous Labyrinth. Work had been begun here in the season previous, and it was now to be crowned with great success. All the underground passages and secret chambers under

[1] See Volume XI., page 248.

the pyramid were examined, and the inscriptions discovered of King Ahmenemhâît III. prove that this was without doubt the pyramid of the monarch of that name. It was discovered that the Romans had broken into the recesses of these secret chambers, and many broken Roman *amphoræ* were unearthed. Later Professor Petrie examined the pyramid of Illahûn, which stands at the gate of the Fayum. It is probable that this was on the site of the ancient locks which regulated the flow of the Nile into Lake Mœris. Many of the antiquities here discovered bore inscriptions of King Usirtasen II., and, in the same locality, was discovered the site of an early Christian cemetery dating from the fifth or sixth centuries. A few miles from Illahûn, the same indefatigable explorer discovered the remains of another town belonging to the eighteenth or nineteenth dynasties. A wall once surrounded the town, and beyond the wall was a necropolis. The place is now called Tell Gurah, and the relics give inscriptions of Thûtmosis III. or Tûtankhamon and of Horemheb.

In the same season of 1888—89, Miss Amelia B. Edwards, who had been sent out by the Egypt Exploration Fund, brought to a conclusion the excavations which had been carried on for several seasons at Bubastis. It was discovered that the temple itself dated back to the reign of the famous Khûfûi (Kheops), the builder of the great Pyramid, since an inscription with his name on it was discovered, together with one inscribed to King Khafrî (Chephren). The monuments discovered on this site were, for the most part, shipped to Europe and America.

The city of Boston, Mass., received a colossal Hâthor-head capital of red granite, part of a colossal figure of a king, an immense lotus-bud capital from the Hypo-style Hall of the temple, a bas-relief in red granite from the Hall of Osorken II., and two bas-reliefs of limestone from the temple of Hâthor, taken from the ancient Termuther. Specimens recovered from here date from the fourth to the twenty-second dynasties, and the relics from Termuther are from the last period of the Ptolemies.

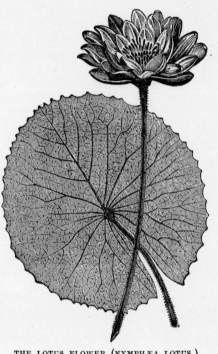

THE LOTUS FLOWER (NYMPHÆA LOTUS.)

Early in 1891, Professor Petrie made his exhaustive examination of the pyramid of Medum, which he declared to be the earliest of all dated Egyptian pyramids, and probably the oldest dated building in the world. Its builder was Snofrui of the third dynasty; and, joined with it, and in a perfect state of preservation, was the pyramid temple built at the same period. From forty to sixty feet of rubbish had accumulated around the buildings, and had to be removed. The front of the temple was thirty feet wide and nine feet high, and a door was discovered at the south end. A wide doorway leads

to the open court built on the side of the pyramid. In
the centre of the court stands the altar of offerings, where
there is also an inscribed obelisk thirteen feet high. The
walls of the temple are all marked with *graffiti* of visitors who belonged to the twelfth and eighteenth dynasties. A statuette was found dedicated to the gods of the
town by a woman.

The tombs at this place had been rifled in ancient
times, but many skeletons of people, who had been buried
in a crouching attitude, were discovered, and Petrie considered that these belonged to a different race from that
which was accustomed to bury the dead recumbent. A
quantity of pottery was also unearthed, dating from the
fourth century. The method by which the plan of a
pyramid was laid out by the ancient Egyptians was discovered in this excavation, and the designs show considerable mechanical ingenuity in their execution, and
afford a perfect system for maintaining the symmetry
of the building itself, no matter how uneven the ground
on which it was to be built.

In the spring of 1891, M. Naville started an excavation on the site of the ancient Heracleopolis Magna at a
place now named Hanassieh. He found here many Roman and Koptic remains, and further discovered the
vestibule of an ancient Egyptian temple. There were
six columns, on which Ramses II. was represented as
offering gifts. The name of Menephtah was also noticed,
and the architraves above the columns were seen to be
cut with cartouches of Usirtasen II. of the twelfth dynasty. This temple was probably one of those to the

service of which Ramses II. donated some slaves, as is described in one of the papyri of the Harris collection.

A stone was discovered by Mr. Wilborn at Luxor, recording a period of seven years' successive failure of the Nile to overflow, and the efforts made by a certain sorcerer named Chit Net to remove the calamity.

During the season of 1895, Professor Petrie and Mr. Quibell discovered homes belonging to paleolithic man on a plateau four thousand feet above the Nile. Thirty miles south of Thebes, there are many large and beautifully worked flints. Their great antiquity is proved by the fact that they are deeply stained, whereas, in the same locality, there are other flints of an age of five thousand years, which show no traces of stains.

Close by this site was discovered the abundant remains of a hitherto unknown race. This race has nothing in common with the true Egyptians, although their relics are invariably found with those of the Egyptians of the fourth, twelfth, eighteenth, and nineteenth dynasties. Petrie declares these men to have been tall and powerful, with strong features, a hooked nose, a long, pointed beard, and brown, wavy hair. They were not related to the negroes, but rather to the Amorites or Libyans. The bodies in these tombs are not mummified, but are contracted, though laid in an opposite direction from those discovered at Medum. The graves are open, square pits, roofed over with beams of wood. This ancient race used forked hunting-lances for chasing the gazelle, and their beautiful flints were found to be like those belonging to an excellent collection already existing in the Ashmolean Museum of Oxford. They also made an abundant use of copper for adzes, harpoons for spearing fish, and needles for sewing garments. They used pottery abundantly, and its variety is remarkable no less than the quality, which, unlike the Egyptian, was all hand-made and never fashioned by aid of the wheel. They entered Egypt about 3,000 B. c., and were probably of the white Libyan race, and possibly may have been the foreigners who overthrew the old Egyptian empire.

The discovery of the name of " Israel " in an Egyptian inscription was in a sense, perhaps, the most remarkable event of the year 1895 in archæology. It was first laid before the public by Professor Petrie,[1] and was treated by Spiegelberg [2] in a communication to the Berlin Academy, and by Steindorff.[3] The name occurs in an inscription dated in the fifth year of Merenptah, the successor of Ramses II., and often supposed to be the Pharaoh of the Exodus. It is there written with the determinative of a people, not of a city or country, and reads in our conventional transliteration *Ysiràar*, but in reality agrees very closely to the Hebrew ישראל, the last portion *àar* being recognised as the equivalent of *el* in several words. Merenptah states that " Israel is fekt (?) without seed (grain or offspring), Syria (*Kharu*) has become widows (*Kharût*) of or to Egypt." We can form no conclusion from these statements as to the relation

[1] Contemporary Review, May 1896.
[2] Sitzberichte, xxv., p 593.
[3] Zeitschrift für deutsch. Alt. test. Wiss., 1896, p. 330.

in which the Israelites stood to Pharaoh and to Egypt, except that they are represented as having been power- less. It is pretty clear, however, from the context that they were then in Palestine, or at least in Syria. Stein- dorff suggests that they may have entered Syria from Chaldæa during the disturbed times in Egypt at the end of the eighteenth dynasty, and connects them with the movements of the Khabiri (Hebrews?) mentioned in the Tel-el-Amarna tablets. On the other hand, it is of course possible, as Professor Petrie points out, that this refer-

THE WORD " ISRAEL " IN HIEROGLYPHS.

ence to the Israelites may have some connection with the Exodus itself. M. Clermont Ganneau thinks that the localities mentioned are all in Southern Palestine.[1]

M. Edouard Naville found at Thebes many remains of the Punt sculptures. The Puntites appear with their aquiline features, their pointed beards, and their long hair; negroes also of black and brown varieties are rep- resented adjoining the Puntites proper. There are wick- erwork huts, and a figure of a large white dog with its ears hanging down. Long-billed birds also appear flying about in the trees. Their nests have been forsaken and robbed, and the men are represented as gathering incense

[1] Revue Archéologique, xxix., p. 127.

from the trees. Altogether, much invaluable information has been gathered concerning the famous people who lived in the Land of Punt, and with whom for a long period the Egyptians held intercommunication. Other discoveries were made near the great temple of Karnak, and the buildings of Medinet-Habu were cleared of rubbish in order to show their true proportions.

From its foundation, the Egypt Exploration Fund has received large pecuniary support from the United States, chiefly through the enthusiasm and energy of Dr. W. C. Winslow, of Boston. In 1880 Doctor Winslow, who had been five months in Egypt, returned to America deeply impressed with the importance of scientific research in Egypt, and, upon hearing of the Exploration Fund in London, he wrote a letter expressive of his interest and sympathy to the president, Sir Erasmus Wilson, which brought a reply not only from him, but also from the secretary, Miss Edwards, expatiating upon the purpose and needs of the society, and outlining optimistically its ultimate accomplishments.

Doctor Winslow was elected honorary treasurer of the Fund for the United States for the year 1883—84.[1] Many prominent residents became interested and added

[1] The American subscriptions from the year 1883 rapidly increased, and by the year 1895 had figured up to $75,800, and the total number of letters and articles written during that time had grown to 2,467. The organisation in America consists of a central office at Boston, together with independent local societies, such as have already been formed in New York, Philadelphia, and Chicago. The Boston office, and any independent local society, which subscribes not less than $750 a year, is entitled to nominate a member of the Committee. At the end of July, 1884, Doctor Winslow had forwarded to London $1,332.20.

their names to its membership, and have given it their effort and their hearty financial support. Among the distinguished American members have been J. R. Lowell, G. W. Curtis, Charles Dudley Warner, and among the chief Canadian members are Doctor Bourinot and Dr. J. William Dawson.

The Fund has always preserved amicable relations with the Government Department of Antiquities in Egypt. Excavations are conducted by skilled explorers, and the results published promptly with due regard to scientific accuracy and pictorial embellishment. The antiquities found are either deposited in the National Museum at Cairo, or distributed among public museums in the United Kingdom and the United States of America and Canada, in strict proportion to the contribution of each locality. Exhibitions are usually held in London in July of each year.

The Fund now consists of three departments, for each of which separate accounts are kept. These departments are: 1. The Exploration Fund, for conducting archeological research generally, by means of systematic excavations. 2. The Archæological Survey, for preserving an accurate pictorial record of monuments already excavated but liable to destruction. 3. The Græco-Roman Branch, for the discovery of the remains of classical antiquity and early Christianity.

The first work of the Græco-Roman Branch was to publish the recently discovered Oxyrrhynchos papyri, of which two volumes, containing many important classical and theological texts, were issued in 1898 and 1899 and

1900. Among its contents are parts of two odes of Pindar, of which one begins with a description of the poet's relation to Xenocritus, the inventor of the Locrian mode of music; a considerable piece of the " Kolax " of Menander, one of the two plays upon which the " Eunuchus " of Terence was based; part of a rhetorical treatise in Doric dialect, which is undoubtedly a work of the Pythagorean school; the conclusion of the eighteenth Κεστός of Julius Africanus, dealing with a question of Homeric criticism; and part of a biography of Alcibiades. A new light is thrown upon some of the less-known departments of Greek literature by a well-preserved papyrus, which contains on one side a prose mime in two scenes, a work of the school of Sophron, having points of resemblance to the fifth mime of Herondas; while on the other side is an amusing farce, partly in prose, partly in verse. The scene is laid on the shores of the Indian Ocean, and the plot turns upon the rescue of a Greek maiden from the hands of barbarians, who speak a non-Greek language with elements apparently derived from Prakrit.[1]

The new Homeric fragments include one of Iliad VI., with critical signs and interesting textual notes. Sappho, Euripides (" Andromache," Archelaus," and " Medea "), Antiphanes, Thucydides, Plato (" Gorgias " and " Republic "), Æschines, Demosthenes, and Xenophon are also represented. Among the theological texts

[1] This is a peculiarly interesting suggestion in view of the fact that there is in the British Museum an unpublished fragment which for some time was considered by Doctor Budge to be a species of Egyptian stenography, but which has also been suggested to be in Pehlevi characters.

are fragments of the lost Greek original of the " Apocalypse of Baruch " and of the missing Greek conclusion of the " Shepherd " of Hermas.

In the winter of 1898—99, Doctors Grenfell and Hunt conducted excavations for the Græco-Roman Branch in the Fayûm. In 1899—1900, they excavated at Tebtunis, in the Fayûm, on behalf of the University of California; and by an arrangement between that university and the Egypt Exploration Fund an important section of the Tebtunis papyri, consisting of second-century B. C. papyri from crocodile mummies, was issued jointly by the two bodies, forming the annual volumes of the Græco-Roman Branch for 1900—01 and 1901—02. Since 1900 Doctors Grenfell and Hunt have excavated each winter on behalf of the Græco-Roman Branch,—in 1900—01 in the Fayûm, and in 1901—02 both there and at Hibeh, with the result that a very large collection of Ptolemaic papyri was obtained. In the winter of 1902—03, after finishing their work at Hibeh, they returned to Oxyrrhynchos. Here was found a third-century fragment of a collection of sayings of Jesus, similar in style to the so-called " Logia " discovered at Oxyrrhynchos in 1897. As in that papyrus, the separate sayings are introduced by the words " Jesus saith," and are for the most part unrecorded elsewhere, though some which are found in the Gospels (*e. g.* " The Kingdom of God is within you " and " Many that are first shall be last, and the last shall be first ") occur here in different surroundings. Six sayings are preserved, unfortunately in an imperfect condition. But the new " Logia " papyrus supplies more evidence concerning its origin than was the case with its predecessor, for it contains an introductory paragraph stating that what follows consisted of " the words which Jesus, the Living Lord, spake " to two of His disciples; and, moreover, one of the uncanonical sayings is already extant in part, the conclusion of it, " He that wonders shall reign and he that reigns shall rest," being quoted by Clement of Alexandria from the Gospel according to the Hebrews. It is, indeed, possible that this Gospel was the source from which all this second series of " Logia " was derived, or they, or some of them, may perhaps have been taken from the Gospel according to the Egyptians, to which Professor Harnack and others have referred the " Logia " found in 1897. But the discoverers are disposed to regard both series as collections of sayings currently ascribed to our Lord rather than as extracts from any one uncanonical gospel.

A SEALING DISCOVERED AT ABYDOS.

CHAPTER VIII

IMPORTANT RESEARCHES IN EGYPT

The Royal Tombs at Abydos: Reconstruction of the First and Second Dynasties : The Ten Temples at Abydos: The statuette of Khûfûi: Pottery
and Pottery Marks: The Expedition of the University of California.

SOME interesting explorations have
been conducted in Egypt by the
Exploration Fund during the four
years 1900—04, under the guidance of
Prof. W. M. Flinders Petrie, whose

PORTRAIT OF DEN. enthusiasm and patience for the work
in this field seem to increase with the years of labour.
In the winter of 1899—1900, Professor Petrie and his
zealous helpers began their investigation of the royal
tombs of the first dynasty at Abydos. Commenting on
this undertaking, Professor Petrie writes:

" It might have seemed a fruitless and thankless task
to work at Abydos after it had been ransacked by

Mariette, and had been for the last four years in the hands of the Mission Amélineau. My only reason was that the extreme importance of results from there led to a wish to ascertain everything possible about the early royal tombs after they were done with by others, and to search even for fragments of the pottery. To work at Abydos had been my aim for years past; but it was only after it was abandoned by the Mission Amélineau that at last, on my fourth application for it, I was permitted to rescue for historical study the results that are here shown.

" Nothing is more disheartening than being obliged to gather results out of the fraction left behind by past plunderers. In these royal tombs there had been not only the plundering of the precious metals and the larger valuables by the wreckers of early ages; there was after that the systematic destruction of monuments by the vile fanaticism of the Kopts, which crushed everything beautiful and everything noble that mere greed had spared; and worst of all, for history, came the active search in the last four years for everything that could have a value in the eyes of purchasers, or be sold for profit regardless of its source; a search in which whatever was not removed was deliberately and avowedly destroyed in order to enhance the intended profits of European speculators. The results are therefore only the remains which have escaped the lust of gold, the fury of fanaticism, and the greed of speculators in this ransacked spot.

" A rich harvest of history has come from the site which was said to be exhausted; and in place of the dis-

ordered confusion of names without any historical connection, which was all that was known from the *Mission
Amélineau*, we now have the complete sequence of kings
from the middle of the dynasty before Mena to probably the close of the second dynasty, and we can trace
in detail the fluctuations of art throughout these
reigns."[1]

At the time when Professor Maspero brought his
history of Egypt to a close, the earliest known historical
ruler of Egypt was King Mena or Menes.[2] Mena is the
first king on the fragmentary list of Manetho, and the
general accuracy of Manetho was supported by the accounts of Herodotus and other ancient writers. For
several centuries these accounts were accepted as the
basis of authentic history. With the rise of the science
of Egyptology, however, search began to be made for
some corroboration of the actual existence of Mena, and
this was found in the inscriptions of a temple wall at
Abydos, which places Mena at the head of the first dynasty; and, allowing for differences of language, the
records of Manetho relating to the earlier dynasty were
established. Mena was therefore accepted as the first
king of the first dynasty up to the very end of the nineteenth century.

As a result of Professor Petrie's recent investigations, however, he has been enabled to carry back the
line of the early kings for three or four generations.

[1] "The Royal Tombs of the First Dynasty," Parts I. — II. (Eighteenth
and Twenty-first Memoirs of the Egypt Exploration Fund), London, 1900–1902.
[2] See Volume I., page 322, *et seq.*

The royal tombs at Abydos lie closely together in a compact group on a site raised slightly above the level of the surrounding plain, so that the tombs could never be flooded. Each of the royal tombs is a large square pit, lined with brickwork. Close around it, on its own level, or higher up, there are generally small chambers in rows, in which were buried the domestics of the king. Each reign adopted some variety in the mode of burial, but they all follow the type of the prehistoric burials, more or less developed. The plain square pit, like those in which the predynastic people were buried, is here the essential of the tomb. It is surrounded in the earlier examples of Zer or Zet by small chambers opening from it. By Merneit these chambers were built separately around it. By Den an entrance passage was added, and by Qa the entrance was turned to the north. At this stage we are left within reach of the early passage-mastabas and pyramids. Substituting a stone lining and roof for bricks and wood, and placing the small tombs of domestics farther away, we reach the type of the mastaba-pyramid of Snofrui, and so lead on to the pyramid series of the Old Kingdom.

The careful manner with which all details of a burial were supervised under the first dynasty enables the modern Egyptologist, by a skilful piecing together of evidence, to reconstruct an almost perfect picture of the life of Egypt at the dawn of civilisation. One of our most valuable sources of information is due to the fact that, in building the walls of the royal tombs, there were deposited in certain parts within the walls objects now

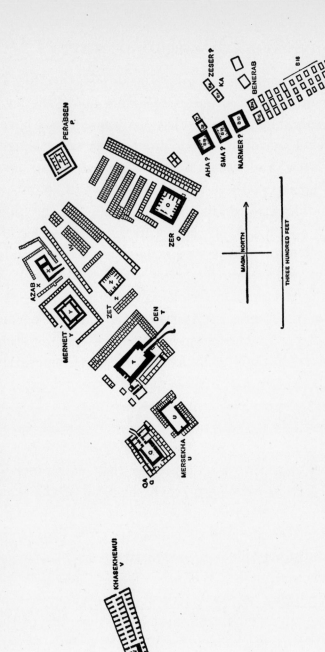

GENERAL PLAN OF THE ROYAL TOMBS AT ABYDOS.

technically known as *deposits*. We do not know whether, in selecting these objects, the ancient Egyptian had regard to what he considered their intrinsic value, or whether, as was most probable, it was some religious motive that prompted his action. Often the objects thus deposited come under the designation of pottery, although the vases were sometimes shaped of stone and not of clay. Within such vases all kinds of objects were preserved. The jar or vase was closed with a lump of clay, either flat or conical, and the clay was impressed, while wet, with a seal.

A detailed and elaborate examination of the relative positions of the tombs, their dimensions, and the objects found in them, compared with the various fragments of historical records of the early dynasties, enables us to reconstruct the exact order of these ancient rulers. This sequence is:

By Tombs.		Table of Abydos	Manetho.
B 7	Ka		
B 9	Zeser [1]		
B 10	Narmer		
B 15	Sma		
B 19	Mena = Aha	Mena	Menes
B 14	Bener-ab		
O	Zer	Teta	Athothis
Z	Zet	Atet	Kenkeens
Y	Merneit	Ata	Uenenfes
T	Den-Setui	Hesepti	Usafais
X	Azab-Merpaba	Merbap	Miebis
U	Mersekha	... ptah ?	Semempses
Q	Qa-Sen	Qebh	Bienekhes

[1] Ka and Zeser were possibly brothers of Mena.

Following the dating tentatively computed by Professor Petrie, the dates of some of these kings are:

			B. C.
Ka	. . . .		4900
Mena	. . .	after	. . 4800
Zer	. . . .		4700
Den-Setui	. . . . . .		4600
Qa	. . . .		4500

Thus we have reconstructed the list of Thinite kings before Mena so far as the facts allow, and perhaps so far as we are ever likely to ascertain them.

The facts about the second dynasty, the kings after Qa, must now be studied. In the tomb of Perabsen it was found that there were buried with him vases of three other kings, which are therefore his predecessors. Their names are Hotepahaui, Raneb, and Neteren; and it is certain that Raneb preceded Neteren, as the latter had defaced and re-used a vase of the former. As on statue No. 1, Cairo Museum, these three names are in the above order, and, as the succession of two of them is now proved, it is only reasonable to accept them in this order. From all the available facts it seems that we ought to restore the dynasty thus:

Tombs.				Seti.				Manetho.
Hotepahaui	.	.	.	Bazau	.	.	.	Bokhos
Raneb	.	.	.	Kakau	.	.	.	Kaiekhos
Neteren	.	.	.	Baneteren .	.	.	.	Binothris
Perabsen	.	.	.	Uaznes	.	.	.	Tlas
(Khashem)	.	.	.	Senda	.	.	.	Sethenes
(Kara)	.	.	.	.	.	.	.	Khaires
Khasekhemui	.	.	.	Zaza	.	.	.	Neferkheres

The oldest tomb that we can definitely assign is that marked B 7, the tomb of King Ka. This is a pit with sloping sides; the thickness of the brick walls is that of the length of one brick, and the soft footing of the wall and pressure of sand behind it has overthrown the longer sides. The broken pottery mixed with the sand, which filled it, largely consisted of cylinder jars, like the later prehistoric form; and these had many inscriptions on them, written in ink with a brush, most of which showed the name of Ka in the usual panelled frame. There can therefore be no doubt of the attribution of this tomb.

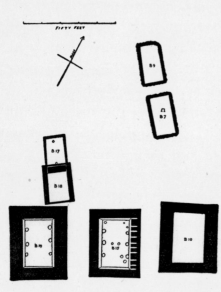

ENLARGED PLAN OF FIRST DYNASTY TOMBS.

The tomb B 9 is perhaps that of King Zeser, who seems to have been a successor of Ka. It is of the same construction as that of Ka. The tomb B 10 appears to be the oldest of the great tombs, by its easternmost position; and the objects of Narmer point to this as his tomb. In both the thickness and the batter of the walls there is a care shown in proportioning the strength of the ends and the sides. The tomb B 15 is probably that of King Sma. Its walls are not quite so thick, being fifty inches at the end. The post-holes in the floor suggest that there were

five on the long side, and one in the middle of each end,
as in the tomb of Narmer. But along the sides are holes
for roofing beams near the top of the wall. These roof
beams do not at all accord with the posts; and this proves
that, here at least, the posts were for backing a wooden
chamber inside the brick chamber. If this be the case
here, it was probably also true in Narmer's tomb; and
hence these brick tombs were only the protective shell
around a wooden chamber which contained the burial.
This same system is known in the first dynasty tombs,
and we see here the source of the chambered tombs of
Zer and Zet. Before the age of Mena, the space around
the wood chamber was used for dropping in offerings
between the framing posts; and then, after Mena, separate brick chambers were made around the wooden
chamber in order to hold more offerings.[1]

The tomb B 19, which contained the best tablet of
Aha-Mena, is probably his tomb; for the tomb with his
vases at Naqada is more probably that of his queen Neit-
hotep. As both the tombs B 17 and 18 to the north of
this contained objects of Mena, it is probable that they
were the tombs of some members of his family.[2]

The great cemetery of the domestics of this age is
the triple row of tombs to the east of the royal tombs;[3]
in all the thirty-four tombs here, no name was found
beside that of Aha on the jar sealings, and the two tombs,

[1] This chamber was burnt; and is apparently that mentioned by M.
Amélineau, *Fouilles, in extenso,* 1899, page 107.

[2] For plan see page 361.

[3] For plan see pages 361 and 364.

B 6 and B 14, seen to be probably of the same age.   In B 14 were found only objects of Aha, and three of them were inscribed with the name of Bener-eb, probably the name of a wife or a daughter of Mena, which is not found in any other tomb.[1]

From the time of Mena has come down to us an ebony tablet, as shown in the illustration.   This is the most

EBONY TABLET OF KING AHA-MENA.

complete of the inscriptions of this king, and was found in two portions in the tombs marked B 18 and B 19.   The

[1] Professor Petrie's arguments, although borne out by the evidence that he produces, have from time to time been criticised.   M. Naville, for example, endeavours to prove that the buildings in the desert are not literally tombs, but rather temples for the cult of their Ka; and that there ought not to be kings anterior to Mena, particularly at Abydos: "Narmer" is really Boethos, the first king of the second dynasty.   According to M. Naville, Boethos, Usaphis, and Miebidos are the only kings as yet identified of the early time.   M. Naville also suggests that Ka-Sekhem and Ka-Sekhemui are two names for one king.

signs upon the tablet are most interesting. On the top
line, after the cartouche of Aha-Mena, there are two
sacred boats, probably of Sokaris, and a shrine and
temenos of Nit. In the line below is seen a man making
an offering, and behind him is a bull running over un-
dulating ground into a net stretched between two poles,
while at the end, standing upon a shrine, is a bird, which
appears to be the ibis of Thot. A third line shows three
boats upon a canal or river, passing between certain
places, and it has been reasonably conjectured that the
other signs in this line indicate these places as being Biu,
a district of Memphis; Pa She (or " the dwelling of the
lake "), the capital of the Fayum; and the Canal of
Mer, or Bahr Yusef. So far this tablet contains picture
signs, but the fourth line gives a continued series of hieroglyphics, and is the oldest line of such characters yet
discovered. Mr. F. Ll. Griffiths translates these characters as " who takes the throne of Horus."

In the north-west corner of the tomb, a stairway of
bricks was roughly inserted in later times in order to
give access to the shrine of Osiris. That this is not an
original feature is manifest: the walls are burnt red by
the burning of the tomb, while the stairs are built of
black mud brick with fresh mud mortar smeared over
the reddened wall. It is notable that the burning of these
tombs took place before their re-use in the eighteenth
dynasty; as is also seen by the re-built doorway of the
tomb of Den, which is of large black bricks over smaller
red burnt bricks. It is therefore quite beside the mark
to attribute this burning to the Kopts.

The tomb of King Zer has an important secondary history as the site of the shrine of Osiris, established in the eighteenth dynasty (for none of the pottery offered there is earlier than that of Amenhôthes III.), and visited with offerings from that time until the twenty-sixth dynasty, when additional sculptures were placed here. Afterwards it was despoiled by the Kopts in erasing

TOMB OF ZER, 4700 B. O.

the worship of Osiris. It is the early state of the place as the tomb of King Zer that we have to study here, and not its later history.

The tomb chamber has been built of wood; and the brick cells around it were built subsequently against the wooden chamber, as their rough, unplastered ends show; moreover, the cast of the grain of the wood can be seen on the mud mortar adhering to the bricks. There are also long, shallow grooves in the floor, a wide one near the west wall, three narrow ones parallel to that, and a short cross groove, all probably the places of beams which supported the wooden chamber. Besides these there was till recently a great mass of carbonised wood along the north side of the floor. This was probably part of the flooring of the tomb, which, beneath the wood-work, was covered with a layer of bricks, which lay on clean sand. But all the middle of the tomb had been cleared to the native marl for building the Osiris shrine, of which some fragments of sculpture in hard limestone are now all that remain.

A strange feature here is that of the red recesses, such as were also found in the tomb of Zet. The large ones are on the west wall, and in the second cell on the north wall. No meaning can yet be assigned to these, except as spirit-entrances to the cells of offerings, like the false doors in tombs of the Old Kingdom.

In spite of the plundering of the tombs in various ages, the work of the Egypt Exploration Fund was so thorough that not a few gold objects have been found in the course of recent excavations. By far the most important discovery of recent years was that of some jewelry in the tomb of King Zer. The story of this find is so entertaining, and illustrates so admirably the method of the modern scientific explorer, that we give the account of it in Professor Petrie's own words:

" While my workmen were clearing the tomb, they noticed among the rubbish which they were moving a piece of the arm of a mummy in its wrappings. It lay in a broken hole in the north wall of the tomb. The party of four who found it looked into the end of the wrappings and saw a large gold bead, the rosette in the second bracelet. They did not yield to the natural wish to search further or to remove it; but laid the arm down where they found it until Mr. Mace should come and verify it. Nothing but obtaining the complete confidence of the workmen, and paying them for all they find, could ever make them deal with valuables in this careful manner. On seeing it, Mr. Mace told them to bring it to our huts intact, and I received it quite undisturbed. In the evening the most intelligent of the party was summoned as a witness of the opening of the wrappings, so that there should be no suspicion that I had not dealt fairly with the men. I then cut open the linen bandages, and found, to our great surprise, the four bracelets of gold and jewelry. The verification of the exact order of threading occupied an hour or two, working with a magnifier, my wife and Mr. Mace assisting. When recorded, the gold was put in the scales and weighed against sovereigns before the workman, who saw everything. Rather more than the value of gold was given to the men, and thus we ensured their good-will and honesty for the future."

The hawk bracelet consists of thirteen gold and fourteen turquoise plaques in the form of the façade with the hawk, which usually encloses the *ka* name of the king. The gold hawks have been cast in a mould with two faces, and the junction line has been carefully removed and burnished. The gold was worked by chisel and burnishing; no grinding or file marks are visible. In the second bracelet, with the rosette, two groups of beads are united at the sides by bands of gold wire and thick hair. The fastening of the bracelet was by a loop and button. This button is a hollow ball of gold with a shank of gold wire fastened in it. The third bracelet is formed of three similar groups, one larger, and the other smaller on either side. The middle of each group consists of three beads of dark purple lazuli. The fastening of this bracelet was by a loop and button. The fourth bracelet is fashioned of hour-glass beads.

In this extraordinary group of the oldest jewelry known, we see unlimited variety and fertility of design. Excepting the plain gold balls, there is not a single bead in any one bracelet which would be interchangeable with those in another bracelet. Each is of independent design, fresh and free from all convention or copying.

The tomb of Zet [1] consists of a large chamber twenty feet wide and thirty feet long, with smaller chambers around it at its level, the whole bounded by a thick brick wall, which rises seven and a half feet to the roof, and then three and a half feet more to the top of the retaining wall. Outside of this on the north is a line of small tombs about five feet deep, and on the south a triple line of tombs of the same depth. And apparently of the same system and same age is the mass of tombs marked W, which are parallel to the tomb of Zet. Later there appears to have been built the long line of tombs, placed askew, in order not to interfere with those which have

[1] For plan see page 361.

been mentioned, and then this skew line gave the direction to the next tomb, that of Merneit, and later on to that of Azab. The private graves around the royal tomb are all built of mud brick, with a coat of mud plaster over it, and the floor is of sand, usually also coated over with mud.

The first question about these great tombs is how

TOMB OF ZET, CIRCA 4700 B. C.

they were covered over. Some have said that such spaces could not be roofed, and at first sight it would seem almost impossible. But the actual beams found yet remaining in the tombs are as long as the widths of the tombs, and therefore timber of such sizes could be procured. In the tomb of Qa the holes for the beams yet remain in the walls, and even the cast of the end of a beam, and in the tombs of Merneit, Azab, and Mersekha are posts and pilasters to help in supporting a roof. The clear span of the chamber of Zet is 240 inches, or 220 if the beams were carried on a wooden lining, as seems likely. It is quite practicable to roof over these great chambers up to spans of twenty feet. The wood of such lengths was actually used, and, if spaced out over only a quarter of the area, the beams would carry their load with full safety. Any boarding, mats, or straw laid over the beams would not increase the load. That there was a mass of sand laid over the tomb is strongly shown by the retaining wall around the top. This wall is roughly built, and not intended to be a visible feature. The outside is daubed with mud plaster, and has a considerable slope; the inside is left quite rough, with bricks in and out.

Turning now to the floor, the basis of it is mud plastering, which was whitewashed. On that were laid beams around the sides, and one down the middle: these beams were placed before the mud floor was hard, and have sunk about one-quarter inch into it. On the beams a ledge was recessed, and on this ledge the edges of the flooring planks rested. Such planks would not bend in the middle by a man standing on them, and therefore made a sound floor. Over the planks was laid a coat of mud plaster. This construction doubtless shows what was the mode of flooring the palaces and large houses of the early Egyptians, in order to keep off the damp of the ground in the Nile valley. For common houses a basis of pottery jars turned mouth down was used for the same purpose. A very striking example of this method was unearthed at Koptos.

The sides of the great central chamber of Zet are not clear in arangement. The brick cross walls, which subdivide them into separate cells, have no finished faces on their ends. All the wall faces are plastered and white-washed; but the ends of the cross walls are rough bricks, all irregularly in and out. Moreover, the bricks project forward irregularly over the beam line. It seems, then, that there was an upright timber lining to the chamber, against which the cross walls were built the walls thus having rough ends projecting over the beams. The foot-ing of this upright plank lining is indicated by a groove left along the western floor beam between the ledge on the beam and the side of the flooring planks. Thus we reach a wooden chamber, lined with upright planks, which stood out from the wall, or from the backs of the beams. How the side chambers were entered is not shown; whether there was a door to each or not. But as they were intended to be for ever closed, and as the chambers in two corners were shut off by brickwork all round, it seems likely that all the side chambers were equally closed. And thus, after the slain domestics and offerings were deposited in them, and the king in the centre hall, the roof would be permanently placed over the whole.

The height of the chamber is proved by the cast of straw which formed part of the roofing, and which comes at the top of the course of headers on edge which copes the wall all around the chamber. Over this straw there was laid one course of bricks a little recessed, and be-yond that is the wide ledge all round before reaching the retaining wall. The height of the main chamber was 90.6 inches from the floor level.

Having examined the central chamber, the chambers at the sides should be next considered. The cross walls were built after the main brick outside was finished and plastered. The deep recesses coloured red, on the north side, were built in the construction; where the top is preserved entire, as in a side chamber on the north, it is seen that the roofing of the recess was upheld by building in a board about an inch thick. The shallow recesses along the south side were merely made in the plastering, and even in the secondary plastering after the cross walls were built. All of these recesses, except that at the south-west, were coloured pink-red, due to mixing burnt ochre with the white.

The tomb of Merneit was not at first suspected to exist, as it had no accumulation of pottery over it; and the whole ground had been pitted all over by the Mission Amélineau making " quelques sondages," without revealing the chambers or the plan. As soon, however, as Petrie began systematically to clear the ground, the scheme of a large central chamber, with eight long chambers for offerings around it, and a line of private tombs enclosing it, stood apparent. The central chamber is very accurately built, with vertical sides parallel to less than an inch. It is about twenty-one feet wide and thirty feet long, or practically the same as the chamber of Zet. Around the chamber are walls forty-eight to fifty-two inches thick, and beyond them a girdle of long, narrow chambers forty-eight inches wide and 160 to 215 inches long. Of these chambers for offerings, Nos. 1, 2, 5, and 7 still contain pottery in place, and No. 3 contains many jar sealings.

At a few yards distant from the chambers full of offerings is a line of private graves almost surrounding the royal tomb. This line has an interruption at the south end of the west side similar to the interruption of the retaining wall of the tomb of Zet at that quarter. It seems, therefore, that the funeral approached it from that direction.

The chamber of the tomb of Merneit shows signs of burning on both the walls and the floor. A small piece of wood yet remaining indicates that it also had a wooden floor like the other tombs. Against the walls stand pilasters of brick; and, although these are not at present more than a quarter of the whole height of the wall, they originally reached to the top. These pilasters are entirely additions to the first building; they stand against the plastering and upon a loose layer of sand and pebbles about four inches thick. Thus it is clear that they belonged to the subsequent stage of the fitting of a roof to the chamber. The holes that are shown in the floor are apparently connected with the construction, as they are not in the mid-line where pillars are likely. At the edge of chamber No. 2 is a cast of plaited palm-leaf matting on the mud mortar above this level, and the bricks are set back irregularly. This shows the mode of finishing off the roof of this tomb.

From the position of the tomb of Den-Setui, it is seen naturally to follow the building of the tombs of

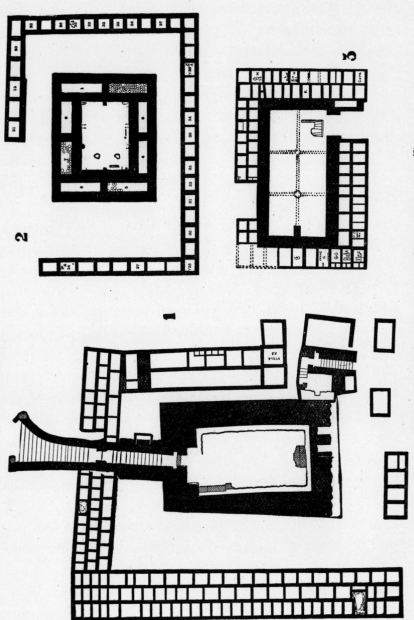

PLANS OF THE TOMBS OF DEN-SETUI (1), MERNEIT (2), AND MERSEKHA (3).

Zet and Merneit. It is surrounded by rows of small chambers for offerings, and for the burial of domestics. The king's tomb appears to have contained a large number of tablets of ivory and ebony, for fragments of eighteen were found, and two others are known, making in all twenty tablets from this one tomb. The inscriptions on stone vases are, however, not more frequent than in previous reigns. This tomb appears to have been one of the most costly and sumptuous. The astonishing feature of this chamber is the granite pavement, such considerable use of granite being quite unknown until the step pyramid of Saqqâra early in the third dynasty. At the south-west corner is a strange annex. A stairway leads down from the west and then turns to the north. At the foot of the first flight of steps is a space for inserting planks and brickwork to close the chamber, like the blocking of the door of the tomb of Azab.[1] This small chamber was therefore intended to be closed. Whether this chamber was for the burial of one of the royal family, or for the deposit of offerings, it is difficult to determine. Of the various rows of graves around the great tomb there is nothing to record in detail. An ebony tablet, presumably of the time of Den, found among the first dynasty tombs, represents a scene in which a king is dancing before Osiris, the god being seated in his shrine. This tablet is the earliest example of those pictorial records of a religious ceremony which, as we now know, was continued almost without change from the

[1] For plan see page 361, and for photograph see page 383.

first dynasty to the thirty-third. It is interesting to note
on this engraving that the king is represented with the
hap and a short stick instead of the oar. It should be
noted also that the royal name, Setui, occurs in the lower
part of the tablet, so that there is a strong presumption
that the tablet is of the time of Den-Setui, and the presumption is almost a certainty when the tablet is compared with some sealings found in its vicinity. Mr. F.
Ll. Griffiths has written at length on this important in-

TABLET OF DEN-SETUI, 4600 B. C.

scription.[1] He thinks that this tablet and two others
somewhat similar were the brief annals of the time, and
record the historic events and the names of government
officials. He translates a portion of the inscription as
" Opening the gates of foreign lands," and in another
part he reads, " The master comes, the King of Upper
and Lower Egypt." Moreover, he translates certain

[1] Royal Tombs of the first dynasty, Part I: Eighteenth Memoir of the
Egypt Exploration Fund, London, 1900, page 42.

signs as "Sheikh of the Libyans," and he identifies a place named *Tny* as This, or the capital of the nome in which Abydos lay.

Of this reign also is an ivory tablet finely polished, but blackened with burning, which has engraved upon it the oldest architectural drawing in the world. The inscription on this precious fragment apparently refers

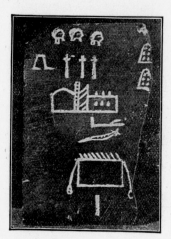

ARCHITECTURAL DRAWING,
B. C. 4600.

to the great chiefs coming to the tomb of Setui, and a picture of a building in the middle of the inscription may be taken as representing on the left the tomb chamber of Den-Setui, with a slight mound over it. The upright strokes represent the steles outside the tombs, adjacent to which is the inclined stairway, while on the right is a diagram of the cemetery, with graves arranged in rows around the tomb,[1] with small steles standing up over the graves.

A small piece of still another ivory tablet[2] gives an interesting portrait of Den-Setui. This king flourished about 4600 B. C., so that this is perhaps the oldest portrait that can be named and dated. It shows the double crown fully developed, and has an additional interest, inasmuch as the crown of Lower Egypt was apparently coloured red, while the crown of Upper Egypt was white

[1] The plan of this tomb, as discovered recently, is given on page 377.
[2] This tablet is illustrated on page 357.

in accordance with the practice that we know existed during the later historic period.

Among the many ivory objects found at Abydos is a small ivory panel from a box which seems to have contained the golden seal of judgment of King Den.

The engraving of this ivory panel is of the finest description, and bears evidence of the magnificent workmanship of the Egyptians 6,500 years ago. It will be seen that enough of the fragment has been preserved to include the cartouche of the monarch, and the snake at the side is the pictograph of judgment. Beneath is the hieroglyph for gold, and at the bottom is a sign which represents a seal cylinder [1] rolling over a piece of clay.

IVORY PANEL OF DEN-SETUI, 4600 B. C.

The tomb of Azab-Merpaba [2] is a plain chamber, with rather sloping sides, about twenty-two feet long and fourteen feet wide. The surrounding wall is nearly five feet thick. The lesser and more irregular chamber on the north is of the same depth and construction, fourteen feet by nine. This lesser chamber had no remains of flooring; it contained many large sealings of jars, and

[1] It was for a long time thought that this hieroglyphic character represented a finger ring, but as it is now positively known that finger rings were not in use until long after the time of Den, this explanation had to be abandoned in favour of the more correct interpretation of a seal cylinder.

[2] For plan see page 361.

seems to have been for all the funeral provision, like the eight chambers around the tomb of Merneit. Around this tomb is a circuit of small private tombs, leaving a gap on the southwest like that of Merneit, and an additional branch line has been added on at the north. All of these tombs are very irregularly built; the sides are wavy in direction, and the divisions of the long trench are slightly

STAIRWAY IN THE TOMB AZAB.

piled up, of bricks laid lengthwise, and easily over-thrown. This agrees with the rough and irregular con-struction of the central tomb and offering chamber. The funeral of Azab seems to have been more carelessly con-ducted than that of any of the other kings here; only one piece of inscribed vase was in his tomb, as against eight of his found in his successor's tomb, and many other of his vases erased by his successor. Thus his palace prop-erty seems to have been kept back for his successor's use, and not buried with Azab himself. In some of the chambers much ivory inlaying was found.

The entrance to the tomb of Azab was by a stairway descending from the east, thus according with the system begun by Den. On the steps, just outside of the door, were found dozens of small pots loosely piled together. These must have contained offerings made after the completion of the burial. The blocking is made by planks and bricks, the whole outside of the planking being covered by bricks loosely stacked, as can be seen in the photograph, the planking having decayed away from before them. The chamber was floored with planks of wood laid flat on the sand, without any supporting beams as in other tombs.

The tomb of Mersekha-Semempses [1] is forty-four feet long and twenty-five feet wide, surrounded by a wall over five feet thick. The surrounding small chambers are only three to four feet deep where perfect, while the central pit is still eleven and one-half feet deep, though broken away at the top. When examined by Professor Petrie few of the small chambers contained anything. Seven steles were found, the inscriptions of which are marked in the chambers of the plan; and other steles were also found here, scattered so that they could not be identified with the tombs. The most interesting are two steles of dwarfs, which show the dwarf type clearly; with one were found bones of a dwarf. In a chamber on the east was a jar and a copper bowl, which shows the hammer marks, and is roughly finished, with the

[1] For plan see pages 361 and 377.

edge turned over to leave it smooth. The small com-
partments in the south-eastern chambers were probably
intended to hold the offerings placed in the graves; the
dividing walls are only about half the depth of the grave.
The structure of the interior of the tomb of Mersekha
is at present uncertain. Only in the corner by the entrance was the wooden flooring preserved; several beams
(one now in Cairo Museum) and much broken wood was

TOMB OF MERSEKHA, SHOWING WOODEN FLOOR.

found loose in the rubbish. The entrance is nine feet
wide, and was blocked by loose bricks, flush with wall
face, as seen in the photograph. Another looser walling
farther out, also seen in the photograph, is probably that
of plunderers to hold back the sand.

The tomb of King Qa, which is the last of the first
dynasty, shows a more developed stage than the others.
Chambers for offerings are built on each side of the

entrance passage, and this passage is turned to the north,
as in the mastabas of the third dynasty and in the pyramids. The whole of the building is hasty and defective.
The bricks were mostly used too new, probably less than
a week after being made. Hence the walls have seriously
collapsed in most of the lesser chambers; only the one
great chamber was built of firm and well-dried bricks.
In the small chambers along the east side the long wall

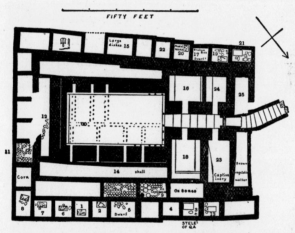

PLAN OF TOMB OF QA, CIRCA 4500 B. C.

between chambers 10 and 5 has crushed out at the base,
and spread against the pottery in the grave 5, and against
the wooden box in grave 2. Hence the objects must have
been placed in those graves within a few days of the
building of the wall, before the mud bricks were hard
enough to carry even four feet height of wall. The
burials of the domestics must therefore have taken place
all at once, immediately after the king's tomb was built,
and hence they must have been sacrificed at the funeral.

The pottery placed in the chambers is all figured in position on the plan.

Only three steles were found in the grave of Qa, but these were larger than those of the earlier graves.   One of them, No. 48, is the longest and most important inscription that has come down to us from the first dynasty. This lay in a chamber [1] on the west side of the tomb. In the preparation of the stele, the block of stone had been ground all over and edges rounded. On its surface the hieroglyphs were then sketched in red ink, and were

1:12

48   Q

STELE OF KING QA.

finally drawn in black, the ground being then roughly hammered out. There the work stopped, and the final scraping and dressing of the figures was never accomplished. The reading of the signs is therefore difficult, but enough is seen to show that the keeper of the tomb bore the name of Sabef. He had two titles which are now illegible, and was also " Overseer of the Sed Festival." This scanty information goes to show how little the official titles were changed between the days of the first dynasty and the time of the building of the pyramids. The stele of the king Qa was found lying over chamber 3; it is like that found by M. Amélineau, carved in black quartzose stone. Near it, on the south, were dozens of large pieces of fine alabaster bowls.

Among various objects found in these chambers should be noted the fine ivory carving from chamber

[1] See chamber No. 21 on the plan, page 385.

23, showing a bound captive; [1] the large stock of painted model vases in limestone in a box in chamber 20; the set of perfect vases found in chamber 21; a fine piece of ribbed ivory; a piece of thick gold-foil covering of a hotep table, patterned as a mat, found in the long chamber west of the tomb; the deep mass of brown vegetable matter in the north-east chamber; the large stock of grain between chambers 8 and 11; and the bed of currants ten inches thick, though dried, which underlay the pottery in chamber 11. In chamber 16 were large dome-shaped jar sealings, with the name of Azab, and on one of them the ink-written signs of the "King's ka."

The entrance passage has been closed with rough brick walling at the top. It is curiously turned askew, as if to avoid some obstacle, but the chambers of the tomb of Den do not come near its direction. After nine steps, the straight passage is reached, and then a limestone portcullis slab bars the way, let into grooves on either side; it was, moreover, backed up by a buttress of brickwork in five steps behind it. All this shows that the rest of the passage must have been roofed in so deeply that entry from above was not the obvious course. The inner passage descends by steps, each about five inches high, partly in the slope, partly in the rise of the step. The side chambers open off this stairway by side passages a little above the level of the stairs.

The interior structure of the tomb of Qa is rather different from any other. Instead of the timber being

[1] The chambers are indicated on the plan on page 385.

an entirely separate structure apart from the brick, the brick sides seem here to have been very loosely built against the timber sides. Some detail yet remains of the wooden floor. The roofing is distinct in this tomb, and it is evident that there was an axial beam, and that the side beam only went half across the chamber. This is the only tomb with the awkward feature of an axial doorway, and it is interesting to note how the beam was placed out of the axis to accommodate it.

The tomb of Perabsen [1] shows a great change in form since the earlier series. A new dynasty with new ideas had succeeded the great founders of the monarchy; the three reigns had passed by before we can again see here the system of the tombs. Even the national worship was changed, and Set had become prominent. The type of tomb which had been developed under Azab, Mersekha, and Qa seems to have given way to the earlier pattern of Zer and Zet. In this tomb of Perabsen we see the same row of small cells separated by cross walls, like those of the early kings; but in place of a wooden central chamber there is a brick chamber, and a free passage is left around it communicating with the cells. What was the form of the south side of that chamber cannot now be traced, as, if any wall existed, it is now entirely destroyed. The entirely new feature is the continuous passage around the whole tomb. Perhaps the object of this was to guard against plunderers entering by digging sideways into the tomb.

[1] For plan see page 361.

The tomb of Khasekhemui[1] is very different from any of the other royal tombs yet known. The total length of the chamber from end to end is two hundred and twenty-three feet, and the breadth in the middle is forty

STONE CHAMBER OF KHASEKHEMUI.

feet, growing wider towards the northern end. The whole structure is very irregular; and, to add to the confusion, the greater part of it was built of freshly made mud bricks, which have yielded with the pressure and flowed out sideways, until the walls are often double their orig-

[1] For plan see page 361.

inal breadth. It was only owing to this flow of the walls over the objects in the chambers, that so many valuable things were found perfect, and in position. Where the whole of the original outline of a wall had disappeared, the form is given in the plan with wavy outline.

The central stone chamber of the tomb of Khasekhemui is the most important part of the whole, as it is the oldest stone construction yet known. The chamber is roughly seventeen by ten feet; the depth is nearly six feet. There is no sign of any roof.

Nearly all the contents of this tomb were removed by the French investigators in 1897. Among the more interesting objects found were sealings of yellow clay, which were curiously enough of different types at opposite ends of the tomb. Copper needles, chisels, axes, and model tools were also found, and a beautiful sceptre of gold and sard was brought to light by Professor Petrie, only an inch or two below a spot that had been cleared by previous explorers.

In chamber 2 of the tomb of Khasekhemui were also found six vases of dolomite and one of carnelian. Two of these are shown in the illustration, and each has a cover of thick gold-foil fitted over the top, and secured with a double turn of twisted gold wire, the wire being sealed with a small lump of clay, the whole operation resembling the method of the modern druggist, in fastening a box of ointment. Near these vases were found two beautiful gold bracelets; one, Number 3, is still in a perfect condition; the other, Number 4, has been, unfortunately, crushed by the yielding of the wall of the tomb in which it was deposited.

Each royal grave seems to have had connected with it two great steles. Two, for instance, were found in the tomb of Merneit, one of which, however, was demolished. There were also two steles at the grave of Qa. So far only one stele had been found of Zet, and one of Mersekha, and none appear to have survived of Zer, Den, or Azab. These steles seem to have been placed

GOLD - CAPPED VASES AND GOLD BRACELETS.

at the east side of the tombs, and on the ground level, and such of them as happened to fall down upon their inscribed faces have generally been found in an excellent state of preservation.

Hence we must figure to ourselves two great steles standing up, side by side, on the east of the tomb; and this is exactly in accord with the next period that we know, in which, at Medum, Snofrui had two great steles and an altar between them on the east of his tomb; and Rahotep had two great steles, one on either side of the offering-niche, east of his tomb. Probably the pair of obelisks of the tomb of Antef V., at Thebes, were a

later form of this system.   Around the royal tomb stood
the little private steles of the domestics, placed in rows,
thus forming an enclosure about the king.

Some of Professor Petrie's most interesting work at
Abydos was commenced in November, 1902.   In the previous season a part of the early town of Abydos had been
excavated, and it was found that its period began at the
close of the prehistoric age, and extended over the first
few dynasties; the connection between the prehistoric
scale and historic reigns was thus settled.   The position
of this town was close behind the site of the old temples
of Abydos, and within the great girdle-wall enclosure
of the twelfth dynasty, which stands about half a mile
north of the well-known later temples of Seti I. and
Ramses II.   This early town, being behind the temples,
or more into the sandy edge of the desert, was higher
up; the ground gently sloping from the cultivated land
upward as a sandy plain, until it reaches the foot of the
hills, a couple of miles back.

The broad result of these new excavations is that ten
different temples can be traced on the same ground,
though of about twenty feet difference of level; each
temple built on the ruins of that which preceded it, quite
regardless of the work of the earlier kings.

In such a clearance it was impossible to preserve all
the structures.   Had Petrie and his companions avoided
moving the foundations of the twenty-sixth dynasty, they
could never have seen much of the earlier work; had
they left the paving of the twelfth dynasty in place,
they must have sacrificed the objects of the Old Kingdom.

Also, had they only worked the higher levels, and left the rest, the inflow of high Nile would have formed a

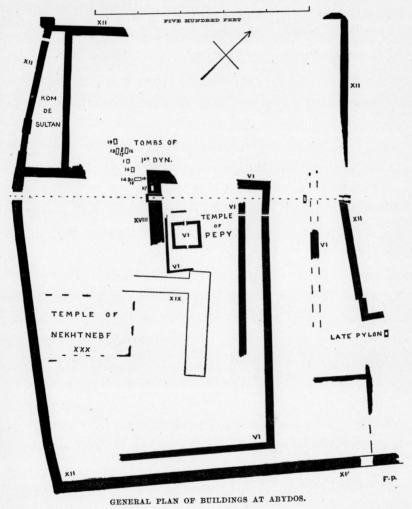

GENERAL PLAN OF BUILDINGS AT ABYDOS.

pond, which would have so rotted the ground that deeper work could not have been carried on in the future. The only course, therefore, was to plan everything fully, and remove whatever stood in the way of more complete exploration. All striking pieces of construction, such as the stone gateways of Papi, were left untouched, and work carried on to deep levels around them; in this way, at the end of the season, the site was bristling with pieces of wall and blocks of stonework, rising ten or fifteen feet above the low level clearances. As the excavations progressed, there was an incessant need of planning and recording all the constructions. Professor Petrie always went about with a large dinner-knife and a trowel in his pocket, and spent much time in cutting innumerable sections and tracing out the lines of the bricks. The top and base level of each piece of wall had to be marked on it; and the levels could then be measured off to fixed points.

An outline of some of the principal buildings is given, to show the general nature of the site of the temple of Abydos. This plan is not intended to show all periods, nor the whole work of any one age; but only a selection which will avoid confusion. The great outer wall on the plan was probably first built by Usirtasen I.; the bricks of the oldest parts of it are the same size as bricks of his foundation deposits, and it rests upon town ruins of the Old Kingdom. But this wall has been so often broken and repaired that a complete study of it would be a heavy task; some parts rest on nineteenth dynasty building, and even Roman patchwork is seen. Its general character is shown with alternating portions, the first set consisting of towers of brickwork built in concave foundations, and then connecting walls between, formed in straight courses. The purpose of this construction has

long been a puzzle. The alternate concave and straight
courses are the natural result of building isolated masses,
on a concave bed like all Egyptian houses, and then connecting them by intermediate walls. The hard face across
the wall, and the joint to prevent the spread of scaling,
are the essential advantages of this construction.

WALL OF USIRTASEN I.

The corner marked Kom-de-Sultan is the enclosure
which was emptied out by Mariette's diggers, because
of the abundance of burials with steles of the twelfth to
eighteenth dynasties. They have removed all the earth
to far below the base of the walls, thus digging in most
parts right through the town of the Old Kingdom, which
stood here before the great walls were built. The inner
two sides of this enclosed corner are later than the outer
wall; the bricks are larger than those of Usirtasen, and
the base of the wall is higher than his. The causeway

line indicated through the site by a dotted line from the east to the west gate is a main feature; but it is later than the sixth dynasty, as the wall of that age cuts it, and it was cut in two by later buildings of the twentieth dynasty. It seems then to begin with Usirtasen, whose gateways it runs through; and to have been kept up by Thûtmosis III., who built a wall with granite pylon for it, and also by Ramses II., who built a great portal colonnade of limestone for the causeway to pass through on entering the cemetery outside the west wall of this plan.

To the north of the causeway are seen the tombs of the first dynasty. One more, No. 27, was found beneath the wall of Thûtmosis; it was of the same character as the larger of the previous tombs. All of these are far below any of the buildings shown on this outline plan.

Of the two long walls, marked vi., the inner is older, but was re-used by Papi. It is probably the temenos of the third dynasty. The outer wall is the temenos of the sixth dynasty, the west side of which is yet unknown, and has probably been all destroyed. The temple of Papi is shown in the middle with the north-west and south sides of the thin boundary wall which enclosed it. The thick wall which lies outside of that is the great wall of the eighteenth dynasty, with the granite pylon of Thûtmosis III. It seems to have followed the line of the sixth dynasty wall on the north. The outline marked xix. shows a high level platform of stone, which was probably for the basement of buildings of Ramses II.

Within the area of these temples was discovered quite a number of historical relics. None is more interesting,

perhaps, than the ivory statuette of the first dynasty
king. This anonymous ruler is figured as wearing the
crown of Upper Egypt, and a thick embroidered robe.

From the nature of the pattern and
the stiff edge represented, it looks
as if this robe were quilted with
embroidery; no such dress is
known on any Egyptian figure yet
found. The work belongs to an
unconventional school, before the
rise of the fixed traditions; it
might have been carved in any age
and country where good natural
work was done. In its unshrink-
ing figuring of age and weakness
with a subtle character, it shows
a power of dealing with individ-
uality which stands apart from all
the later work.

IVORY STATUETTE OF FIRST
DYNASTY KING.

Of greater interest, however,
is the ivory statuette of Khûfûi,
which is the first figure of that monarch that has
come to light. The king is seated upon his throne,
and the inscription upon the front of it leaves no
doubt as to the identity of the figure. The work is
of extraordinary delicacy and finish; for even when mag-
nified it does not suggest any imperfection or clumsi-
ness, but might have belonged to a life-sized statue.
The proportion of the head is slightly exaggerated; as,
indeed, is always the case in minute work; but the char-

acter and expression are as well handled as they might be
on any other scale, and are full of power and vigour. The
idea which it conveys to us of the personality of Khûfûi
agrees with his historical position. We see the energy,
the commanding air, the indomitable will, and the firm

ability of the man who stamped
for ever the character of the Egyptian monarchy and outdid all time
in the scale of his works. No other
Egyptian king that we know resembled this head; and it stands
apart in portraiture, though perhaps it may be compared with the
energetic face of Justinian, the
great builder and organiser.

Two ivory lions were also found
in one of the private tombs around
that of Zer. It is evident that these
lions were used as playing pieces,
probably for the well-known prehistoric game of Four Lions and a

IVORY STATUETTE OF KHÛFÛI.

Hare, for the bases of the lions are
much worn, as if by sliding about upon a smooth surface,
and the pelt of the lion, as originally carved, is also worn
off as if by continued handling. The lion shown in the
illustration is of a later style than those of Zer or of
Mena. Near the place where this was found were a few
others. One of them, apparently a lioness, is depicted
with a collar, indicating that the animal had been tamed,
and yet another had inserted within the head an eye

accurately cut in chalcedony. Another valuable object
unearthed at Abydos was the sceptre of King Khasekhemui. This consisted of a series of cylinders of sard
embellished at every fourth cylinder with double bands
of thick gold, and com-
pleted at the thinner end
with a plain cap of gold,
copper rod, now corroded,
binding the whole together.

During the reign of
King Zer the ivory arrow
tip began to be commonly

CARVED IVORY LION.

used; hundreds were gathered from his tomb, and the
variety of forms is greater than in any other reign. Besides the plain circular points, many of them have reddened tips; there are also examples of quadrangular
barbed tips, and others are pentagonal, square, or oval.
Only the plain circular tips appear in succeeding reigns
down to the reign of Mersekha, except a single example
of the oval forms under Den.

Some flint arrow-heads were also found around the
tomb of Zer, mostly of the same type as those found in
the tomb of Mena.[1] Two, however, of these arrow-heads,
Numbers 13 and 14, are of a form entirely unknown as
yet in any other age or country. The extreme top of the
head is of a chisel form, and this passes below into the
more familiar pointed form. The inference here is almost
inevitable, and it seems as if the arrow-heads had been
made in this peculiar way with a view to using the arrow

[1] For plan see page 361.

a second time after the tip was broken in attacking an animal. Another curious object dating from this reign and classed among the arrows is a small portion of flint set perpendicularly into the end of a piece of wood. This, in the opinion of Professor Giglioli, is not an arrow at all, but a tattooing instrument. If this explanation be correct, then this instrument is an extremely interesting find, for the fact has been recently brought to light that

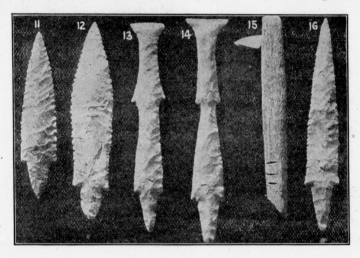

ANCIENT EGYPTIAN ARROWS.

tattooing was in vogue in prehistoric times, and there is, moreover, at Cairo, the mummy of a priestess of the twelfth dynasty having the skin decorated in this manner.

Among the domestic articles is an admirable design of pair of tweezers, made with a wide hinge and stiff points. Of analogous interest are two copper fish-hooks, which, however, have no barbs. Needles also, which we know were used in prehistoric days, appear in the relics of the tomb of Zer and of subsequent rulers. Of the reign of Zer are also found copper harpoons cut with a second fang, similar forms being found among the remains of Mersekha and of Khasekhemui. In the centre

MISCELLANEOUS COPPER OBJECTS.

of the illustration is seen the outline of a chisel of the time of Zer, very similar to those used in the early prehistoric ages. The same continuity from prehistoric to first dynasty times is shown in the shape of the copper pins dating from Zer, Den, Mersekha, and Qa.

At various times quite a considerable number of articles relating to intimate daily life has been discovered. An exceedingly fortunate find was that of an ivory comb of crude but careful workmanship, and which, even after the lapse of sixty-seven centuries, has only lost three of its teeth. This comb, according to the inscription on it, belonged to Bener-ab, a distinguished lady, whose tomb has been already mentioned, and who was either the wife or the daughter of King Mena of the first dynasty.

Of the class of domestic objects is the primitive but doubtless quite effective corn-grinder shown in the illustration. This was found in an undisturbed tomb in the Osiris temenos, where also was a strangely shaped three-sided pottery bowl, similar in shape to a stone bowl of the same period, but otherwise unknown in antiquity. This three-sided bowl may be regarded as a freak of the

IVORY COMB, B. C. 4800.

workman rather than as having any particular value along the line of evolution of pottery forms; and it is interesting to note that bowls of this form have been quite recently made by the modern English potters in South Devonshire, as the result of the inventive fancy of a village workman.

During the course of the excavations at Abydos many thousands of fragments of pottery were collected. Those that appeared to be of historic value were sorted and classified, and, as a result of minute and extended labours, it is now possible for the reader to see at a glance the principal types of Egyptian

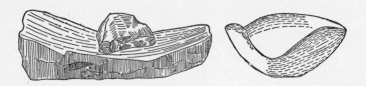

CORN- GRINDER AND THREE - SIDED BOWL.

pottery from prehistoric times, and to view their relationship as a whole. The diagram exhibits an unbroken series of pottery forms from s. D. 76 to B. C. 4400. The forms in the first column are those classified according to the chronological notation devised by Professor Petrie, enabling a " sequence date " (s. D.) to be assigned to an object which cannot otherwise be dated. In the second column are forms found in the town of Abydos, and in the last column are those unearthed in the tombs. Most

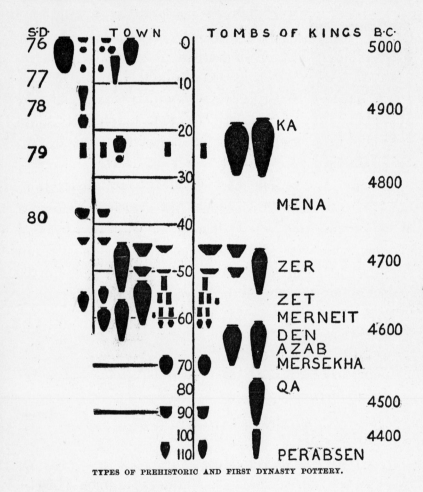

TYPES OF PREHISTORIC AND FIRST DYNASTY POTTERY.

of the large jars bear marks, which were scratched in the moist clay before being baked; some few were marked after the baking. Some of the marks are un-questionably hieroglyphs; others are probably connected with the signs used by the earlier prehistoric people; and many can scarcely be determined. A typical instance of these pottery marks is shown in the illustration.

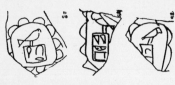

POTTERY MARKS.

These signs appear to be distinctly of the time of Mersekha, and the fortified enclosure around the name may refer to the tomb as the eternal fortress of the king. These marks can be roughly classified into types according to the skill with which they were drawn. The first example illustrates the more careful workmanship, and the others show more degraded forms, in which the outline of the hawk and the signs in the cartouche become gradually more debased.

It is tolerably certain that what are known as the Mediterranean alphabets were derived from a selection of the signs used in these pottery marks.

An undisturbed tomb was found by accident in the Osiris temenos. The soil was so wet that the

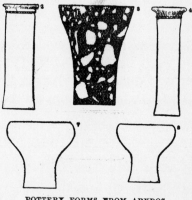

POTTERY FORMS FROM ABYDOS.

bones were mostly dissolved; and only fragments of the skull, crushed under an inverted slate bowl, were preserved. The head had been laid upon a sandstone corn-grinder. Around the sides of the tomb were over two dozen jars of pottery, most of them large. And near the body were sixteen stone vases and bowls. Some of the forms, such as are shown in the illustration, Nos. 3, 7, 8, are new to us. A strange three-sided pottery bowl [1] was also found here, but since there is no museum in England where such a complete tomb can be placed, it was sent to Philadelphia, in order that the whole series should be arranged as originally found.

The sealings, the general description of which has been already given, have come to light in such consid-

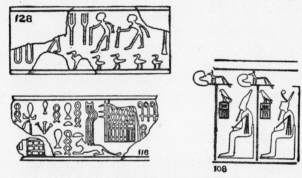

THREE TYPES OF SEALINGS.

erable quantities during the past few years that their study became a special branch of Egyptology. As to the earliest sealings, it was not until the time of Den that a broad informity of style was established. The seals of the second dynasty are generally of a smaller style and more elaborately worked than those of the first dynasty. It is reasonable, therefore, to conclude that the later seals were made in stone or metal rather than in wood.

The illustration given of sealing No. 128, of the Egypt Exploration Fund collection, shows a very fair type of

[1] See page 402.

the figuring of men and animals at the time of the first dynasty as a survival of the prehistoric manner of engraving. Here, then, at the very dawn of history, we find a spirited depiction of the human form, for, rude though it is, there can be no doubt but that it is a representation of the human figure, and stiff and ungainly though the action of the drawing be, there can be no doubt as to the progressive movement intended by the artist. On a sealing, No. 116, is seen the leopard with the bent bars on his back. The shrine upon the same seal is of the general form, and is like the early huts with reed sides, and an interwoven palm-rib roof. This is a specimen of an intermediate manner of workmanship. The most advanced stage of art in the sealings of the first dynasty, is No. 108. This is the royal seal of King Zer, B. C. 4700, showing him seated and wearing the crowns of Upper and Lower Egypt. By his side are the royal staff and his cartouches. It was workmanship of this character which survived in Egypt almost as late as Roman times; that is to say, the same style engraving was current in the Valley of the Nile for forty-six centuries.

A SEALING SHOWING JARS.

A particularly interesting sealing is a representation of two jars with the flat seals across their tops. These jars, moreover, are depicted as bound around with a network of rope in a manner which corresponds with some fragments of rope found around some jars of this character.

A small fragment of pottery originally forming the base of a brown earthenware dish had inscribed upon it some accounts, and is the oldest of such business records yet found in Egypt. The exact import of the figures is not yet entirely intelligible, but they seem to refer to quantities of things rather than to individuals, as the numbers, although mostly twenty, are sometimes one hundred and two hundred. This interesting fragment was found at the tomb of Zet, and thus establishes the use of arithmetic before 4600 B. C.

ACCOUNTS ON POTTERY, B. C. 4600.

The expedition supported by Mrs. Hearst, in the name of the University of California, has done some useful work at El-Ahaiwah, opposite Menshiyeh. The main cemetery at this place is an archaic one, containing about a thousand graves or more, of which about seven hundred had already been plundered. Between these plundered graves, about 250 were found untouched in modern times. The graves yielded a good collection of archaic pottery, pearl and ivory bracelets, hairpins, carnelian, garnet, gold, blue glaze and other beads, etc.

About this cemetery was a cemetery of the late New Empire, containing a number of vaulted tombs built of unburned brick. These yielded a large number of necklaces, and several fine pieces of faïence and ivory, and other objects. A second cemetery, farther north, contained a few late archaic graves and about fifteen large tombs, usually with one main chamber and two small chambers at each end. These tombs were of two types (1) roofed over with wood, without a stairway, (2) roofed over with a corbelled vault and entered from the

UNIQUE INSTANCE OF A DISSECTED BURIAL.

west by a stairway. The burials in these tombs are in the archaic position, head to south. Dissected, or secondary, burials occur in these cemeteries, but only rarely. Only one indisputable case was found, as shown in the illustration.

It would require several volumes adequately to deal with the results of the excavations of the present century. Further discoveries, all throwing new light upon the life of ancient Egypt, are being made each season, and the number of enthusiastic workers gathered from every nation constantly increases. Notwithstanding the heroic and splendid work of past investigators, for many years to come the valley of the Nile promises to yield important results, not only in actual field work, but also in the close study and better classification of the thousands of objects that are continually being brought to light.

Six thousand years of history have been unrolled; tomb and tablet, shard and papyrus have told their story, and the vista stretches back to the dawn of human history in that inexhaustible valley watered by the perennial overflow of the grandest river in the world. But there is much still to be accomplished by the enthusiastic spirit, the keen and selective mind, in the study of this ancient land, the cradle and the grave of nations.

THE END.

INDEX

INDEX

INDEX

INDEX

INDEX